Risk Management in Crisis

Risk management is a domain of management which comes to the fore in crisis. This book looks at risk management under crisis conditions in the COVID-19 pandemic context.

The book synthesizes existing concepts, strategies, approaches and methods of risk management and provides the results of empirical research on risk and risk management during the COVID-19 pandemic. The research outcome was based on the authors' study on 42 enterprises of different sizes in various sectors, and these firms have either been negatively affected by COVID-19 or have thrived successfully under the new conditions of conducting business activities. The analysis looks at both the impact of the COVID-19 pandemic on the selected enterprises and the risk management measures these enterprises had taken in response to the emerging global trends. The book puts together key factors which could have determined the enterprises' failures and successes.

The final part of the book reflects on how firms can build resilience in challenging times and suggests a model for business resilience. The comparative analysis will provide useful insights into key strategic approaches of risk management.

Piotr Jedynak is Professor of Management. He works at Jagiellonian University in Cracow, Poland, where he holds the positions of Vice-Rector for Financial and HR Policy and Head of the Management Systems Department. He specializes in risk management, strategic management and management systems. He is the author of numerous publications, an auditor and consultant to many public and business organizations.

Sylwia Bąk holds a PhD in Management Sciences. She works as a Researcher and Lecturer in the Management Systems Department of Jagiellonian University in Cracow, Poland. In her interests, research and publications, she focuses on issues related to risk management, strategic management and standardized management systems.

Routledge Advances in Risk Management

Forecasting Air Travel Demand
Looking at China
Yafei Zheng, Kin Keung Lai and Shouyang Wang

Supply Chain Risk Management in the Apparel Industry
Peter Cheng, Yelin Fu and Kin Keung Lai

Risk Management in Supply Chains
Using Linear and Non-linear Models
Mohammad Heydari, Kin Keung Lai and Zhou Xiaohu

Risk Management in Public–Private Partnerships
Mohammad Heydari, Kin Keung Lai and Zhou Xiaohu

Renminbi Exchange Rate Forecasting
Yunjie Wei, Shouyang Wang and Kin Keung Lai

Candlestick Forecasting for Investments
Applications, Models and Properties
Haibin Xie, Kuikui Fan and Shouyang Wang

Risk Management in Crisis
Winners and Losers during the COVID-19 Pandemic
Piotr Jedynak and Sylwia Bąk

Corruption, Infrastructure Management and Public–Private Partnership
Optimizing through Mathematical Models
Mohammad Heydari, Kin Keung Lai and Zhou Xiaohu

For more information about this series, please visit: www.routledge.com/Routledge-Advances-in-Risk-Management/book-series/RM001

Risk Management in Crisis

Winners and Losers during the COVID-19 Pandemic

Piotr Jedynak and Sylwia Bąk

Routledge
Taylor & Francis Group
LONDON AND NEW YORK

First published 2021
by Routledge
2 Park Square, Milton Park, Abingdon, Oxon OX14 4RN

and by Routledge
605 Third Avenue, New York, NY 10158

Routledge is an imprint of the Taylor & Francis Group, an informa business

British Library Cataloguing-in-Publication Data
A catalogue record for this book is available from the British Library

Library of Congress Cataloging-in-Publication Data
Names: Jedynak, Piotr, author. | Bąk, Sylwia, author.
Title: Risk management in crisis: winners and losers during the COVID-19 pandemic/Piotr Jedynak and Sylwia Bąk.
Description: Abingdon, Oxon; New York, NY: Routledge, 2022. | Series: Routledge advances in risk management series | Includes bibliographical references and index. |
Identifiers: LCCN 2021017834 | ISBN 9780367674540 (hbk) | ISBN 9780367674557 (pbk) | ISBN 9781003131366 (ebk)
Subjects: LCSH: Risk management. | Organizational resilience. | COVID-19 (Disease)
Classification: LCC HD61 .J44 2022 | DDC 658.15/5–dc23
LC record available at https://lccn.loc.gov/2021017834

ISBN: 978-0-367-67454-0 (hbk)
ISBN: 978-0-367-67455-7 (pbk)
ISBN: 978-1-003-13136-6 (ebk)

DOI: 10.4324/9781003131366

Typeset in Galliard
by Deanta Global Publishing Services, Chennai, India

Contents

Figures

Tables

Preface

Risk management is an approach to management that works particularly well in difficult and turbulent times when the comfort of planning an enterprise's activities is significantly disrupted. Such a situation that has made management difficult on an unprecedented scale is the COVID-19 pandemic. The book addresses the issue of risk management in crisis situations, with a particular focus on the circumstances caused by the COVID-19 pandemic. The book consists of seven chapters. We first synthesize existing concepts, strategies, approaches and methods of risk management. This is followed by an identification of challenges to risk management as they emerge in crisis situations. The second part of the book (Chapters 4, 5, 6, 7) already deals directly with the COVID-19 pandemic situation. We present a series of case studies illustrating the following categories: (1) the main business risks that emerged as a result of the pandemic, (2) the behaviours of enterprises that appear to be losers because they lost a lot in the crisis situation associated with the pandemic and (3) the behaviours of enterprises that, despite emerging risks, transformed their business in such a way that in the end they at least did not lose, and sometimes benefited from the crisis situation. Due to the great diversity of the identified behaviours of the selected enterprises, we divided them into particular categories, which allowed us to identify the dominant profiles of risk exposure under the pandemic conditions, indicating the key factors of failure and success. The final part of the book is our attempt to develop an original model of resilience to crisis based on the experiences of the discussed enterprises during the COVID-19 pandemic. The book is addressed to academics, students of many specializations (especially business studies), as well as practitioners employed as managers and specialists in enterprises of various sizes and sectors.

Piotr Jedynak and Sylwia Bąk

Credits

The publication was funded by the Priority Research Area Society of the Future under the programme "Excellence Initiative – Research University" at the Jagiellonian University in Krakow.

Introduction

In this book, we attempt to answer the question of what risk management has to offer enterprises that find themselves in a crisis situation. We take into special consideration the specifics of the crisis caused by the COVID-19 pandemic. We confront existing risk management approaches and tools with the practical actions of the enterprises that we studied in a pandemic situation. On the basis of case studies of dozens of enterprises, we try to identify what actions their managers took in the face of the pandemic and what factors determined their successes or failures. The book consists of seven chapters.

Chapter 1 entitled “Uncertainty and risk in the modern world” is a synthesis of research on the issues of uncertainty and risk. We present the genesis of such research and analyse the approaches to and ways of defining these two concepts in various fields and disciplines of science, with particular emphasis on management sciences. Additionally, we categorize the risks relevant to the activities of enterprises and attempt to chronologically map tendencies in their development, in both a practical dimension – in terms of the impact of the particular risk categories on the activities of enterprises – and a theoretical dimension – in terms of the indication of the first scientific texts to have used the names of these categories. In this chapter we also present the main directions of research on uncertainty and risk established by Nobel Prize Laureates in economic sciences.

Entitled “Concepts and standards of risk management”, Chapter 2 aims to present contemporary concepts and standards of risk management. In the first part we define the place of risk management in enterprise management systems. Next we characterize the role of risk in modern management concepts, including Lean management, outsourcing, CSR, supply chain management and value-based management. As risk and the extent to which it interferes with business activities have led to the emergence of professional domains of risk management, we present a review of these approaches. Our analysis focuses on enterprise risk management and business continuity management. Chapter 2 concludes with an identification and comparison of existing risk management standards, both holistic and specific ones.

The aim of Chapter 3 entitled “Challenges of risk management during crisis situations” is to identify challenges that enterprises have to confront and deal with by means of their risk management systems in crisis situations. At all stages of the

DOI: 10.4324/9781003131366-101

course of a crisis there occur interdependencies between risk management and crisis management. Therefore, in this chapter crisis is discussed as a specific management situation and types of crisis are classified and described. Furthermore, we identify approaches and strategies used in crisis management, which is one of the specialist fields of risk management. The final part of this chapter comprises an analysis of experiences from selected crises relevant for enterprise management.

Entitled "Dominant business risks during the COVID-19 pandemic", Chapter 4 aims to show the types of risks that emerged the most strongly and were the most common during the COVID-19 pandemic. The conducted analyses reveal a specific nature of various types of risk determined by a wide range of their sources, as well as the consequences of their occurrence for enterprises. The analyzed types include financial risks, organizational risks, strategic risks and global risks.

"'Risk losers' during the COVID-19 pandemic: case studies" is the title of Chapter 5. Its objective is to show cases of enterprises that, for various reasons, failed in confrontation with the challenges of the COVID-19 pandemic. Based on the conducted case studies, in this chapter we analyse the position of selected enterprises, indicating the causes and consequences of their failures. We focus on representatives of different sectors and different sizes, also diversified in terms of the local or global character of their business activities. In particular, we examine those managerial actions that are of key importance in a crisis situation and determine failure or lack thereof in the effective adaptation of enterprises to a crisis situation, for example a strategic reflection and an adjustment in the strategy and business model, decision-making processes, change management, resource policies, relations with stakeholders and communication with the market.

Entitled "'Risk winners' during the COVID-19 pandemic: case studies", Chapter 6 discusses a group of enterprises successful in confrontation with the COVID-19 pandemic. Based on the conducted case studies, the chapter analyses the position of the selected enterprises, focusing on the sources and consequences of their management success. We focus on representatives of different sectors and different sizes, also diversified in terms of the local or global character of their business activities. In particular, we examine those managerial actions that are of key importance in a crisis situation and determine success or lack thereof in the effective adaptation of enterprises to a crisis situation, for example a strategic reflection and an adjustment in the strategy and business model, decision-making processes, change management, resource policies, relations with stakeholders and communication with the market.

The purpose of Chapter 7 entitled "Building enterprises' resilience to crisis: lessons learned during the COVID-19 pandemic" is a synthesis of the previous deliberations oriented towards the development of a model for building enterprises' resilience to crisis and a procedure for its implementation, based on the conclusions of the conducted empirical research. The chapter outlines two main areas of enterprises' activities aimed at building their resilience to crisis situations: (1) reducing threats and combating weaknesses, and (2) exploiting opportunities and developing strengths. In both areas, we indicate groups of concrete actions that should help enterprises to build and strengthen their resilience. The chapter concludes with the authors' original model of the enterprise resilient to crisis together with a procedure for its implementation. The framework is based on the following pillars: (1) a culture of preparedness, (2) business continuity and (3) disaster resilience. The application of the model leads to the development of features of resilience, for example redundancy, adaptive capacity, agility, flexibility, diversity and efficiency.

In the conclusions, we present a summary of the conducted research, as well as resultant managerial, theoretical and methodological implications. We also outline further, in our opinion attractive, research directions.

In the book, we use a number of research methods, for example a literature review, an analysis of management standard or various types of reports. On the other hand, in the empirical part (Chapters 5 and 6), we apply a triangulation of research techniques, using, among others, a case study, a content analysis, a comparative analysis technique, exploratory techniques and exemplification. The sources of data for the empirical research include: (1) information obtained directly from the selected enterprises, in the form of communications posted on their official websites, periodic and current reports and on social media, official statements of their representatives and provided internal documents, (2) professional reports analyzing the impact of the COVID-19 pandemic on the activities of enterprises (e.g. reports of consulting firms), (3) statements of economic and social experts, as well as (4) thematic scientific papers and specialist industry periodicals.

The book is addressed to all readers interested in how risk management practices should be followed in crises of such an unprecedented scale as the COVID-19 pandemic.

1 Uncertainty and risk in the modern world

1.1. History of research on uncertainty and risk

Over time and as a result of dynamic technological, social and economic changes, uncertainty and risk have begun to emerge in all spheres of activity of national economies and societies on a macroeconomic scale as well as business entities and individuals on a microeconomic scale, becoming subjects of research in many fields and disciplines of science (Banse and Bechmann, 1998; Zinn, 2006; 2010; Elahi, 2013; Schiliro, 2017). Below we outline the genesis of research on uncertainty and risk from the perspective of economic and social sciences.

1.1.1. Uncertainty and risk from the perspective of economics

The need for research on uncertainty and risk was recognized in modern times. These concepts were introduced into economic terminology by Cantillon in the 18th century (Cantillon, 1755). This researcher noted inherent insecurity accompanying business activities and a major impact of risk on income formation. His theories (the long-term general equilibrium theory, the price theory, the exit theory, the quantity theory of money) formed the basis for the subsequent understanding of uncertainty and risk in the theory of economics (Cantillon, 1938). Moreover, the historical research of Laplace and Poincare allowed, among other things, to identify the relationship between access to information and risk assessment as well as the cause-and-effect relationships of risky business decisions, thus becoming a starting point for the development of subsequent methods and techniques of analysis and assessment of uncertainty and risk in the activities of business entities (Kaczmarek, 2010).

1.1.1.1. Uncertainty and risk in classical and neoclassical economics

In economic theory, the importance of uncertainty and risk was initially reflected in explaining the functioning of mechanisms governing the conduct of business activities. Economists such as Willet, Knight, Keynes and Arrow studied the possibilities of forecasting economic phenomena and safeguarding enterprises against their negative effects.

DOI: 10.4324/9781003131366-1

In his book *The Economic Theory of Risk and Insurance*, Willet (1901) differentiated between the degree of probability and the degree of uncertainty that a particular event would happen. On this basis, he formulated a rule indicating that an increase in the probability of loss occurrence is inextricably accompanied by an increase in uncertainty as to the expected end result. Willet's research constituted a basis for further studies conducted within the scope of classical, and subsequently neoclassical, economics.

In classical economics, risk was regarded as one of the sources of costs. Smith and Ricardo repeatedly emphasized that the risk-bearing entity expects in return relevant remuneration, which was considered a component of fair profit (Pivetti, 1987). However, early economic research did not focus on different categories of risk or its interaction with market participants, so risk was understood as a natural component of operating costs (Klimczak, 2008) generated due to the fact that a business entity is never able to operate in absolute certainty. Costs can then be divided into losses and own costs. An extreme cost of uncertainty may be the necessity to discontinue operations. What contributes to the occurrence of costs of risk and uncertainty is errors in situation assessment, fear of loss or misallocation of resources (Williams et al., 2002).

The issue of risk in the light of classical economics and its links with neoclassical economics were considered by Knight (1921) in his groundbreaking work *Risk, Uncertainty and Profit.* Neoclassical economics does not explain the importance of risk in the activities of economic entities. Knight, however, took up a discourse in which, on the one hand, he argued that measurable risk does not undermine the assumptions of neoclassical economics, and on the other hand, he pointed out that these assumptions could not be applied in situations of uncertainty. In assessing uncertainty and risk, the author recommended relying on past experience. A slightly different approach in this respect was presented by Keynes, the initiator of Keynesianism, the leading 20th-century macroeconomic theory. In his groundbreaking work *A Treatise on Probability*, Keynes (1921) claimed that in the assessment of future economic events one should assume the existence of the present state as lasting indefinitely. Knight (1921) also referred to the impact of uncertainty on investors' decisions, claiming that their decisions are necessarily accompanied by fundamental uncertainty. He also studied the relationships among uncertainty, risk and reward, and his key findings were extensively used in other disciplines (Nishimura and Ozaki, 2017).

1.1.1.2. Genuine uncertainty, benefits and costs of risk

The findings resulting from Knight's and Keynes's observations were also followed up in research conducted in the later periods, including that on genuine uncertainty. It was related to the need to accept the thesis that economic operators, despite various ways of hedging against negative consequences of risk, must take into account the occurrence of unexpected, previously unknown situations whose course will not be interrupted by previously taken economic decisions (Shackle, 1972).

In addition to analyzing uncertainty and risk as sources of cost, economic theory also focuses on the benefits of uncertainty and risk. Knight (1921) was the first to notice the possibility of generating profit under conditions of genuine uncertainty, calling them occasional benefits. The catalogue of benefits includes, in particular, the variety and increased attractiveness of actions taken. Other conclusions from studies aimed at identifying the benefits of uncertainty and risk in business indicate a division into benefits gained and benefits lost (Minc, 1975). The benefits and costs of risk occurrence are associated with the emergence of two categories of risk: pure risk (incurring loss without the possibility to gain benefits) and speculative risk (the possibility to either incur loss or gain benefits in the form of profit) (Williams et al., 2002).

Uncertainty and risk were also recognized as determinants of the proper functioning of economic mechanisms by Arrow, an eminent researcher in this field, for example in his theory of choice under conditions of uncertainty and risk. Thanks to the numerous works of this author, combined in the series entitled *Essays in the Theory of Risk Bearing* (Arrow, 1971), taking into account the importance of uncertainty and risk in economic research undoubtedly influenced the development of this field of science. According to the theory of choice in the conditions of risk, it was considered that one of the key problems was to describe its uncertain consequences. It was explained that uncertainty about consequences exists in the mind of the person making a choice and regulates their behaviour. In market relationships, the consequences of uncertainty may involve the occurrence of goods or cash payments at certain points in the future. The main conclusion of Arrow's research is the thesis of the existence of economic entities bearing the burden of risk occurrence. In principle, these are enterprises that assume the risk of uncertainty and thus incur unexpected losses or gain unexpected benefits (Arrow, 1971).

1.1.1.3. Uncertainty, risk and decision-making

Uncertainty and risk also became the subject of research in the process of formulating the theory of expected utility maximization. This theory was developed on the basis of so-called Bernoulli's (1738) Petersburg paradox. The principle of maximizing expected utility should be followed by those participants of economic life who, according to Arrow, in their decision-making processes have only knowledge determined by so-called subjective probability. Then the principle of utility maximization becomes a key criterion optimizing choices made in conditions of uncertainty (Kasprzak, 1979). The development of the theory of expected utility maximization was also enriched by the contributions made by von Neumann and Morgenstern (1947) as well as Savage (1954), who developed the concept of subjective expected utility, taking into account personalistic probability. Savage's concept of utility was contradicted in experimental economics by the Ellsberg (1961) paradox, which indicates that patterns of choice cannot be explained by the probability of action assessment.

One of the cornerstones of mainstream economics is the theory of the rationality of business entities, which takes into account uncertainty and risk as factors influencing the rationality of decisions made by individuals or businesses, i.e. the microeconomic dimension of economic life. Economic phenomena are most often analyzed with the assumption of limited rationality of human beings as decision-makers. However, this assumption does not mean that the rationality of the choices is called into question, but rather that the rationality of individuals is more intentional than real (Simon, 1965). In mainstream economics, the theory of rationality is directly related to the theory of economic choice, which analyses the uncertainty of economic phenomena as a basic variable. The cognitive aspect of uncertainty in the theory of economic choice began to be taken into account in the 1950s, when uncertainty was perceived as the subjective probability of the rationality of economic factors. Attempts to extend this approach can be seen, for example, in the research conducted by Simon (1955) and subsequently by Gigerenzer (2002).

1.1.1.4. Uncertainty and risk and the state of economies

Another area of research on uncertainty and risk in economics is their role in the shaping of real economic life in the macroeconomic dimension, and thus an analysis of their impact on the functioning of national economies. There is a strong trend which makes economic successes dependent on the extent to which state authorities are aware of the substantial influence of uncertainty and risk on the growth of the welfare of modern societies (Williams et al., 2002). According to Drucker (1968; 1993), the ability of societies to cope with problems resulting from states of uncertainty can be treated as a criterion distinguishing between developed and developing countries because skilful control of unforeseeable events and elimination of their negative consequences is a confirmation of effective use of economic potential. According to this author, uncertainty is inextricably linked to macroeconomic phenomena, affecting the continuity of the world economy and technology, economic policy, the development of particular industries and society as a whole.

Uncertainty and risk are also objects of research in evolutionary economics. Among others, Nelson and Winter (1982; 2002) carried out cognitive and structural analyses of the foundations of technological innovations, using risk as one of their determinants.

1.1.1.5. Towards holistic and applied research on uncertainty and risk

However, the economic theories presented above analyse uncertainty and risk fragmentarily. This means that, in each case, uncertainty and risk are included in chains of cause-and-effect relationships confirming the validity of a given theory, but are not implemented at the level of fundamental economic laws and mechanisms. Research on uncertainty and risk resulting in the formulation of models and holistic economic theories was developed at the end of the 20th century and confirmed the need for an interdisciplinary approach to their analysis (Klimczak, 2008). The importance of the ability to analyse, assess and control risk in business from an economic point of view is nowadays emphasized in research, which is the most often a continuation, development or current commentary to the primary theories (Taylor, 2003; Toma et al., 2012).

Extensive connections can also be seen between uncertainty and risk on the one side and institutional economics and entrepreneurship on the other. Indeed, uncertainty in the economic space has a direct link to institutional asymmetry, and institutional solutions are key to supporting entrepreneurship, which is inherently risky, including in terms of the profitability or unprofitability of undertakings (Hall and Woodward, 2010) at the micro level for enterprises and at the macro level for entrepreneurial economies (Williams et al., 2017). According to Schumpeter (1934), entrepreneurship constitutes a fundamental phenomenon of economic development. Kanbur (1980) also analyzed relationships between entrepreneurship and risk-taking. On the other hand, commenting on such an approach to entrepreneurship, Baumol (2010) adds that entrepreneurship is conditioned by an individual approach of an economic entity to risk-taking.

The economic dimension of research on uncertainty and risk also concerns the impact of uncertainty on enterprises' investing (Dixit and Pindyck, 1994) and thus on their growth (Lensink et al., 2005), as well as the impact of risk on innovation (Bowers and Khorakian, 2014), which is the subject of research on innovation economics.

1.1.1.6. Research on uncertainty and risk in financial theory

Risk and uncertainty are also an important subject of financial research. Professional analysis of processes related to the measurement and control of business risk started to appear in the mid-20th century. Research conducted, among others, by Galton allowed the creation of instruments which are still used nowadays in risk assessment and monitoring processes, mainly in the theory of financial risk (Kaczmarek, 2010). This theory was developed as a result of treating uncertainty and risk as conditions determining the functioning of companies. However, the direct cause of the development of the financial risk theory was the recognition of the relationship between the occurrence of risk and the formation of income, the generation of profits and the recording of financial losses. As a result, uncertainty and risk became the drivers of a number of financial analysis concepts.

One of the foundations of financial theory is the concept of probabilistic risk (Miller and Modigliani, 1958), which identifies uncertainty with objective risk. This concept was mainly applied to large enterprises with the capacity to process more data than small entities and to use advanced decision-making support methods and tools with a view to reducing the occurrence of risk.

The issues of risk and uncertainty explored from the perspective of financial analysis also contributed to research into developing risk measures to make enterprises' financial decisions more transparent. The result of this work was, among others, the Markowitz (1952) portfolio theory. He proposed the first fully mature measure of financial risk and a research programme called *modern portfolio theory* which established a new direction in the perception of risk in financial markets.

As a result of the work on *modern portfolio theory*, a catalogue of risk measuring and forecasting methods was developed to create financial instrument valuation models dedicated to financial institutions and supervisory bodies. Portfolio theory also constituted a basis for the development of the concept of knowledge of the distribution of future wealth which considered the standard deviation of expected future wealth as a measure of risk (Sharpe, 1964). A particular type of risk measure, developed over the years to enable multidimensional characterization of a company's financial position and to simplify the risk assessment process, is financial ratios such as financial liquidity, debt, profitability, management efficiency and market value. Along with the development of research on risk and uncertainty measures, the subject of research was simultaneously the shortcomings and disadvantages of these measures mainly created on the basis of statistical tools only. In response to the identified weaknesses, the most satisfactory risk measures were sought, from not only a financial, but also a strategic or management perspective. Among other things, the theory of multi-variable alternative characterization of risk increase was developed in such a way as to obtain comparable results in different situations (Rothschild and Stiglitz, 1970; 1971).

In the 1970s uncertainty and the resulting limited decision-making rationality became the subject of research in financial theory. An analysis of the impact of various decision-making factors on mutual relations among creditors, shareholders and corporate management bodies, taking into account the phenomenon of incomplete information, resulted in the formulation of agency cost theory by Jensen and Meckling (1976). According to these authors, incomplete access to information prevents effective valuation of companies' assets, i.e. it has exactly the same effect as the occurrence of uncertainty in conducting business activities. The agency cost theory also identified ways of reducing uncertainty by obtaining additional information, which involves additional costs called monitoring and control costs. It was subsequently applied in the contract theory and adapted in the new institutional economics theory represented by Williamson (1998; 2002). The theory of new institutional economics was derived from the earlier transaction cost theory, which had added an analysis of the costs of using a price system to the neoclassical theory (Coase, 1937). The assumptions of the new institutional economics were also related to uncertainty resulting from incomplete access to information and limiting the rationality of individuals, but in the context of financial and non-financial methods of solving conflicts of interest in the contract performance process.

Research on risk was and is also being conducted with the aim of identifying causes of crises. A breakthrough in the study of relations between risk and financial crises was *Madness, panic, crash: History of financial crises* by Kindleberger (1999), in which the author points to the irrationality of market participants and the resulting uncertainty of market behaviours as factors triggering crisis mechanisms. Moreover, on the basis of the analysis of major economic crises, starting from 1618, he identified risk factors causing the escalation of a crisis and its rapid spread on an international and even global scale. Research on the risk of financial crises was intensified after the global crisis in early 2007. Among other things, new possibilities for measuring and analyzing risk were recognized, enabling earlier preparation, mainly of financial institutions, for the possible effects of a forecast collapse (Claessens et al., 2009).

Uncertainty and risk identified in the activities of individuals, businesses, societies and national economies became motivators for singling insurance out as a sub-discipline within finance. The emergence of insurance is a consequence of the identification of uncertainty and risk as key determinants of economic decisions. The development of insurance was parallel to the development of entrepreneurship, which was originally recognized as efforts aimed at overcoming uncertainty in the economic space (Diebold et al., 2010). In research on uncertainty and risk in the context of insurance, emphasis was placed on risk control and management in processes that can reduce the negative consequences of risk materialization. Planned risk management increases benefits and provides the opportunity to insure against those risks that can be predicted to occur by estimating probability. Thus, research on insurance focused on risk that could be easily measured (Williams et al., 2002). However, it should be noted that, despite the existence of scientific research on measurable risk in the context of insurance activity, the first contracts of this type were generally not based on a quantitative assessment of risk in the probabilistic sense (Masci, 2011). Johann Heinrich von Thünen (1910) was the first economist to draw attention to the possibility of calculating and insuring business risk. The author also pointed out that there are business decisions with unpredictable results that are uninsurable. However, it is precisely thanks to decisions with unpredictable consequences that entrepreneurs are able to generate significantly higher profits, i.e. receive a risk premium. Thanks to the development of insurance activity, from the first small institutions to modern insurance companies, the uncertainty of the world of economy and business and the resulting extensive catalogue of risks contributed to the development of risk measurement methods using quantitative tools. The most common quantitative tools include those derived from the exact sciences, mainly statistical measures and the probability calculus. While the measurement of measurable risks did not raise any doubts among researchers, over time attempts were being made to predict, at least theoretically, nonmeasurable risks, i.e. those subject to uncertainty. To this end, researchers started to use a number of optimization criteria determining decision-making functions. They include criteria proposed by Laplace, Wald, Savage, Bayes and Hurwicz (Williams et al., 2002). The subjects of research on risk in the context of insurance also included the issues of rational purchase of forms of insurance cover (Mossin, 1968) and shaping of optimal terms and conditions of insurance contracts depending on the nature and scale of the identified risk (Raviv, 1979).

Uncertainty and risk are also the subjects of research in banking. Events that may have a negative impact on the position of banks and their development prospects, as well as the increasing probability of the occurrence of such events resulted in the necessity to prepare a detailed categorization of banking risk and to develop effective methods of its prevention, estimation, measurement and evaluation (Iwanicz-Drozdowska, 2018). Banking risk issues are also widely linked to financial crisis mechanisms. The risk factors that cause significant instability in key financial institutions can be referred to as destabilizing factors. Furthermore, research covers the sensitivity and vulnerability of banking systems to crisis-related risks as well as the impact of banking crises on economic growth, financial stability indicators and inflation (Apătăchioae, 2014).

1.1.2. Uncertainty and risk from a psychological and sociological perspective

Uncertainty and risk are also the subjects of research in psychology and sociology. They appear in research on psychological and sociological determinants of risk-taking, behaviours in situations involving uncertainty and the influence of risk factors on the behaviour of individuals (the psychological aspect) and societies (the sociological aspect).

1.1.2.1. Uncertainty and risk in psychology

The main theory related to the behavioural perspective of uncertainty is the psychological theory of decision-making, which indicates the mind of the decision-maker, or the manager in the case of an economic entity, as the source of uncertainty (Nosal, 2001; Kozielecki, 2004). The scientific basis for the psychological decision-making theory in conditions of uncertainty and risk is the prospect theory (Kahneman and Tversky, 1979). As far as the issue of making decisions in conditions of risk is concerned, the prospect theory contradicts the theory of expected utility. The prospect theory assumes that risky decisions are made on the basis of subjective decision weights (characterized by overestimating low probabilities of risk occurrence and underestimating high ones) and the values of profit and loss measures (indicating the degree of satisfaction felt by decision-makers in taking risk compared to the initial state). Kahneman and Tversky (1992) developed the prospect theory into the cumulative prospect theory creating a model of decision-makers' attitude towards risk. The model indicates that risk-taking is conditioned by individual tendencies and preferences to bear it. This theory was also applied in further research aimed at explaining mental pathways in choice-making processes, for example in the model of buyers' mental accounting (Thaler, 1999).

The psychological aspect of risk continued to appear in research concerning, among other things, preference for risk bearing in the current of the so-called psychometric paradigm using psychophysical scaling techniques and multidimensional analytical techniques for creating attitudes towards risk, as well as explaining the perception of risk (Fischhoff et al., 1978; Fischhoff et al., 1981; Slovic et al., 1982). Analyses also covered propensity to take risk depending on expected benefits or losses (Edwards, 1961; Wilson et al., 1987; Barbosa et al., 2007) as well as so-called decision-making subjectivism and subjective risk (Jonas et al., 2001; Slovic, 2001; Gospodarek, 2012). The psychological research approach to uncertainty and risk also shows links to the theory of choice and the question of rationality of choices. The subjects of analysis in this area include the voluntary character of choices and mental habits in the processes of risky or uncertain choices (Gliszczyńska, 1979; Aarts et al., 2006) and the multifacetedness of the psychological background of risk and rationality of choices (Vlek and Stallen, 1980; Kiev, 2016).

Psychological factors determine certain attitudes towards risk (Elliott and Archibald, 1989). Attitudes towards risk include aversion, neutrality, propensity, avoidance, withholding. An individual's attitude towards risk determines their behaviour, investment decisions, actions taken in conditions of instability or crisis, or willingness to purchase insurance cover (Wärneryd, 1996).

Risk as a determinant of psychological conditions for decision-making became a subject of interest in economic psychology. The application of psychological theories provides a basis for understanding economic decisions that are inevitably connected with risk (Zaleśkiewicz, 2012), as well as consumer decisions (Falkowski and Tyszka, 2009). The approach to risk from the point of view of social psychology is particularly important in conditions characterized by complexity and instability (Kossowska et al., 2018).

At present, with regard to the negative consequences of uncertainty and risk, research on the borderline between psychology and sociology is dominated by the social cognition approach aimed at explaining the conditions for making decisions concerning the social world and the rationality of behaviour, including economic behaviour, of individuals in the face of growing threats (Frith and Blakemore, 2006). The socio-cognitive perspective of economic behaviours allows one to discover psychological mechanisms that shape the ways of interpreting risky situations (Crusius et al., 2012). In the social cognition approach, an important research area is the issue of psycho-social risk and safety management (Guadix et al., 2015) in response to growing psycho-social risks in the broadly understood business sphere, including employment reduction and work intensification (Langenhan et al., 2013).

The importance of the psychological dimension of decision-making in conditions of uncertainty and risk as well as the rationality of choices has become so important for organizations that risk psychology (Slovic, 2001) can be considered a permanent subject of research in the areas of modern management, particularly psychology in management or psychological risk management. The topic of risk psychology in relation to management is also linked to occupational health and safety, business ethics and social responsibility (Leka and Cox, 2008; Jain et al., 2011).

1.1.2.2. Uncertainty and risk in sociology

Uncertainty and risk became the subject of sociological research relatively late. It was only the emergence of intensified climate threats, financial crises or terrorism on an international scale that triggered the need to investigate their causes in the social field. Works by Beck are considered to be pioneering contributions to research on risk in the sociological context. This researcher conducted a discourse on a distinction between measurable risk and its social awareness and explained the blurring of boundaries between the industrial society and the risk society (Beck, 1987; 2002). The author also recognized the need to take into account globalization processes in the analysis of growing social uncertainty, changing basic terminology in his later works: the previously defined risk society became the world risk society (Beck, 2012). The author noted that the progressing globalization of social and economic processes did not remain neutral to the nature of risk occurring in the environment of individuals and organizations.

The area of interest of sociologists remains far removed from the measurable calculation of risk or the rationalization of the perspective of decision-makers. Therefore, research in this area is linked, among other things, to the theory of action and the systematization of risk in sociology. The main subjects of research have therefore become: the analysis of the social approach to uncertainty, the theory of a sense of decreasing security in the modern society (and the analysis of the impact of this phenomenon on the social perception of risk), as well as the analysis of the causes of social conflicts as the main risks concerning intra-social integration (Kaczmarek, 2003). The culturalist concept of risk (otherwise referred to as constructivist), which treats risk as a certain social construct, also derives from sociology (Douglas and Wildavsky, 1982). Although chronologically this concept was developed earlier than the publication of Beck's first works, it was only critics of his theory who became more interested in the constructivist approach to risk (Krohn and Krücken, 1993). The culturalist concept of risk involves the spread of risk culture as a relatively new concept in the area of organizational management. A low level or absence of risk culture is indicated as one of the major causes of spectacular collapses of business entities during the global crisis of 2008 (Korombel, 2013).

Beck's work initiated further research in the current known as the sociology of uncertainty and risk. In this perspective, future identifiable states of risk are considered in three different ways (Zinn, 2009) as: the effects of the risk of making irrational social decisions, the effects of calculating-probabilistic risk, and part of the contemporary worldview. The sociology of uncertainty and risk also allows one to consider them from the cultural (Douglas, 1992), political (Dean, 1999) and systemic (Luhmann, 1993) points of view. Furthermore, theoretical reflections on the role of risk in the shaping of social change became a foundation for empirical research on the perception and management of disasters, decisions affecting the general public, social regulations, the voluntary character of risk-taking at the level of national economies and behaviours towards the essentially uncertain future (Zinn, 2009).

Many authors (e.g. Latour, 1993; Eisenstadt, 2000) point to the development of modernity as the cause of a new quality and structure of social risk. Social risk is indicated as the direct cause of intensifying socio-cultural inequalities (Bourdieu, 1979). Power (2004) argues that social problems are the result of too much focus on the prevention of immediate foreseeable risks and the simultaneous neglect of the main responsibilities to society, i.e. social work, health care, crime prevention.

According to the theory of social risk, risk should be considered in a flexible manner going beyond generally accepted standards and the probability calculus. The real social world cannot be transformed into an artificial world of measurable risk factors (Hacking, 1991) because in addition to predictable and measurable social risk areas, there is a systematic increase in uncontrolled areas that are the source of a significant proportion of social problems (Power, 2004). Much earlier similar conclusions were reached by Weber (1948), an eminent sociologist, who noted that the rationality of people as representatives of society in shaping the worldview cannot be conditioned only by mathematical estimations because the sources of social threats are so extensive that they cannot be put into any measurable framework. Therefore, in principle there is no basis for estimating the probability of events.

In the sociological approach, risk is also related to theories considered in other areas of science, e.g. the choice theory and the decision theory. In this area, the impact of social learning on decision-making and choices in conditions of uncertainty is analyzed (Bursztyn et al., 2014; Lahno and Serra-Garcia, 2015). Another theory referring to risk and uncertainty is the social justice theory (Rawls, 1971). It is used to analyse aspects of social injustice and justice in terms of risk allocation (Cettolin and Riedl, 2016).

1.2. The understanding of uncertainty and risk in management

In view of the fact that uncertainty and risk play an important role in the development of many fields and disciplines of science, they are interdisciplinary concepts. The proper understanding, analysis and interpretation of uncertainty and risk, both theoretically and practically, are determinants of effective management (Tchankova, 2002). Uncertainty and risk are treated as two of the key determinants of the activity of enterprises, regardless of their size or activity profile, and therefore they should be analyzed in a multidimensional manner in the context of management. Also, the research area of management sciences, which constitutes the theoretical basis for the implementation of management practices in various types of organizations, bears the hallmarks of interdisciplinarity. Therefore, management sciences are most often understood as the cumulative value of all areas of an organization's activity, where numerous disciplines interweave (Czakon and Komańda, 2011; van Baalen and Karsten, 2012). Due to the factors presented above justifying the interdisciplinary character of management, the concepts of uncertainty and risk are defined separately in many areas of science.

1.2.1. The defining of uncertainty

Uncertainty is usually treated as a concept with a broader substantive scope than risk. Our review of the major definitions of uncertainty based on the types of identified methodological approaches is presented in Table 1.1.

Table 1.1 Approaches to defining uncertainty

Approach to defining	*Definitions*
With respect to the causes of occurrence	Metacognitive awareness of ignorance of the source of knowledge about a given phenomenon (Smithson, 1999) Lack of complete information on future events (Krickx, 2000) A situation in which decision-makers have limited knowledge to accurately describe the results of future events (Carbonara and Caiazza, 2010)
With respect to the possibility of assessing probability	The possibility of event occurrence presented by means of a cause-and-effect chain of reasoning, characterized by the impossibility of estimating the probability of such occurrence (van der Heijden, 2000) Events about which no reliable data can be obtained and for which the likelihood of occurrence cannot be estimated (Holton, 2004) Inevitable unpredictability of the future due to unpredictable factors expressed by means of classical probabilities (Spiegelhalter, 2017)
With respect to the role in the decision-making process	Cognitive limitations (ontological uncertainty) and incomplete knowledge (epistemological uncertainty) in the market decision-making process (Schumpeter, 1934) Incompleteness of information in the decision-making process (dispersion of knowledge) (von Hayek, 1945)
With respect to forecast consequences	Possibility of the occurrence of a potentially harmful event (Freeston et al., 1994) Possibility of the occurrence of a negative event (Dugas et al., 2001) Possibility of the occurrence of unforeseeable negative events (Carleton et al., 2010)

As can be seen from Table 1.1, uncertainty is the most often equated with events characterized by unpredictability, with negative consequences being the most frequently expected results. Context-sensitive proposals can also be found among the definitions examined, for example with respect to decision-making processes or available knowledge resources, which results in the lack of an unambiguous definition of uncertainty within the context of management.

Uncertainty is also quite often used when defining risk, as a concept with a narrower scope, a higher level of concretization and a more real character.

1.2.2. The defining of risk

Risk in itself is regarded as a universal concept, applicable in both science and all dimensions of business life: economic, social and political (Śliwiński, 2002). Similarly to the case of uncertainty, the ways in which risk is defined in the scientific literature are characterized by great diversity, which can be justified by the number and diversity of scientific disciplines on the basis of which risk is interpreted and attempts at its operationalization are made (Spekman and Davis, 2004; Elahi, 2013). With regard to management sciences, it is possible to indicate attempts to define risk both conceptually and in the area of sub-disciplines of management science, such as quality management, strategic management or risk management – a sub-discipline directly dedicated to the role of risk in business management (Kaczmarek, 2006).

The results of the conducted review of the major definitions of risk, including approaches to risk definition, are presented in Table 1.2.

The review of the definitions of risk included in Table 1.2 reflects and confirms the different understandings of this concept. A chronological analysis of the emerging definitions also indicates that over time there occurred a significant shift in the understanding of the concept, from a narrow approach identifying risk most often with the probability of the occurrence of negative events, to a broad approach emphasizing a catalogue of the real consequences of risk materialization.

1.2.3. Differences between uncertainty and risk

The analysis of the definitions of uncertainty and risk allows one to conclude that due to many common elements (Pablo, 1999) there is a strong relationship of meaning between these concepts, but they are not identical (Jedynak and Bąk, 2020). This is evidenced by the definitions of uncertainty and risk formulated by the same authors by way of demonstrating significant differences between them. On this basis, it is possible to identify their distinguishing criteria (Table 1.3).

The analysis of the definitions of uncertainty and risk compiled on a contrasting basis (Table 1.3) allowed the development of a catalogue of criteria that clearly distinguish between the two concepts in terms of meaning. On the basis of these criteria, it is therefore possible to define uncertainty as a nonmeasurable, subjective, unpredictable, irrational and uninsurable cause of risk, of a negative or neutral nature. Risk, on the other hand, is a relatively measurable, objective, predictable (estimable), rational and (partially) insurable result of uncertainty of a negative or positive nature.

1.2.4. Perception of uncertainty and risk in management

Risk in management is usually perceived in the organizational dimension. This perception refers to management at every level of an organizational structure, in terms of allocating responsibility for risk management (DeLoach, 2004), as well as management processes, in terms of allowing leaders to identify and track threat signals (Calandro, 2015).

Due to the scale and intensity of negative (financial, functional, personal) effects they may cause, uncertainty and risk are also understood in management as factors determining the conditions for making economic decisions, including managerial ones, differentiated with respect to the range of information available

Table 1.2 Approaches to defining risk

Approach to defining	*Definitions*
With respect to the source of occurrence	A situation where at least one of its constituent elements is unknown, but the probability of its occurrence is known (Pasieczny, 1981) The threat of failure to achieve planned profit due to possessing incomplete information (Holscher, 1987) A situation where, in conditions of incomplete information, decisions made are not optimal in terms of the objective pursued (Kreim, 1988) A situation or event where material or human value is endangered and whose outcome is uncertain (Rosa, 1998)
With respect to the possibility of achieving established objectives	Uncertainty about a specific event under the conditions of two or more possibilities. This is a measurable uncertainty as to whether the intended objective of the action will be achieved (American Risk and Insurance Association, 1966) The threat of failure to achieve the intended objective (Gruszka and Zawadzka, 1992) The threat of failure to achieve the intended objective or incurring losses (Sierpińska and Jachna, 1993) Uncertainty about the occurrence of deviations from the intended results (Johanning, 1999) Probability that the process results will not meet expectations (Knechel, 2002) The threat of failure of undertaken actions (Damodran, 2002) Uncertainty about future results (Doerig, 2003) The degree of variability or uncertainty about achieving the intended economic or organizational result (Stabryła, 2006) The degree of uncertainty about the achievement of the organization's objectives (ISO Guide 73 …, 2009) Impact (expressed in terms of deviation from the intended state) of uncertainties on objectives (which may have different aspects and categories, and can be applied at different levels of management) (ISO 31000 …, 2018)
With respect to the role in the decision-making process	One of the conditions for making managerial decisions requiring the ability to determine the probability of the expected effects of decisions made (Raiffa and Luce, 1957) Uncertainty about the future events or results of decisions made (Sinkey Jr, 1992) Possibility of the occurrence of deviations in the factual results of made decisions from the intended results (Buschgen, 1997) A factor whose evaluation and minimization are a key condition for effective strategic management (Urbanowska-Sojkin, 2013)

(*Continued*)

Table 1.2 (Continued) Approaches to defining risk

Approach to defining	*Definitions*
With respect to expected results	The possibility of failure, in particular the occurrence of independent events which are unforeseeable and unpreventable, and which may render undertaken actions ineffective, unfavourable and uneconomical by reducing utility or increasing expenditures (Zieleniewski and Szczypiorski, 1963)
	The uncertainty of loss is treated as a mainly psychological phenomenon that is important in people's relationships and experiences (Denenberg, 1964)
	The measure of the probability and seriousness of adverse consequences of an event (Lawrence, 1976)
	The product of the occurrence probability and severity of the effects of an event (Wilson and Crouch, 1982)
	The combination of the result, probability, significance, cause-and-effect scenario of an event and the affected population (Kumamoto and Henley, 1996)
	A deviation from the expected income level (Gardner and Mills, 1988)
	The possibility of incurring damage or loss (Kendall, 1998)
	The possibility of the occurrence of events or adverse trends resulting in future losses or fluctuations in future income levels (Marshall, 2001)
	Anticipated damage resulting from the occurrence of an event (Campbell, 2005)
	A threat of incurring a quantifiable loss (Buła, 2003)
	Uncertainty about the occurrence of a loss (Regda, 2007)
	The uncertainty and severity of events and their consequences in terms of value (Aven and Renn, 2009)
With respect to the possibility of value estimation	The variation of the rate of return from investments on the capital market (Markowitz, 1959)
	Changeability measured by the standard deviation of net cash flows generated by a given undertaking (Uyemura and Deventer, 1993)
	A situation in which results are likely to be better or worse than expected, provided that the distribution of the probability of deviations of these results from their expected value is also known (Marsh, 1995)

to a decision-maker or a group of decision-makers in a given situation (Ugur, 2005). Thus, it is possible to distinguish decision-making (Harrison, 1977):

- under the conditions of certainty (very rare in the case of business decisions),
- under the conditions of risk (the manager has information allowing them to forecast the effects of the available choice options, but these are uncertain effects that are more or less likely to occur),

Table 1.3 A catalogue of criteria to distinguish between uncertainty and risk

Author	*Understanding of uncertainty*	*Understanding of risk*	*Distinguishing criterion between uncertainty (U) and risk (R)*
Willet (1901)	Subjective feeling about the occurrence of an undesirable event	Objectivized uncertainty about the occurrence of an undesirable event	U – subjectivism R – objectivism
Knight (1921)	Nonmeasurable events of a qualitative nature, often with positive consequences (uncertainty of profit)	Uncertainty expressed in a measurable manner and concerning adverse events (risk of loss)	U – nonmeasurability R – measurability
Keynes (1921)	The possibility of the occurrence of events whose probability cannot be precisely determined	The possibility of the occurrence of events with a predictable probability	U – nonmeasurability, unpredictability R – measurability, predictability
Pfeffer (1956)	A combination of gambling measured by the degree of conviction, a state of mind	A combination of gambling measured by probability, a state of the real world	
Lange (1967)	A case that cannot be examined using the probability calculus	A case that can be examined using the probability calculus	
Arrow (1971)	The irrationality of the state of the world	One of the rational dimensions of uncertainty (subjective uncertainty)	U – irrationality R – rationality
Jedynak and Szydło (1997)	A source of risk, a universal and complex phenomenon of a negative or neutral nature	A frequent and dynamic phenomenon (related to human activity) of a negative or positive nature (profits or losses)	U – negative or neutral nature R – negative or positive nature
Snowdon et al. (1998)	A situation whose probability cannot be quantified (measured), uninsurable, open to potential unexpected events	A characteristic feature of a situation whose probability is known, can be quantified (measured), is insurable, complete and closed	U – nonmeasurability, uninsurability R – measurability, insurability
Williams et al. (2002)	A nonmeasurable aspect of subjective risk	Measurable and objective uncertainty	U – nonmeasurability, subjectivism R – measurability, objectivism
Bodie and Merton (2003)	A necessary but insufficient condition for risk to arise (cause of risk)	The result of uncertainty (uncertainty affecting the well-being of the persons concerned)	U – cause of risk R – effect of uncertainty

- under the conditions of uncertainty (the manager usually does not have information allowing them to forecast the effects of the available choice options, and if they have such information, it is not possible to estimate the degree of the probability of their occurrence, so the effects of decisions made under such conditions are usually unforeseeable),
- under the conditions of extreme uncertainty (mainly during crises, the manager has no way of predicting the outcome of their decisions).

Since the alleged objective of the sub-discipline of management dedicated to risk is to provide decision-makers with a theoretical and practical basis for systematically coordinating the process of managing identified risks and dealing with inherent uncertainty (Williams et al., 2006), the making of business decisions under the conditions of uncertainty or risk is permanently embedded in the competence areas of managers, regardless of the industry or size of a business entity. Taking into account the basic catalogue of managerial tasks (Nogalski and Śniadecki, 2001), including team management, decision-making, continuous improvement and adjustment of the organization to changes in the environment, the risk management function seems to be dedicated to the fulfilment of the last of these tasks, i.e. the adaptation of the entity to dynamic changes in the near and more distant environment.

Furthermore, risk is taken into account in all dimensions of management: strategic, tactical and operational. Besides its perception in the context of different types of threats to conducted business activities, the understanding of the concept of risk in relation to management clearly outlines its importance in the following two contexts: the shaping organizational objectives and managerial attitudes, as well as conditions under which business decisions are made.

The perception of risk can significantly influence the formulation and pursuit of organizational objectives adopted in the management process. A proper approach to risk allows the enterprise to define threats to its activities in an autonomous and adequate manner as well as to manage them optimally (Sargeant and Jen, 2016). The perception of risk also supports the process of shaping attitudes to specific threats appropriate to a given situation (Ulbert and Csanaky, 2004), which translates into managerial attitudes and decisions determining the process of effective risk management. Risk management is currently an obligatory managerial function. Moreover, thanks to a skilful adaptation of risk management in various areas of the organization's activity, it is possible to maintain a balance between rationality in taking risky actions and subjectivity in terms of their perception (Hámori, 2003). It is also easier to properly assess the sources of risk, especially their reversibility/irreversibility, to assess the consequences of their materialization and to make decisions concerning voluntary or obligatory compensation for such consequences (Kasperson et al., 1988).

1.3. Trends in the development of enterprise risk

In parallel with the development of management sciences, the specific character of risks identified in business organizations was changing. The basis for the various enterprise risk typologies which have developed over the years is sources of risk. Sources of risk can be found in the business environment, particularly in its physical, social, political, operational, economic and legal dimensions (Tchankova, 2002). The most important types of risks that directly affect the core business of enterprises, distinguished on the basis of a field criterion, include: financial risk, production risk, organizational risk, personnel risk, logistical risk, investment risk, regulatory risk, political risk, technological risk, marketing risk, reputational risk and business risk.

1.3.1. *Business risk*

Business risk is the type of risk that very early on began to determine business activities of enterprises. This concept appeared in scientific texts as early as the second decade of the 20th century. In a text by Reed (1916), weather conditions were seen as a business risk for production activities on agricultural farms in the USA. Later in the 1960s business risk began to appear in analyses of the psychological approach to management. What researchers were looking for at that time was psychological factors conditioning the taking of business risk (Phelan et al., 1961). In scientific literature, the formal separation of business risk as one of the categories of risk faced by enterprises took place in relation to financial activities. At that time, business risk occurred as an inherent component of investment risk, related to production conditions, but independent of the method of financing enterprise resources (Mayer, 1965). Thus, the category of business risk and the beginnings of the awareness of its importance in the activities of enterprises are the result of the dynamic volatility of the economic environment, which shed new light on the issue of risk management in business. The approach to business risk became one of the determinants of an enterprise's survival on the market, regardless of the represented industry (Kot and Dragon, 2015). Business risk is closely related to macroeconomic risk factors (including political risk), most often having a strategic dimension.

1.3.2. *Financial risk*

Another important type of risk in the activities of enterprises is financial risk. Although the idea of financial risk, and thus the first scientific texts using this term, dates back to the 1920s (Foster and Catchings, 1925), the origins of its fundamental conceptualization could only be seen in the 1950s, when Miller, Modigliani and Markowitz published their groundbreaking works. The dynamic development of the theory of financial risk and its measures lasted until the 1990s, which witnessed the first crisis manifesting itself in mass bankruptcies of significant entities, despite the use of hedging tools in financial management (e.g. the British Barings bank or the Long-Term Capital Management hedging fund established, among others, by the aforementioned Nobel Prize Laureates Myron and Scholes) (Bouchaud and Potters, 2000; Flood, 2012). These events caused a decline in confidence in the financial risk theory. They were followed by a period of transition whose hallmark was *The Black Swan* by Taleb (2007), in which the author defined and explained the causes of financial market events characterized by great impact and simultaneously the impossibility of estimating the probability of their occurrence. The period ended in 2007 with another, this time catastrophic, collapse in the form of the global financial and banking crisis that forced enterprises to reorganize their internal financial systems (Toarna and Cojanu, 2015).

1.3.3. Technological risk

Technological risk is also of no small importance in the activities of enterprises. The very concept of technological risk has been present in economic literature since the 1940s. The first text comes from 1941 and concerns a theory of production in conditions of technological risk (Tintner, 1941). In the era of dynamic technological progress manifesting itself, among other things, in production mechanization and innovation, changes in production potential, shortened production cycles (Çalışkan, 2015), IT and information technology development (Teymouri and Ashoori, 2011), knowledge and technology transfer in R&D (Akcali and Sismanoglu, 2015), the development of artificial intelligence and the application of technological solutions in management processes (Phillips-Wren and Jain, 2006), enterprises in all sectors of the economy face the challenge of coping with new threats related to uneven economic development and intensifying competition (Firszt, 2014). A characteristic subcategory of technological risk is cyber risk. The first means of protection against cyber risk were already available in the 1970s and the 1980s, but only for major financial institutions and blue-chip companies. This type of risk started to play a more significant role in the activities of average enterprises in the 1990s, in parallel to the intensive development of the internet. Threats resulting from conducting business activities in cyberspace may cause serious losses, starting from interruptions in business activities and consequent additional costs, through the potential possibilities of disclosing confidential information or personal data and the consequences of non-compliance with legal regulations, and ending at the loss of reputation and the necessity of implementing technologically advanced and expensive protections against cybercrime, including additional costs of insurance (Camillo, 2017). Cyber risk takes a particular form in financial sector enterprises (mainly banks), where the provision of services through electronic channels (e-banking), besides generating many new threats, forces enterprises to reorganize themselves and to adjust their functioning systems to the requirements of risk management (Bąk, 2017).

1.3.4. Investment risk

The 1920s witnessed the beginning of the rapid development of stock exchanges. At that time, loans secured by shares became commonplace among companies. However, the first individual markets of this type had been established a little bit earlier, in the period of industrialization (e.g. the New York Stock Exchange in

1792 and the London Stock Exchange in 1773). The world's stock trading institutions achieved the peak of their growth in the 1960s. It was then that threats related to stock exchange trading started to be identified as a new category of risk, i.e. investment risk. The first publication on this risk category dates back to 1953 (Bagley, 1953). New opportunities to make profits outside the core business, in the form of investments in securities, in a way forced enterprises to include the new form of risk in the catalogue of identified risks in order to minimize the possibility of financial losses. In fact, investment risk constitutes a danger that the actual rate of return on stock investments may differ from the expected rate of return, which may be caused by fortuitous factors such as fluctuations in stock exchange quotations (Fleckner, 2006; Fleckner and Hopt, 2013). Investment risk also includes macroeconomic risk factors (Grinols and Turnovsky, 1993).

1.3.5. Regulatory risk

With the development of stock markets, investing enterprises also had to meet the requirements of stock exchange rules and legal regulations, which resulted in the creation of strategies aimed at dealing with regulatory risk. The formalization of regulatory risk with respect to legal regulations applicable to business activities varies depending on structural, political and legislative changes in individual countries (United Nations Economic Commission for Europe, 2012). The first publication addressing the importance of regulatory risk in business activities was *Regulatory Risk, Investment and Welfare* (Woroch, 1988).

1.3.6. Marketing risk

Marketing risk is another category of risk playing an important role in determining the position, performance and competitive advantage of enterprises. According to Drucker, the first reasons for treating marketing as a universal corporate function could be seen in the events of the first half of the 19th century (Cohen, 2014). The beginnings of the development of research on the role of marketing risk in management are the works by Bauer (1960), who introduced the concept of risk into marketing literature, and Cox (1967). Marketing activities often determine an enterprise's competitive position. Jacoby and Kaplan (1972) and Roselius (1971) presented the first attempts at developing a holistic approach to marketing risk, focusing on identifying a catalogue of its negative consequences. The consequence of their work was the development of marketing risk analysis and assessment methods integrated with other functional areas and adapted to the conditions of the environment (Boutang and De Lara, 2016).

1.3.7. Political risk

The 1960s were a time of an increasing influence of political changes on the functioning of enterprises. Due to increasing political instability, a new type of risk, i.e. political risk (Usher, 1965), emerging in academic literature at that time became and continues to be a serious threat to and challenge for mainly foreign investments of enterprises. Since 1980, the impact of political risk on foreign direct investment flows has become so great that the processes of assessing this risk and seeking investor protection measures have become routine elements of managers' decision-making processes, mainly in manufacturing companies operating on a global scale (Jodice, 1985; Sottilotta, 2013). As a result of the wide variety of definitions of political risks, there is a consensus in the scientific literature on the subject that a precise and uniform definition is rather difficult to formulate (Kobrin, 1979; Sottilotta, 2013) due to the fact that it is not an individual risk, but a set of related types of risk (Graham et al., 2016).

1.3.8. Personnel risk

Because of the high degree of influence of human resources on the functioning of an enterprise, personnel risk is analyzed as a separate category of risk. The first publication examining in detail the role of personnel risk is *Guide to Personal Risk Taking* (Byrd, 1978). Professional analyses of personnel risk and work on the development of its measuring methods started to be performed in parallel with the dynamic growth of research in the area of human resources management in the penultimate decade of the 20th century (Hussain and Ahmad, 2012; Neves and Eisenberger, 2014). Personnel risk is defined as the probability of a negative event occurring as a result of personal decisions and the scale of negative consequences of that event on the proper functioning of the enterprise (Lipka, 2002).

1.3.9. Production risk

Production risk is the type of risk that has accompanied business enterprises since the beginning of their production activities. It is related to the changing efficiency of production processes. Such changes may result from inadequate quality of raw and intermediate materials, equipment failures or human errors (Wrodarczyk, 2011). Despite the fact that problems related to the aforementioned causes were appearing simultaneously with the development of industrial production activities in the 19th century, it was only the period after World War II that witnessed a dramatic growth in a wide range of production activities. At that time, the awareness of the role of production risk in generating results was considerably raised, which resulted in a formalized approach to production risk and its initial categorization at the turn of the 1960s (Freeman and Louçã, 2001; Kumbhakar, 2002). In scientific literature, this concept began to appear in the early 1980s (Britto, 1980).

1.3.10. Logistical risk

Due to strict requirements concerning customer service, as well as increasing costs of capital, warehousing and transport, logistics management started to play a major role in the operations of enterprises (Ciesielski, 1999). Although not defined and not managed, logistical risk has accompanied manufacturing companies since the launch of sales processes. The importance of logistical risk in business management was analyzed in literature for the first time in 1980 (Wright, 1980). However, the professionalization of the approach to logistical risk and its comprehensive definition in management theory and practice were only a consequence of imposing more stringent logistical requirements on enterprises due to the dynamically progressing globalization process in the 1990s, which considerably facilitated international trade and contributed to the intensification of international cooperation in the form of supply chains (Finch, 2004; Chang et al., 2015).

1.3.11. Organizational risk

Business activities are also accompanied by organizational risk, initially equated with potential dangers resulting from errors in the harmonization of processes taking place in the enterprise, in the functioning of machinery and equipment as well as the resulting possibility of disturbances in the continuity of business operations (Bizon-Górecka, 2004). However, over time, the meaning of organizational risk as understood by enterprises was broadened to include risks related to employees (i.e. the aforementioned personnel risk), legal procedures and requirements, technical and logistical issues, as well as any irregularities in organizational and control processes taking place within the enterprise (Kaczmarek, 2010). This broadening of the scope of organizational risk took place during the intensive development of management methods and concepts in the 1970s (Penc, 2002). The first scientific publications analyzing this category of risk date back to the late 1980s (Morris, 1987).

1.3.12. Reputational risk

Another type of risk important in the activities of enterprises, and especially for their competitive position and ability to survive is reputational risk. Reputation is a multidimensional concept (Pineiro-Chousa et al., 2016) that can be a source of both direct reputational risk and indirect growth risk (Comeig et al., 2015). Despite enterprises' awareness of the sources of reputational risk, the formal identification of reputational risk factors and the implementation of professional forms of image protection began to appear in the second half of the 1990s. The first scientific publication on this topic focused on the need to include the new category of reputational risk in management (Goddard, 1998), while a significant increase in its use and its formal definitions formulated on the basis of management sciences were observed after a series of reputation scandals in international corporations (e.g. Enron, WorldCom, Tyco) at the beginning of the 21st century. Reputational risk results mainly from the interference of the mass media in the shaping of opinions about business organizations and the phenomenon of the widespread exchange of information in the business environment. Reputational risk lies in the gap between the socially expected and actual behaviour of an enterprise (Brady and Honey, 2007), and its existence is directly related to the development of technology (including social media) and ongoing globalization processes (Eckert, 2017). The degree of an enterprise's exposure to reputational risk is determined by (Eccles et al., 2007): the consistency/inconsistency of opinions about the enterprise's activities with the factual state of affairs, the external expectations of interest groups regarding the enterprise and the quality of intra-organizational management.

1.3.13. Global risk

The 1990s were a period of great acceleration in globalization processes. The liberalization of trade, the removal of barriers to the movement of capital and labour, the development of international organizations, the emergence of knowledge-based economies, and the increased complexity of the functioning of economic entities are just some of the factors determining the distinction of a new, multidisciplinary category of global risk that is important not only on a macro scale for national economies, but also on a micro scale for individual enterprises operating on international markets (Hossu et al., 2009; Marginean, 2015; Okoye and Nwaigwe, 2015). The very concept of global risk appeared in scientific literature in a publication summarizing the conclusions of the Forum on Global Change and Our Common Future (Mlot, 1989). The term "global risk" can be used to describe an uncertain event or condition that, if it occurs, could have a significant negative impact on several countries or sectors over the next ten years (World Economic Forum, 2017). Global risk is also a category of risk where dynamic changes can be observed due to transformations in the economic environment. Therefore, international organizations periodically provide economic operators with comprehensive information on the directions of these changes in the form of numerous analytical reports. Such reports include *The Global Risks Reports*, which are prepared annually by the World Economic Forum. Global risk constitutes an integrated set of economic, environmental, geopolitical, social and technological risks. Besides its considerable impact on individual enterprises (Gleason et al., 2006), it is also an important factor in enterprises' cooperation within international supply chains, strategic alliances or global networks (Christopher et al., 2011; Manuj and Mentzer, 2008; Tse et al., 2011). Furthermore, the impact of global risk on modern companies may have a number of consequences for management processes (Jedynak and Bąk, 2018):

- the large variety of types of global risk contributes to the complexity of functioning of modern businesses,
- the possibilities of measuring the scale of threats where different types of global risk coexist are limited, especially taking into account the analytical potential of individual enterprises,
- the level of uncertainty in the processes of measuring and assessing the impact of global risk justifies a flexible approach to management,

- management processes taking into consideration global risk should take place particularly at the level of strategy.

1.3.14. Strategic and operational risk

The way of categorizing risk on the basis of the time horizon criterion is also important in the activities of enterprises. Thanks to this, the literature on the subject distinguishes the following categories of risk: strategic risk related to an enterprise's long-term activities on the market, growth, development dynamics, achievement of long-term business goals (Gregorczyk, 2013) and operational risk related to ongoing operations involving internal procedures, systems or employees (Tedford and Hämmerle, 2008). Strategic risk was defined as a distinct type of risk relatively late, due to business organizations' excessive concentration on financial risk and risk resulting from changes in the economic environment. The concept of strategic risk in economic sciences began to function in the 1980s (Aivazian and Callen, 1983). With regard to management, however, it was analyzed and defined in a comprehensive manner by Porter (1987) as a risk of failure to achieve objectives arising from the company's strategy, and then by Frigo and Anderson (2011) as internal and external factors that could potentially jeopardize the achievement of objectives arising from a strategy. Meanwhile, operational risk, due to its significant role in corporate governance, began to appear in economic literature in the 1960s (Schwartz and Aronson, 1967). However, this category of risk was only defined and explained fully and uniformly by the Basel Committee on Banking Supervision for financial institutions in Basel II in 2004 and in a document clarifying the principles formulated at that time (Basel Committee on Banking Supervision, 2011).

1.3.15. Evolution of risk

The effect of mapping the pace and character of changes in risk formation is the positioning of the key types of business risk on a timeline (Figure 1.1). As it results from the above analyses, the tendencies in the development of risk over the indicated period determined the strategies and resulting objectives of enterprises, causing changes in the nature and priorities of their business activities in particular periods. Thus, Figure 1.1 is an attempt to graphically represent the trends in the development of business risk, with an indication of scientific publications that were the first to use the terms referring to particular types of risk.

As can be seen from the risk overview in Figure 1.1, the types of risk that are of key importance in the activities of enterprises started to appear and be identified in the second decade of the 20th century. Subsequently, the emergence of new categories of risk in scientific literature intensified in the 1950s and 1960s, when the achievements of the classical management theories caused the necessity to formulate a certain synthesis of previous deliberations, which in turn resulted

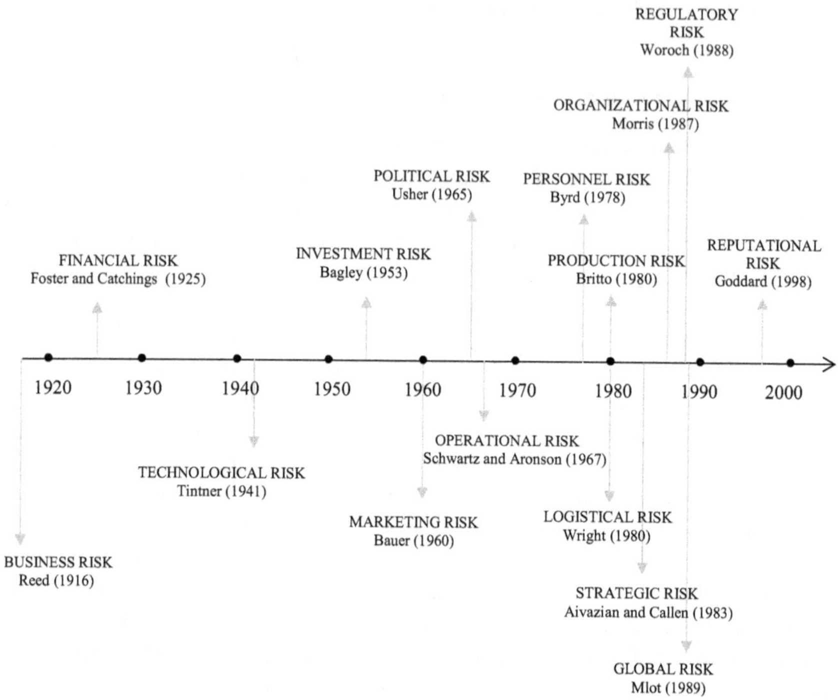

Figure 1.1 A chronological development of risks regarding business activities. Note: The publications were selected on the basis of a systematic review of the scientific literature available in the EBSCO and Web of Science databases.

in the emergence of the so-called integrating trends in management sciences, such as the systemic and situational approaches (Lachiewicz and Matejun, 2012).

1.4. Directions of research on uncertainty and risk indicated by Nobel Prize Laureates

Uncertainty and risk as concepts of an interdisciplinary nature are an important research area for scientists whose breakthrough achievements have been confirmed by the award of the Bank of Sweden Prize in Economic Sciences in memory of Alfred Nobel. An analysis of the award-winning achievements of all Laureates to date (1969–2020) shows that research on risk and uncertainty is conducted by them in many disciplines and sub-disciplines of economic sciences, including: macroeconomics, microeconomics, financial economics, econometrics, management sciences, general equilibrium theory, game theory, institutional economics, information economics, behavioural economics and international economics (Bąk, 2020). Table 1.4 presents a list of the Nobel Prize Laureates who carried out scientific research on risk and uncertainty and the disciplines of science represented by the awarded achievements.

Table 1.4 Nobel Prize Laureates in economic sciences conducting research on risk and uncertainty

Laureate	*Year*	*Scientific discipline of the awarded achievement*
MACROECONOMICS		
Friedrich von Hayek	1974	Theory of money and economic fluctuations and analysis of interdependence among economic, social and institutional phenomena
Milton Friedman	1976	Analysis of consumption, monetary history and theory and demonstration of complexity of stabilization policies
Franco Modigliani	1985	Analyses of saving and financial markets
Robert Lucas Jr	1995	Theory of reasonable expectations in macroeconomic analysis
Paul Romer, William Nordhaus	2018	Role of technological innovation and climate change in macroeconomic analysis
MICROECONOMICS		
Leonid Hurwicz, Eric S. Maskin, Roger B. Myerson	2007	Fundamentals of mechanism design theory
Paul R. Milgrom Robert B. Wilson	2020	Improving auction theory and inventing new auction formats that benefit sellers, buyers and taxpayers worldwide
FINANCIAL ECONOMICS		
James M. Buchanan Jr	1986	Theory of making political and economic decisions
Harry Markowitz, Merton Miller, William Sharpe	1990	Financial economics theory, mainly in the area of corporate finance, including contributions to the development of general financial asset valuation theory and portfolio theory
Robert Merton, Myron Scholes	1997	New methods for determining the value of derivatives
ECONOMETRICS		
Lawrence Klein	1980	Econometric models and their application to analysis of economic fluctuations and economic policies
MANAGEMENT SCIENCES		
Herbert Simon	1978	Decision-making processes in economic organizations
Elinor Ostrom	1990	Analysis of economic governance, especially the common good
Oliver E. Williamson		Analysis of management with respect to selection of economic operators
GENERAL EQUILIBRIUM THEORY		
Paul Samuelson	1970	Development of static and dynamic economic theory, analytical and methodological development in economic sciences

(*Continued*)

Table 1.4 (Continued) Nobel Prize Laureates in economic sciences conducting research on risk and uncertainty

Laureate	*Year*	*Scientific discipline of the awarded achievement*
John Hicks, Kenneth Arrow	1972	General economic equilibrium theory and social welfare theory
Maurice Allais	1988	Market theory and efficient use of resources in partial and general equilibrium theory
GAME THEORY		
Reinhard Selten, John Nash Jr, John Harsanyi	1994	Analysis of equilibrium in game theory
Thomas C. Schelling	2005	Understanding of conflict and cooperation by means of game theory analysis
INSTITUTIONAL ECONOMICS		
Ronald Coase	1991	Importance of transaction costs and property rights for the institutional structure and functioning of the economy
Oliver Hart, Bengt Holmström	2016	Contract theory
ECONOMICS OF INFORMATION		
George A. Akerlof, A. Michael Spence, Joseph E. Stiglitz	2001	Analysis of markets characterized by information asymmetry
BEHAVIOURAL ECONOMICS		
Gary S. Becker	1992	Extending microeconomic analysis to a wide range of human behaviours and interactions, including extra-market behaviours
Daniel Kahneman	2002	Integration of psychological research with economic sciences, in particular that relating to human judgement and decision-making in conditions of uncertainty
Vernon L. Smith		Methodology of laboratory experimentation as a tool for empirical economic analysis, particularly useful for the study of alternative market mechanisms
Richard Thaler	2017	Development of behavioural economics
INTERNATIONAL ECONOMICS		
Paul Krugman	2008	Analysis of trade patterns and locations of business activities (international commercial and economic geography)

Source: the authors' own work based on: The Sveriges Riksbank Prize in Economic Sciences in Memory of Alfred Nobel, 2020.

1.4.1. Macroeconomic research on uncertainty and risk

In the field of macroeconomics, research on uncertainty and risk was carried out, among others, by Fredrich von Hayek, a representative of the Austrian school. Developing the theory of decision-making, the author referred to the uncertainties of the surrounding world. He defined uncertainty as a situation in which a decision-maker has only a fragmentary part of the needed information, while the existing uncertainty can only be eliminated by the entire necessary knowledge held by a set of all decision-makers involved in a specific decision-making process. Hayek also pointed out that the market understood as a mechanism for coordinating the exchange of information can effectively deal with the phenomenon of uncertainty and the resultant dispersed knowledge (von Hayek, 1945; Brady, 2011). Uncertainty was also an important area of scientific interest for Robert Lucas Jr., who regarded it as an important element in the development of John Muth's theory of rational expectations. Lucas analyzed prices of assets in a changing economy and developed the scientific achievements of Friedman and Phelps, whose main research focused on connections and relationships between unemployment and inflation. Lucas stressed that only uncertain changes in the supply of money can have a real impact on changes in unemployment, and the unpredictability of a monetary policy in the fight against unemployment is a factor determining its effectiveness (Lucas, 1972; 1978). Milton Friedman, on the other hand, treated risk and uncertainty as dichotomous concepts, seeing the economy as a domain of risk, not uncertainty. He also analyzed the effectiveness and consequences of choice in conditions of risk (Friedman and Savage, 1948). Another Nobel Prize winner, Franco Modigliani, is a co-author of research analyzing consumer decisions in conditions of uncertainty (Drèze and Modigliani, 1972) and, in addition, together with another Nobel Prize winner, Merton Miller, he developed a theorem on the impact of investment decisions and capital structure on the valuation of enterprises and on their ability to generate positive financial results under conditions of free competition. The assumptions for this theorem are closely linked to business risk and indicate that such risk can be estimated using the standard deviation of expected earnings before interest and tax. Thus, according to these assumptions, enterprises with the same level of standard deviation should be classified as belonging to the same risk classes (Czekaj and Dresler, 1995). William Nordhaus and Paul Romer are other Nobel Prize Laureates whose scientific work addresses the issue of risk in macroeconomics. Romer was involved in explaining interactions between economic growth and the development of innovations for which risk is one of the characteristic features (Romer, 1990). William Nordhaus, on the other hand, dealt with the impact of environmental risk on economic conditions (Nordhaus, 1993).

1.4.2. Microeconomic research on uncertainty and risk

Uncertainty and risk are also a major research problem for specialists in microeconomics. Leonid Hurwicz developed one of the optimization criteria (the Hurwicz optimism index criterion) used in the process of forecasting economic phenomena of a nonmeasurable nature. This criterion applies to the decision-making process in conditions of uncertainty and recommends the choice of such a decision variant whose maximum usefulness of the result is the greatest

(Gaspars-Wieloch, 2014). Research on risk in the area of microeconomics was also conducted by Eric Maskin in cooperation with John Riley. It focused on risk associated with auctioning and resulting from uncertainty as to the buying preferences of bidders (Maskin and Riley, 1984). Roger Myerson also contributed to the development of microeconomic research on risk by analyzing the possibility of its optimization from the seller's perspective and the buyer's neutral position with respect to risk (Myerson, 1981). In this area of economics, Paul Milgrom and Robert Wilson also contributed to the development of research on risk and uncertainty, developing auction theory and creating new auction formats that can be beneficial to sellers, buyers and taxpayers all over the world. The achievements of these researchers will facilitate the development of measures aimed at minimizing the risk of price collusion. They also developed a theory of auctioning items of common value. It is assumed that such auctions are characterized by uncertainty, but eventually they are the same for all participants (Wilson, 1992; Milgrom, 2010).

1.4.3. Research on uncertainty and risk conducted by representatives of financial economics

Quite a few Nobel Prize Laureates were researchers specializing in financial economics. James M. Buchanan Jr conducted research on the relationship between a system of government and uncertainty and risk. Its result was a social theory integrating political and economic decisions as well as elements of the legal system. However, the most connections between financial economics and risk can be seen in the works by Markowitz, Miller and Sharp. One of their achievements was the development of a general theory of financial assets valuation. Another success of these three researchers was proving the existence of risk-free financial assets and making a contribution to the theory of investment risk (Varian, 1993). Harry Markowitz is the author of the so-called portfolio theory dealing with the optimization of financial investments. In particular, he studied the effects of asset risk as well as asset correlation and diversification in relation to expected returns on the investment portfolio. In addition, Markowitz significantly developed the optimal investment theory, important for managers and concerning assets that differ in their expected rate of return and risk level (Markowitz, 1952; 1987). Merton Miller developed economic methods to reduce corporate risk, including net assets diversification and maximization (Varian, 1993). William Sharpe co-authored the Capital Asset Pricing model based on Markowitz's theory and constituting an important contribution to the theory of market equilibrium under conditions of risk (Sharpe, 1964; 1970). The issue of risk can also be seen in Robert Merton's research. One of his research objectives was to facilitate more effective risk management in financial markets (Merton, 1973; 1977). Myron Scholes contributed substantially to improving economic valuation in many areas of the economy by creating new financial instruments burdened with less risk. The result was smoother risk management processes (Scholes, 1976).

1.4.4. Research on uncertainty and risk in econometrics

Risk and uncertainty are also important determinants of econometric research, mainly in the area of the modelling of economic phenomena. This fact can be observed, for example, in the scientific achievements of Lawrence Klein. The author focused primarily on exchange rate risk, but also liquidity risk and credit risk. He emphasized that an appropriate measure of exchange rate risk is the discrepancy between the forecasts of exchange rates and their actual values; hence, exchange rate risk can be gradually reduced by improving forecasting methods (Herring, 1983; Morris and Shin, 2016).

1.4.5. Research on uncertainty and risk in management

Another discipline of economic sciences with a considerable range of research on risk and uncertainty is management. Herbert Simon dealt, among other things, with the impact of uncertainty on decision-making processes in organizations. In this respect, he was the creator of a rational model of decision-making and a concept of the limited rationality of a human being as a decision-maker in conditions of uncertainty. His numerous works (Simon, 1965; 1977; 1979; 1989) influenced the development of the theory of organization and management, as well as the psychology of research in management sciences. Oliver E. Williamson has undertaken research on certain and uncertain choices of business entities, their rationality, investment risk, opportunistic behaviours, as well as the risk related to the phenomenon of information asymmetry (Williamson, 2015). Elinor Ostrom contributed to the emergence of a new economic trend, i.e. the economics of the common good. She formulated a set of principles of communal management which assume the existence of the risk of unforeseen crisis situations and the necessity to develop low-cost and effective mechanisms for dealing with both unforeseeable and probable problems (Ostrom, 1990).

1.4.6. Research on uncertainty and risk in the theory of general equilibrium

The theory of general equilibrium is another area of economic sciences where risk and uncertainty need to be taken into account. Paul Samuelson's research on risk and its probability significantly influenced the development of the theory of expected utility (Samuelson, 1952). In his numerous works (Hicks, 1939; 1973; 1979), John R. Hicks, one of the most outstanding representatives of the mathematical trend in economics, dealt also with economic risk, proving that risk can be insured, assuming the reliable functioning of the law of large numbers. Kenneth J. Arrow was also an outstanding author of risk research. He is a co-author of the general equilibrium theory and a researcher of the decision theory, the uncertainty and risk theory, as well as information asymmetry. He contributed to the development of insurance economics by dealing, among other things, with the problem of risk in the analysis of moral hazard (Arrow, 1951;

1965; 1974). He is also the author of a series of essays on the theory or risk-bearing (Arrow, 1971). Maurice Allais (the author of the Allais paradox) used risk as a determinant of the implemented methodology of his experiment. The main method used was checking the relationship between certain and risky choices in the decision theory. The author also focused on the causes and risk of the occurrence of economic crises (Allais, 1965; 1966; 1969).

1.4.7. Research on uncertainty and risk in game theory

Uncertainty and risk are dominant factors in the game theory. This theory is directly linked to the rationality of making appropriate decisions in various situations, including risky ones. John Nash Jr, Reinhard Selten and John C. Harsanyi analyzed equilibrium in the theory of games, which is inextricably linked to the theory of decision-making under conditions of risk. The last of these three researchers dealt particularly with game theory analysis under conditions of risk and incomplete information, providing a theoretical basis for a new area of research that would be known as information economics (Harsanyi, 1967). Awarded the Nobel Prize for achievements in the development of the game theory, Thomas Schelling researched the issue of uncertainty of economic phenomena, focusing on the methods of solving international conflicts. To this end, he analyzed certain and uncertain determinants of retaliation, as well as numerous aspects of their credibility and effectiveness (Schelling, 1981).

1.4.8. Research on uncertainty and risk in information economics

Expanding the topic of the importance of risk research in information economics, it is necessary to highlight the work of Akerlof, Spence and Stiglitz. These three economists made considerable contributions to the development of research on information risk. Among other things, they analyzed the impact of information asymmetry on the risk of failure in relations among different market participants. Another area of their research was the determination of the course of microeconomic and macroeconomic phenomena by the disproportionate distribution of market information (Lofgren et al., 2002).

1.4.9. Research on uncertainty and risk in institutional economics

Institutional economics is also an area that provides a background for research on economic risk. As a precursor of the transaction cost theory, Ronald Coase formulated a theorem in relation to ownership, adapted subsequently to the economic contract theory. He also addressed the issue of the rationality of risky choices, arguing that an analysis of transaction costs is necessary in the process of forecasting and determining market behaviours, and thus also in estimating the level of risk and its consequences (Coase, 1937). Oliver Hart analyzed the risk of incomplete contracts, thus contributing with his research to the evolution of the contract theory. The result theory of incomplete contracts takes into account uncertainties related to executed contracts and resulting from the impossibility of foreseeing all potential variants of contract terms (Hart and Moore, 1998). Bengt Holström, who was awarded the Nobel Prize together with Hart, claimed that contracts safeguard against uncertainty and have a positive impact on the security of economic and social relations (Schmidt, 2017).

1.4.10. Research on uncertainty and risk in behavioural economics

Risk and uncertainty also became important objects of study for scientists representing behavioural economics. Daniel Kahneman and Vernon L. Smith carried out innovative research on decision-making under conditions of uncertainty. Kahneman (who wrote a number of works on this subject with Tversky) (Kahneman and Tversky, 1979; 1992) applied cognitive psychology in economic analysis. In his research, he paid special attention to the behaviours of individuals in conditions of uncertainty. This became a foundation for a new field, i.e. economic psychology. Smith, meanwhile, is the creator of laboratory experimentation methods that became a breakthrough in the understanding of economic behaviours in conditions of uncertainty and risk (Smith, 1962; 1965). Gary Becker is another scientist representing behavioural economics, whose research on risk was focused on market insurance conditions (Ehrlich and Becker, 1972). Another representative of behavioural economics is Richard H. Thaler, who researched, among other things, the impact of cognitive errors on the economic decisions of individuals under risk conditions and on the functioning of markets (Thaler, 1994; 1999; 2015).

1.4.11. Research on uncertainty and risk in international economics

International economics is another area of economic sciences where risk and uncertainty constitute an important research object and are regarded as phenomena inherent in international transactions and business relations, among both individual enterprises and countries. Paul Krugman, whose research focused mainly on the geographical and economic aspects of mostly international trade, analyzed the risk of economic crises and recessions, as well as their impact on market relations and management processes, on the basis of observations of globalization processes and the functioning of global markets. He also dealt with the economics of market information and related uncertainty (Krugman et al., 2018).

References

Aarts, H., Verplanken, B., van Knippenberg, A. (2006). Predicting behavior from actions in the past: Repeated decision making or a matter of habit? *Journal of Applied Social Psychology*, 28(15), pp. 1355–1374.

Aivazian, V.A., Callen, J.L. (1983). Reorganization in bankruptcy and the issue of strategic risk. *Journal of Banking & Finance*, 7(1), pp. 119–133.

Akcali, B.Y., Sismanoglu, E. (2015). Innovation and the effect of research and development (R&D) expenditure on growth in some developing and developed countries. *Procedia – Social and Behavioral Sciences*, 195, pp. 768–775.

Allais, M. (1965). *The Role of Capital in Economic Development. In The Econometric Approach to Development Planning*. Amsterdam: North-Holland.

Allais, M. (1966). A restatement of the quantity theory of money. *American Economic Review*, 56, pp. 1123–1157.

Allais, M. (1969). Growth and inflation. *Journal of Money, Credit and Banking*, 1(3), pp. 355–426.

American Risk and Insurance Association. (1966). *Bulletin of the Commission on Insurance Terminology*, Malvern, PA, 2(1).

Apătăchioae, A. (2014). New challenges in the management of banking risks. *Procedia Economics and Finance*, 15, pp. 1364–1373.

Arrow, K.J. (1951). *Social Choice and Individual Values*. New York: Wiley.

Arrow, K.J. (1965). *Aspects of the Theory of Risk-Bearing*. Helsinki: Y.H. Foundation.

Arrow, K.J. (1971). *Essays in the Theory of Risk Bearing*. Amsterdam: North-Holland.

Arrow, K.J. (1974). *The Limits of Organization*. New York: Norton.

Aven, T., Renn, O. (2009). On risk defined as an event where the outcome is uncertain. *Journal of Risk Research*, 12, pp. 1–11.

van Baalen, P., Karsten, L. (2012). The evolution of management as an interdisciplinary field. *Journal of Management History*, 18(2), pp. 219–237.

Bagley, D.E. (1953). Reports on maturing research – some observation recent studies of investment risk. *Journal of Finance*, 8(2), pp. 99–112.

Banse, G., Bechmann, G. (1998). *Interdisziplinre Risikoforschung. Eine Bibliographie*. Opladen/Wiesbaden: Westdeutscher Verlag.

Barbosa, S., Gerhardt, M., Kickul, J. (2007). The role of cognitive style and risk preference on entrepreneurial self-efficacy and entrepreneurial intentions. *Journal of Leadership & Organizational Studies*, 13(4), pp. 86–104.

Basel Committee on Banking Supervision. (2011). *Principles for the Sound Management of Operational Risk*. Switzerland: Bank for International Settlements.

Bauer, R.A. (1960). Consumer behavior as risk taking [in:] R.S. Hancock (ed.), *Dynamic Marketing for a Changing World. Proceedings of the 43rd Conference of the American Marketing Association*. Chicago, IL: American Marketing Association, pp. 389–398.

Baumol, W. (2010). *The Microtheory of Innovative Entrepreneurship*. Princeton, NJ: Princeton University Press.

Bąk, S. (2017). Bankowość elektroniczna jako nowy wymiar zarządzania ryzykiem operacyjnym w sektorze bankowym. *Przedsiębiorczość i Zarządzanie*, XVIII, 10(1), pp. 139–150.

Bąk, S. (2020). The problem of uncertainty and risk as a subject of research of the Nobel Prize Laureates in economic sciences. *Journal of Economics and Management*, 39(1), pp. 21–40.

Beck, U. (1987). *Społeczeństwo ryzyka*. Warszawa: Wydawnictwo Naukowe PWN.

Beck, U. (2002). *Społeczeństwo ryzyka. W drodze do innej nowoczesności*. Warszawa: Wydawnictwo Naukowe Scholar.

Beck, U. (2012). *Społeczeństwo światowego ryzyka. W poszukiwaniu utraconego bezpieczeństwa*. Warszawa: Wydawnictwo Naukowe Scholar.

Bernoulli, D. (1738). Specimen theoriae novae de mensura sortis. *Papers of the Imperial Academy of Sciences in Petersburg*, 5, pp. 175–192.

Bizon-Górecka, J. (2004). Koszty w przedsiębiorstwie w ujęciu komplementarnym. *Rynek Terminowy*, 2, pp. 48–54.

Bodie, Z., Merton, R.C. (2003). *Finanse*. Warszawa: PWE.

Bouchaud, J.P., Potters, M. (2000). *Theory of Financial Risk: From Statistical Physics to Risk Management*. Cambridge: Cambridge University Press.

Bourdieu, P. (1979). *La Distinction: Critique Sociale du Jugement*. Paris: Les Éd. DeMinuit.

Boutang, J., De Lara, M. (2016). Risk marketing. *Journal of Centrum Cathedra*, 9(1), pp. 27–51.

Bowers, J., Khorakian, A. (2014). Integrating risk management in the innovation project. *European Journal of Innovation Management*, 17(1), pp. 25–40.

Brady, A., Honey, G. (2007). *Corporate Reputation: Perspectives of Measuring and Managing a Principal Risk*. London: The Chartered Institute of Management Accountants.

Brady, M.E. (2011). Comparing J.M. Keynes's and F. Von Hayek's differing definitions of uncertainty as it relates to knowledge: Keynes's unavailable or missing knowledge concept versus Hayek's dispersal of knowledge concept. *International Journal of Applied Economics and Econometrics*, 19(3), pp. 1–20.

Britto, R. (1980). Resource allocation in a sample, two-sector, model with production risk. *Economic Journal*, 90(358), pp. 363–370.

Buła, P. (2003). *Zarządzanie ryzykiem w jednostkach gospodarczych. Aspekt uniwersalistyczny*. Kraków: Akademia Ekonomiczna w Krakowie.

Bursztyn, L., Ederer, F., Ferman, B., Yuchtman, N. (2014). Understanding mechanisms underlying peer effects: Evidence from a field experiment on financial decisions. *Econometrica*, 82(4), pp. 1273–1301.

Buschgen, H. (1997). *Przedsiębiorstwo bankowe*, 2. Warszawa: Poltext.

Byrd, R.E. (1978). *Guide to Personal Risk Taking*. New York: AMACOM.

Calandro, J. (2015). A leader's guide to strategic risk management. *Strategy & Leadership*, 43(1), pp. 26–35.

Çalışkan, H.K. (2015). Technological change and economic growth. *Procedia – Social and Behavioral Sciences*, 195, pp. 649–654.

Camillo, M. (2017). Cyber risk and the changing role of insurance. *Journal of Cyber Policy*, 2(1), pp. 53–63.

Campbell, S. (2005). Determining overall risk. *Journal of Risk Research*, 8, pp. 569–581.

Cantillon, R. (1755). *Essai sur la nature du commerce en general*. Ballyheigue: Fletcher Gyles.

Cantillon, R. (1938). *Ogólne rozważania nad naturalnymi prawami handlu* (Essai sur la nature du commerce en général). W. Zawadzki (ed. and translate). Warszawa: Szkoła Główna Handlowa w Warszawie – Skład Główny Biblioteka Polska.

Carbonara, G., Caiazza R. (2010). How to turn crisis into opportunity: Perception and reaction to high level of uncertainty in banking industry. *Foresight*, 12(4), pp. 37–46.

Carleton, R.N., Gosselin, P., Asmundson, G.J.G. (2010). The intolerance of uncertainty index: Replication and extension with an english sample. *Psychological Assessment*, 22(2), pp. 396–406.

Cettolin, E., Riedl, A. (2016). Justice under uncertainty. *Management Science*, 63(11), pp. 3739–3759.

Chang, C.H., Xu, J., Song, D.P. (2015). Risk analysis for container shipping: From a logistics perspective. *The International Journal of Logistics Management*, 26(1), pp. 147–171.

Christopher, M., Mena, C., Khan, O., Yurt, O. (2011). Approaches to managing global sourcing risk. *Supply Chain Management: An International Journal*, 16(2), pp. 67–81.

Ciesielski, M. (1999). *Logistyka w strategiach Firm*. Warszawa-Poznań: PWN.

Claessens, S., Demirgüç-Kunt, A., Moshirian, F. (2009). Global financial crisis, risk analysis and risk measurement. *Journal of Banking & Finance*, 33(11), pp. 1949–1952.

Coase, R.H. (1937). The nature of the firm. *Economica*, 4(6), pp. 386–405.

Cohen, W.A. (2014). *Drucker o marketingu. Nauczanie najbardziej wpływowego teoretyka biznesu*. Lublin: Słowa i Myśli.

Comeig, I., Holt, C.A., Jaramillo-Gutiérrez, A. (2015). *Dealing with Risk: Gender, Stakes, and Probability Effects*. Spain: University of Valencia, ERI-CES Valencia.

Cox, D.F. (1967). *Risk Taking and Information Handling in Consumer Behavior*. Boston, MA: Harvard University, Graduate School of Business Administration.

Crusius, J., van Horen, F., Mussweiler, T. (2012). Why process matters: A social cognition perspective on economic behavior. *Journal of Economic Psychology*, 33(3), pp. 677–685.

Czakon, W., Komańda, M. (2011). *Interdyscyplinarność w naukach o zarządzaniu*. Katowice: Wydawnictwo Uniwersyteu Ekonomicznego w Katowicach.

Czekaj, J., Dresler, Z. (1995). *Podstawy zarządzania finansami firm*. Warszawa: PWN.

Damodran, A. (2002). *Investment Valuation: Tools and Techniques for Determining the Value of Any Asset*. New York: Wiley Finance.

Dean, M. (1999). *Governmentality: Power and Rule in Modern Society*. London: Sage.

DeLoach, J. (2004). The new risk imperative – An enterprise-wide approach. *Handbook of Business Strategy*, 5(1), pp. 29–34.

Denenberg, H.S. (1964). *Risk and Insurance*. Englewood Cliffs, NJ: Prentice Hall.

Diebold, F.X., Doherty, N.A., Herring, R.J. (2010). *The Known, the Unknown, and the Unknowable in Financial Risk Management: Measurement and Theory Advancing Practice*. Princeton, NJ: Princeton University Press.

Dixit, A.K., Pindyck, R.S. (1994). *Investment under Uncertainty*. Princeton, NJ: Princeton University Press.

Doerig, H. (2003). *Operational Risk in Financial Services*. NewYork: Credit Suisse Group.

Douglas, M. (1992). *Risk and Blame: Essays in Cultural Theory*. London: Routledge.

Douglas, M., Wildavsky, A. (1982). *Risk and Culture: An Essay on the Selection of Technical and Environmental Dangers*. Berkeley, CA: University of California Press.

Drèze, J.H., Modigliani, F. (1972). Consumption decisions under uncertainty. *Journal of Economic Theory*, 5(3), pp. 307–335.

Drucker, P.F. (1968). *The Age of Discontinuity: Guidelines to Our Changing Society*. New York: Harper & Row.

Drucker, P.F. (1993). *Post-Capitalist Society*. New York: Harper Business.

Dugas, M.J., Gosselin, P., Ladouceur, R. (2001). Intolerance of uncertainty and worry: Investigating specificity in a nonclinical sample. *Cognitive Therapy and Research*, 25(5), pp. 551–558.

Eccles, R.G., Newquist, S.C., Schatz, R. (2007). Reputation and its risks. *Harvard Business Review*, 85(2), pp. 104–114.

Eckert, C. (2017). Corporate reputation and reputation risk: Definition and measurement from a (risk) management perspective. *The Journal of Risk Finance*, 18(2), pp. 145–158.

Edwards, W. (1961). Behavioral decision theory. *Annual Review of Psychology*, 12, pp. 473–498.

Ehrlich, I., Becker, G.S. (1972). Market insurance, self-insurance, and self-protection. *Journal of Political Economy*, 80(4), pp. 623–648.

Eisenstadt, S.N. (2000). Daedalus. *Multiple modernities*, 129(1), pp. 1–29.

Elahi, E. (2013). Risk management: The next source of competitive advantage. *Emerald*, 15(2), pp. 117–131.

Elliott, C.S., Archibald, R.B. (1989). Subjective framing and attitudes towards risk. *Journal of Economic Psychology*, 10(3), pp. 321–328.

Ellsberg, D. (1961). Risk, ambiguity, and the savage axioms. *Quarterly Journal of Economics*, 75, pp. 643–669.

Falkowski, A., Tyszka, T. (2009). *Psychologia zachowań konsumenckich*. Gdańsk: Gdańskie Wydawnictwo Psychologiczne.

Finch, P. (2004). Supply chain risk management. *Supply Chain Management: An International Journal*, 9(2), pp. 183–196.

Firszt, D. (2014). Postęp technologiczny jako element zintegrowanego rozwoju polskiej gospodarki. *Nierówności Społeczne a Wzrost Gospodarczy*, 37(1), pp. 258–275.

Fischhoff, B., Slovic, P., Lichtenstein, S. (1981). *Acceptable Risk*. New York: Cambridge.

Fischhoff, B., Slovic, P., Lichtenstein, S., Read, S., Combs, B. (1978). How safe is safe enough? A psychometric study of attitudes toward technological risk and benefits. *Policy Science*, 9, pp. 127–152.

Fleckner, A.M. (2006). Stock exchanges at the crossroads. *Fordham Law Review*, 74(5), pp. 2541–2620.

Fleckner, A.M., Hopt, K.J. (2013). Stock exchange law: Concept, history, challenges. *Virginia Law and Business Review*, 7(3), pp. 513–559.

Flood, M.D. (2012). A brief history of financial risk and information [in:] M. Brose, M. Flood, D. Krishna, W. Nichols (eds.), *Handbook of Financial Data and Risk Information*. Cambridge: Cambridge University Press, pp. 1–32.

Foster, W.F., Catchings, W. (1925). Why not do away with profits? *Harvard Business Review*, 3(2), pp. 141–149.

Freeman, C., Louçã, F. (2001). *As Time Goes By. From the Industrial Revolution to the Information Revolution*. Oxford: Oxford University Press.

Freeston, M.H., Rhéaume, J., Letarte, H., Dugas, M.J., Ladouceur, R. (1994). Why do people worry? *Personality and Individual Differences*, 17(6), pp. 791–802.

Friedman, M., Savage, L. (1948). The utility analysis of choice involving risk. *Journal of Political Economy*, 56(4), pp. 279–304.

Frigo, M., Anderson, R.J. (2011). Strategic risk management: A foundation for enterprise risk management and governance. *Journal of Corporate Accounting & Finance*, 22(3), pp. 81–88.

Frith, U., Blakemore, S.J. (2006). Social cognition [in:] R. Morris, L. Tarassenko, M. Kenward (eds.), *Cognitive Systems – Information Processing Meets Brain Science*. Amsterdam, Boston, Heidelberg, London, New York, Oxford, Paris, San

Diego, San Francisco, Singapore, Sydney, Tokyo: Elsevier Academic Press, pp. 138–162.

Gardner, M., Mills, D. (1988). *Managing Financial Institutions.* Chicago, IL: The Dryden Press.

Gaspars-Wieloch, H. (2014). Modifications of the Hurwicz's decision rule. *Central European Journal of Operations Research*, 22(4), pp. 779–794.

Gigerenzer, G. (2002). *Bounded Rationality: The Adaptive Toolbox.* Cambridge, MA: MIT Press.

Gleason, K.C., Madura, J., Wiggenhorn, J. (2006). Operating charakteristics, risk and performance of born-global firms. *International Journal of Managerial Finance*, 2(2), pp. 96–120.

Gliszczyńska, X. (ed.). (1979). *Psychologia pracy. Podstawowe twierdzenia psychologicznej teorii decyzji.* Warszawa: PWN.

Goddard, S. (1998). Reputational risk needs managing. *Business Insurance*, 32(49), pp. 39–44.

Gospodarek, T. (2012). *Aspekty złożoności i filozofii nauki w zarządzaniu.* Wałbrzych: Wydawnictwo Wałbrzyskiej Wyższej Szkoły Zarządzania i Przedsiębiorczości.

Graham, B.A., Johnston, N.P., Kingsley, A. (2016). A unified model of political risk [in:] J.M. de Figueiredo, M. Lenox, F. Oberholzer-Gee, R.G. Vanden Bergh (eds.), *Strategy Beyond Markets, Advances in Strategic Management*, 34, Emerald Group Publishing Limited, pp. 119–160.

Gregorczyk, S. (2013). Globalizacja a zarządzanie ryzykiem strategicznym w przedsiębiorstwie [in:] R. Bartkowiak, P. Wachwiak (eds.), *Wiedza i bogactwo narodów.* Warszawa: Wydawnictwo SGH, pp. 34–45.

Grinols, E.L., Turnovsky, S.J. (1993). Risk, the financial market, and macroeconomic equilibrium. *Journal of Economic Dynamics and Control*, 17(1–2), pp. 1–36.

Gruszka, B., Zawadzka, Z. (1992). *Ryzyko w działalności bankowej.* Warszawa: Oficyna Wydawnicza Szkoły Głównej Handlowej.

Guadix, J., Carillo-Castrillo, J., Onieva, L., Lucena, D. (2015). Strategies for psychosocial risk management in manufacturing. *Journal of Business Research*, 68(7), pp. 1475–1480.

Hacking, I. (1991). How should we do the history of statistics? [in:] G. Burchell, C. Gordon, P. Miller (eds.), *The Foucault Effect. Studies in Governmentality.* London: Harvester Wheatsheaf, pp. 181–195.

Hall, R.E., Woodward, S.E. (2010). The burden of the nondiversifiable risk of entrepreneurship. *American Economic Review*, 100, pp. 1163–1194.

Hámori, B. (2003). Experiments and prospects – In connection with Daniel Kahneman's Nobel Prize. *Economic Review*, L, pp. 779–799.

Harrison, F.L. (1977). Decision-making in conditions of extreme uncertainty. *Journal of Management Studies*, 14(2), pp. 169–178.

Harsanyi, J. (1967). Games with incomplete information played by Bayesian players. Part I. *Managment Science*, 14(3), pp. 159–183, Part II. *Managment Science*, 14(5), pp. 320–334, Part III. *Managment Science*, 14(7), pp. 486–502.

Hart, O., Moore, J. (1998). *Foundations of Incomplete Contracts* (NBER Working Paper Series No. 6726). Cambridge, MA: National Bureau of Economic Research.

von Hayek, F.A. (1945). The use of knowledge in society. *American Economic Review*, 35(4), pp. 519–530.

van der Heijden, K. (2000). *Planowanie scenariuszowe w zarządzaniu strategicznym.* Kraków: Oficyna Ekonomiczna.

Herring, R.J. (ed.). (1983). *Managing Foreign Exchange Risk*. Pennsylvania: The Wharton School University.

Hicks, J.R. (1939). *Value and Capital: An Inquiry Into Some Fundamental Principles of Economic Theory*. Oxford: Clarendon Press.

Hicks, J.R. (1973). *Capital and Time: A New-Austrian Theory*. Oxford: Clarendon Press.

Hicks, J.R. (1979). *Causality in Economics*. New York: Basic Books.

Holscher, R. (1987). *Risikokosten-Management in Kreditinstituten*. Frankfurt: F. Knapp.

Holton, G. (2004). Defining risk. *Financial Analysts Journal*, 60(6), pp. 19–25.

Hossu, D., Humaila, H., Mocanu, S., Saru, D. (2009). Complex networks to model the economic globalization process. *IFAC Proceedings Volumes*, 42(25), pp. 62–67.

Hussain, M., Ahmad, M. (2012). Mostly discussed research areas in human resource management (HRM) – A literature review. *International Journal of Economics and Management Sciences*, 2(3), pp. 10–17.

ISO Guide 73. (2009). *Risk Management – Vocabulary*. Geneva.

ISO 31000. (2018). *Risk Management – Guidelines*. Geneva.

Iwanicz-Drozdowska, M. (2018). *Zarządzanie ryzykiem bankowym*. Warszawa: Poltext.

Jacoby, J., Kaplan, L.B. (1972). The components of perceived risk [in:] M. Venkateran (ed.), *SV – Proceedings of the Third Annual Conference of the Association for Consumer Research, Advances in Consumer Research*, Chicago, IL, pp. 382–393.

Jain, A., Leka, S., Zwetsloot, G. (2011). Corporate social responsibility and psychosocial risk management in Europe. *Journal of Business Ethics*, 101(4), pp. 619–633.

Jedynak, P., Bąk, S. (2018). The global risk landscape – Its shape, tendencies and consequences for management. *Journal of Economics and Management*, 32(2), pp. 48–59.

Jedynak, P., Bąk, S. (2020). Understanding uncertainty and risk in management. *Journal of Intercultural Management*, 12(1), pp. 12–35.

Jedynak, P., Szydło, S. (1997). *Zarządzanie ryzykiem*. Wrocław–Warszawa–Kraków: Zakład Narodowy im. Ossolińskich – Wydawnictwo.

Jensen, M., Meckling, W. (1976). Theory of the firm: Managerial behavior, agency costs, and ownership structure. *Journal of Finance Economics*, 4, pp. 305–360.

Jodice, D.A. (1985). *Political Risk Assessment: An Annotated Bibliography, Bibliographies and Indexes in Law and Political Science*, 3. Westport, CT: Greenwood Press.

Johanning, L. (1999). *Value-at-Risk zur Marktrisikosteuerung und Eigenkapitallokation*. Reihe: Risikomanagement und Finanzcontrolling, 1, Bad Soben, Uhlenbruch.

Jonas, E., Schulz-Hardt, S., Frey, D., Thelen, N. (2001). Confirmation bias in sequential information search after preliminary decisions. *Journal of Personality and Social Psychology*, 80, pp. 557–571.

Kaczmarek, T.T. (2003). Interdyscyplinarne badanie zdywersyfikowanego ryzyka. Typologia i semantyka. *Ekonomia. Rynek, Gospodarka, Społeczeństwo*, 11, pp. 87–115.

Kaczmarek, T.T. (2006). *Ryzyko i zarządzanie ryzykiem. Ujęcie interdyscyplinarne*. Warszawa: Difin.

Kaczmarek, T.T. (2010). *Zarządzanie ryzykiem ujęcie interdyscyplinarne*. Warszawa: Difin.

Kahneman, D., Tversky A. (1979). Prospect theory: An analysis of decision under risk. *Econometrica*, 47(2), pp. 263–292.

Kahneman, D., Tversky, A. (1992). Advanced in prospect theory, cumulative representation of uncertaint. *Journal of Risk and Uncertainty*, 5, pp. 297–323.

Kanbur, S.M. (1980). A note on risk taking, entrepreneurship, and schumpeter. *History of Political Economy*, 12(4), pp. 489–498.

Kasperson, R.E., Renn, O., Slovic, P., Brown, H.S., Emel, J., Goble, R., Kasperson, J.X. Ratick, S. (1988). The social amplification of risk: A conceptual framework. *Risk Analysis*, 8(2), pp. 177–187.

Kasprzak, T. (1979). Wstęp do wydania polskiego [in:] K.J. Arrow (ed.), *Eseje z teorii ryzyka*. Warszawa: Państwowe Wydawnictwo Naukowe, p. 7.

Kendall, R. (1998). *Zarządzanie ryzykiem dla menedżerów*. Warszawa: Liber.

Keynes, J.M. (1921). *A Treatise on Probability*. London: Macmillan and Co.

Kiev, A. (2016). *Psychologia ryzyka*. Ożarów Mazowiecki: Wydawnictwo Linia.

Kindleberger, C.P. (1999). *Szaleństwo, panika, krach. Historia kryzysów finansowych*. Warszawa: WIG PRESS.

Klimczak, K. (2008). Ryzyko w teorii ekonomii. *Master of Business Administration*, 6, pp. 64–69.

Knechel, W.R. (2002). The role of the independent accountant in effective risk management. *Review of Business and Economic*, 27(1), pp. 65–86.

Knight, F.H. (1921). *Risk, Uncertainty and Profit*. Boston, MA: Houghton Mifflin.

Kobrin, S. (1979). Political risk: A review and reconsideration. *Journal of International Business Studies*, 19, pp. 39–52.

Korombel, A. (2013). Istota i znaczenie kultury ryzyka dla funkcjonowania organizacji. *Zeszyty Naukowe Uniwersytetu Szczecińskiego*, 761(60), pp. 471–478.

Kossowska, M., Szumowska, E., Szwed, P. (2018). *Tolerancja w czasach niepewności*. Sopot: Smak Słowa.

Kot, S., Dragon, P. (2015). Business risk management in international corporations. *Procedia Economics and Finance*, 27, pp. 102–108.

Kozielecki, J. (2004). *Społeczeństwo transgresyjne. Szansa i ryzyko*. Warszawa: Wydawnictwo Żak.

Kreim, E. (1988). *Zukunftsorientierte Kreditentscheidung*. Wiesbaden: Gabler.

Krickx, G.A. (2000). The relationship between uncertainty and vertical integration. *The International Journal of Organizational Analysis*, 8(3), pp. 309–329.

Krohn, W., Krücken, G. (1993). Riskante Technologien: Reflexion und Regulation. Einführung in die sozialwissenschaftliche Risikoforschung Frankfurt/Main: Suhrkamp.

Krugman, P.R., Obstfeld, M., Melitz, M. (2018). *International Economics: Theory and Policy*. Global Edition, Upper Saddle River, NJ: Prentice Hall.

Kumamoto, H., Henley, E. (1996). *Probabilistic Risk Assessment and Management for Engineers and Scientists*. New York: Wiley-IEEE Press.

Kumbhakar, S.C. (2002). Specification and estimation of production risk, risk preferences and technical efficiency. *American Journal of Agricultural Economics*, 84(1), pp. 8–22.

Lachiewicz, S., Matejun, M. (2012). Ewolucja nauk o zarządzaniu [in:] A. Zakrzewska-Bielawska (ed.), *Podstawy zarządzania*. Warszawa: Oficyna a Wolters Kluwer Business, pp. 85–141.

Lahno, A., Serra-Garcia, M. (2015). Peer effects in risk taking: Envy or conformity? *Journal of Risk and Uncertainty*, 50(1), pp. 73–95.

Lange, O. (1967). *Optymalne decyzje. Zasady programowania*. Warszawa: PWN.

Langenhan, M.K., Leka, S., Jain, A. (2013). Psychosocial risks: Is risk management strategic enough in business and policy making? *Safety and Health at Work*, 4(2), pp. 87–94.

Latour, B. (1993). *We Have Never Been Modern*. Cambridge, MA: Harvard University Press.

Lawrence, W.W. (1976). *Of Acceptable Risk*. Los Altos, CA: William Kaufman Inc.

Leka, S., Cox, T. (2008). *The European Framework for Psychosocial Risk Management*. Nottingham: I-WHO publications.

Lensink, R., van Steen, P., Sterken, E. (2005). Uncertainty and growth of the firm. *Small Business Economics*, 24, pp. 381–391.

Lipka, A. (2002). *Ryzyko personalne. Szanse i zagrożenia zarządzania zasobami ludzkimi*. Warszawa: Poltext.

Lofgren, K.G., Persson, T. and Weibull, J.W. (2002). Markets with asymmetric information: The contributions of George Akerlof, Michael Spence and Joseph Stiglitz. *Scandinavian Journal of Economics*, 104(2), pp. 195–211.

Lucas, R.E. (1972). Expectations and the neutrality of money. *Journal of Economic Theory*, 4, pp. 103–124.

Lucas, R.E. (1978). Asset prices in an exchange economy. *Econometrica*, 46(6), pp. 1429–1446.

Luhmann, N. (1993). *Risk: A Sociological Theory*. New York: A. de Gruyter.

Manuj, I., Mentzer, J.T. (2008). Global supply chain risk management strategies. *International Journal of Physical Distribution & Logistics Management*, 38(3), pp. 192–223.

Marginean, S. (2015). Economic globalization: From microeconomic foundation to national determinants. *Procedia Economics and Finance*, 27, pp. 731–735.

Markowitz, H. (1952). Portfolio selection. *Journal of Finance*, 7(1), pp. 77–91.

Markowitz, H. (1959). *Portfolio Selection. Efficient Diversification of Investments*. New Haven, CT: Yale University Press.

Markowitz, H. (1987). *Mean-Variance Analysis in Portfolio Choise and Capital Markets*. Cambridge: Blackwell Publishers.

Marsh, W.H. (1995). *Basic Financial Management*. Cincinnati, OH: South-Western College Publishing.

Marshall, C. (2001). *Measuring and Managing Operational Risk in Financial Institutions*. Singapore: John Wiley & Sons.

Masci, P. (2011). The history of insurance: Risk, uncertainty and entrepreneurship. *Business and Public Administration Studies*, 6(1), pp. 25–68.

Maskin, E., Riley, J. (1984). Optimal auctions with risk averse buyers. *Econometrica*, 52 (6), pp. 1473–1518.

Mayer, R.W. (1965). Business risk and the earnings multiplier. *Financial Analysts Journal*, 21(5), pp. 19–21.

Merton, R.C. (1973). Theory of rational option pricing. *Bell Journal of Economics and Management Science*, 4(1), pp. 141–183.

Merton, R.C. (1977). An analytic derivation of the cost of loan guarantees and deposit insurance: An application of modern option pricing theory. *Journal of Banking and Finance*, 1, pp. 3–11.

Milgrom, P. (2010). *Putting Auction Theory to Work*. Cambridge: Cambridge University Press.

Miller, M.H., Modigliani, F. (1958). The cost of capital and the theory of investment. *American Economic Review*, 48, pp. 261–297.

Minc, B. (1975). *Systemy ekonomiczne.* Warszawa: PWN.
Mlot, C. (1989). Global risk assessment. *BioScience*, 39(7), pp. 428–430.
Morris, R.M. (1987). Defining risk levels: A matter of degrees. *Industrial Management*, 29(5), pp. 2–8.
Morris, S., Shin, H.S. (2016). Illiquidity component of credit risk – The 2015 Lawrence R. Klein lecture. *International Economic Review*, 57(4), pp. 1135–1148.
Mossin, J. (1968). Aspects of rational insurance purchasing. *Journal of Political Economy*, 76(4), pp. 533–568.
Myerson, R. (1981). Optimal auction design. *Mathematics of Operations Research*, 6, pp. 58–73.
Nelson, R., Winter, S. (1982). *An Evolutionary Theory of Economic Change.* Cambridge, MA: Harvard University Press.
Nelson, R., Winter, S. (2002). Evolutionary theorizing in economics. *Journal of Economic Perspectives*, 16(2), pp. 23–46.
von Neumann, J., Morgenstern, O. (1947). *Theory of games and economic behavior.* 2nd edition. Princeton, NJ: Princeton University Press.
Neves, P., Eisenberger, R. (2014). Perceived organizational support and risk taking. *Journal of Managerial Psychology*, 29(2), pp. 187–205.
Nishimura, K.G., Ozaki, H. (2017). *Economics of Pessimism and Optimism. Theory of Knightian Uncertainty and Its Applications.* Chiyoda First Bldg. East, Nishi-Kanda, Chiyoda-ku, Tokyo: Springer Japan KK.
Nogalski, B., Śniadecki, J. (2001). *Umiejętności menedżerskie w zarządzaniu przedsiębiorstwem.* Bydgoszcz: Oficyna Wydawnicza Ośrodka Postępu Organizacyjnego.
Nordhaus, W.D. (1993). Reflections on the economics of climate change. *Journal of Economic Perspectives*, 7(4), pp. 11–25.
Nosal, C. (2001). *Psychologia myślenia i działania menedżera.* Wrocław: AKADE.
Okoye, H.N., Nwaigwe, L.C. (2015). The impact of globalization to business and the world economy. *International Journal of Business and Management Review*, 3(5), pp. 17–32.
Ostrom, E. (1990). *Governing the Commons: The Evolution of Institutions for Collective Action.* Cambridge: Cambridge University Press.
Pablo, A.L. (1999). Management risk interpretations: Does industry make a difference? *Journal of Managerial Psychology*, 14(2), pp. 92–107.
Pasieczny, L. (1981). *Encyklopedia organizacji i zarządzania.* Warszawa: PWE.
Penc, J. (2002). Nowe koncepcje zarządzania. *Ekonomika i Organizacja Przedsiębiorstwa*, 7, pp. 3–13.
Pfeffer, I. (1956). *Insurance and Economic Theory.* Huebner Foundation for Insurance Education. Philadelphia, PA: University of Pennsylvania.
Phelan, J.G., Stein, D.D., Weissman, H. (1961). An exploration of some personality – Correlates to business risk taking behavior. *Amercian Psychologist*, 16(7), pp. 400–401.
Phillips-Wren, G., Jain, L. (2006). Artificial intelligence for decision making [in:] B. Gabrys, R.J. Howlett, L.C. Jain (eds.), *Knowledge-Based Intelligent Information and Engineering Systems*, Lecture Notes in Computer Science, KES, 4252, Berlin, Heidelberg: Springer, pp. 531–536.
Pineiro-Chousa, J., Vizcaíno-González, M., López-Cabarcos, M. (2016). Reputation, game theory and entrepreneurial sustainability. *Sustainability*, 8(1196), pp. 1–13.

Pivetti, M. (1987). Interest and profit in Smith, Ricardo and Marks. *Political Economy Studies in the Surplus Approach*, 3(1), pp. 63–74.
Porter, M.E. (1987). From competitive advantage to corporate strategy. *Harvard Business Review*, 65(3), pp. 43–59.
Power, M. (2004). *The Risk Management of Everything*. London: DEMOS.
Raiffa, H., Luce, E.S. (1957). *Games and Decisions*. New York: John Wiley & Sons.
Raviv, A. (1979). The design of an optimal insurance policy. *American Economic Review*, 69(1), pp. 84–96.
Rawls, J. (1971). *A Theory of Justice*. Cambridge, MA: Harvard University Press.
Reed, W.G. (1916). Weather as a business risk in farming. *Geographical Review*, 2(1), pp. 48–53.
Regda, G.E. (2007). *Principles of Risk Management and Insurance*. New York: Prentice Hall.
Romer, P.M. (1990). Endogenous technological change. *Journal of Political Economy*, 98(5), pp. 71–102.
Rosa, E. (1998). Meta theoretical foundations for post-normal risk. *Journal of Risk Research*, 1, pp. 15–44.
Roselius, T. (1971). Consumer rankings of risk reduction methods. *Journal of Marketing*, 35, pp. 56–61.
Rothschild, M., Stiglitz, J.E. (1970). Increasing risk: A definition. *Journal of Economic Theory*, 2(3), pp. 225–243.
Rothschild, M., Stiglitz, J.E. (1971). Increasing risk: Its economic consequences. *Journal of Economic Theory*, 3(1), pp. 66–84.
Samuelson, P.A. (1952). Probability, utility, and the independence axiom. *Econometrica*, 20(4), pp. 670–678.
Sargeant, A., Jen, S. (2016). Risk perception and management in development philanthropy. *Voluntary Sector Review*, 7(3), pp. 251–267.
Savage, L. (1954). *The Foundations of Statistics*. New York: John Wiley & Sons.
Schelling, T.C. (1981). *The Strategy of Conflict*. Boston, MA: Harvard University Press.
Schiliro, D. (2017). Economics versus psychology. Risk, uncertainty and the expected utility theory. *Munich Personal RePEc Archive*, MPRA Paper No. 83366.
Schmidt, K.M. (2017). Contributions of Oliver Hart and Bengt Holmström to contract theory. *Scandinavian Journal of Economics*, 119(3), pp. 489–511.
Scholes, M.S. (1976). Taxes and the pricing of options. *Journal of Finance*, 31, pp. 319–332.
Schumpeter, J.A. (1934). *Theory of Economic Development: An Inquiry into Profits, Capital, Credit, Interest and the Business Cycles*. Cambridge, MA: Harvard University Press.
Schwartz, E., Aronson, J.R. (1967). Some surogate evidence in support of the concept of optimal financial structure. *Journal of Finance*, 22(1), pp. 10–18.
Shackle, G.L.S. (1972). *Epistemics and Economics: A Critique of Economic Doctrines*. Cambridge: Cambridge University Press.
Sharpe, W. (1964). Capital assets prices: A theory of market equilibrium under conditions of risk. *Journal of Finance*, 19(3), pp. 425–442.
Sharpe, W. (1970). *Portfolio Theory and Capital Market*. New York: McGraw-Hill.
Sierpińska, M., Jachna, T. (1993). *Ocena przedsiębiorstwa według standardów światowych*. Warszawa: PWN.

Simon, H.A. (1955). A behavioural model of rational choice. *The Quarterly Journal of Economics*, 69(1), pp. 99–118.

Simon, H.A. (1965). *Administrative Behavior: A Study of Decision Making Processes in Administrative Organisation*. Toronto, ON: Free Press.

Simon, H.A. (1977). *Models of Discovery and Other Topics in the Methods of Science*. Dordrecht: Kluwer Academic Publishers.

Simon, H.A. (1979). *Models of Thought*, 1. New Haven, CT: Yale University Press.

Simon, H.A. (1989). *Models of Thought*, 2, New Haven, CT: Yale University Press.

Sinkey, J.F. Jr. (1992). *Commercial Bank Financial Management in the Financial Services Industry*. New York: Macmillan Publishing Company.

Slovic, P. (2001). *Smoking: Risk, Perception Policy*. Thousand Oaks, CA: Sage.

Slovic, P., Fischhoff, B., Lichtenstein, S. (1982). Facts versus fears: Understanding perceived risk [in:] D. Kahneman, P. Slovic, A. Tversky (eds.), *Judgment under Uncertainty: Heuristics and Biases*. Cambridge: Cambridge University Press, pp. 463–489.

Smith, V. (1962). An experimental study of competitive market behavior. *Journal of Political Economy*, 70, pp. 111–137.

Smith, V. (1965). Experimental auction markets and the Walrasian hypothesis. *Journal of Political Economy*, 70, pp. 387–393.

Smithson, M. (1999). Conflict aversion: Preference for ambiguity vs conflict in sources and evidence. *Organizational Behavior and Human Decision Processes*, 79(3), pp. 179–198.

Snowdon, B., Vane, H., Wynarczyk, P. (1998). *Współczesne nurty teorii makroekonomii*. Warszawa: Wydawnictwo Naukowe PWN.

Sottilotta, C.E. (2013). *Political Risk: Concepts, Definitions, Challenges*. Working Paper Series, SOG-WP6/2013, Luiss School of Government, Roma.

Spekman, R.E., Davis, E.W. (2004). Risky business: Expanding the discussion on risk and extended enterprise. *International Journal of Physical Distribution & Logistics Management*, 34(5), pp. 414–433.

Spiegelhalter, D. (2017). Risk and uncertainty communication. *Annual Review of Statistics and Its Application*, 4, pp. 31–60.

Stabryła, A. (2006). *Zarządzanie projektami ekonomicznymi i organizacyjnymi*. Warszawa: PWN.

Śliwiński, A. (2002). *Ryzyko ubezpieczeniowe. Taryfy, budowa i optymalizacja*. Warszawa: Poltext.

Taleb, N. (2007). *The Black Swan*. New York: Random House.

Taylor, C.R. (2003). The role of risk versus the role of uncertainty in economic systems. *Agricultural Systems*, 75(2–3), pp. 251–264.

Tchankova, L. (2002). Risk identification – Basic stage in risk management. *Environmental Management and Health*, 13(3), pp. 290–297.

Tedford, D., Hämmerle, E. (2008). Managing operational risks in small – and Medium-sized enterprises (SMEs) engaged in manufacturing – An integrated approach. *International Journal of Technology Policy and Management*, 8(4), pp. 420–441.

Teymouri, M., Ashoori, M. (2011). The impact of information technology on risk management. *Procedia Computer Science*, 3, pp. 1602–1608.

Thaler, R.H. (1994). *Quasi Rational Economics*. New York: Russell Sage Foundation.

Thaler, R.H. (1999). Mental accounting matters. *Journal of Behavioral Decision Making*, 12, pp. 183–206.

Thaler, R.H. (2015). *Misbehaving: The Making of Behavioral Economics.* New York: W.W. Norton & Company.

The Sveriges Riksbank Prize in Economic Sciences in Memory of Alfred Nobel. (2020). All Prizes in Economic Sciences. https://www.nobelprize.org/prizes/lists/all-prizes-in-economic-sciences/ (Access: 10.09.2020).

von Thünen, J.H. (1910). *Der isolierte Staat in Beziehung auf Landwirtschaft und Nationalökonomie.* Jena: Verlag von Gustav Fischer.

Tintner, G. (1941). The pure theory of production under technological risk and uncertainty. *Econometrica*, 9(3–4), pp. 305–312.

Toarna, A., Cojanu, V. (2015). The 2008 crisis: Causes and future direction for the academic research. *Procedia Economics and Finance*, 27, pp. 385–393.

Toma, S.V., Chiriță, M., Şarpe, D. (2012). Risk and uncertainty. *Procedia Economics and Finance*, 3, pp. 975–980.

Tse, Y.K., Tan, K.H., Chung, S.H., Lim, M.K. (2011). Quality risk in global supply network. *Journal of Manufacturing Technology Management*, 22(8), pp. 1002–1013.

Ugur, M. (2005). Risk, uncertainty and probabilistic decision making in an increasingly volatile world. *Handbook of Business Strategy*, 6(1), pp. 19–24.

Ulbert, J., Csanaky, A. (2004). Risk perception and risk behaviour. *Economic Review*, LI, pp. 235–258.

United Nations Economic Commission for Europe. (2012). *Risk Management in Regulatory Frameworks: Towards a Better Management of Risk.* New York and Geneva.

Urbanowska-Sojkin, E. (2013). *Ryzyko w wyborach strategicznych w przedsiębiorstwach.* Warszawa: PWE.

Usher, D. (1965). Political risk. *Economic Development & Cultural Change*, 13(4), pp. 453–463.

Uyemura, D.G., van Deventer, D.R. (1993). *Financial Risk in Banking Management: The Theory and Application of Asset and Liabilities Management.* Irwin: Burr Ridge.

Varian, H. (1993). A portfolio of Nobel Laureates: Markowitz, Miller and Sharpe. *Journal of Economic Perspectives*, 7(1), pp. 159–169.

Vlek, C., Stallen, P.J. (1980). Rational and personal aspects of risk. *Acta Psychologica*, 45(1–3), pp. 273–300.

Wärneryd, K.E. (1996). Risk attitudes and risky behavior. *Journal of Economic Psychology*, 17(6), pp. 749–770.

Weber, M. (1948). Science as a vocation [in:] H.M.C.W. Gerth (ed.), *Weber, Max: Essays in Sociology.* London: Routledge & Kegan Paul, pp. 129–156.

Willett, A.W. (1901). *The Economic Theory of Risk and Insurance, Studies in History, Economics and Public Law.* New York: The Columbia University Press.

Williams Jr., C.A., Smith, M.L., Young, P.C. (2002). *Zarządzanie ryzykiem a ubezpieczenia.* P. Wdowiński (translate), Warszawa: Wydawnictwo Naukowe PWN.

Williams, N., Vorley, T., Williams, C. (2017). *Entrepreneurship and Institutions. The Causes and Consequences of Institutional Asymmetry.* Lanham, MD: Rownan & Littlefield International.

Williams, R., Bertsch, B., Dale, B., van der Viele, T., van Iwaarden, J., Smith, M., Visser, R. (2006). Quality and risk management: What are the key issues? *The TQM Magazine*, 18(1), pp. 67–86.

Williamson, O.E. (1998). *Ekonomiczne instytucje kapitalizmu.* Warszawa: PWN.

Williamson, O.E. (2002). The theory of the firm as governance structure: From choice to contract. *Journal of Economic Perspective*, 16(3), pp. 171–195.

Williamson, O.E. (2015). Ekonomia kosztów transakcyjnych: naturalne etapy rozwoju. Nobel lecture given on December 8, 2009 with an introduction by Bob Jessop. *Zarządzanie Publiczne*, 2(32), pp. 67–90.

Wilson, D.R., Kaplan, R.M., Schneiderman, L.J. (1987). Framing of decisions and selection of alternatives in health care. *Social Behavior*, 2, pp. 51–59.

Wilson, R. (1992). Strategic analysis of auctions [in:] R. Aumann, S. Hart (eds.), *Handbook of Game Theory*, Volume 1, Chapter 8. Amsterdam: North-Holland/ Elsevier Science Publishers, pp. 227–279.

Wilson, R., Crouch, E.A.C. (1982). *Risk – Benefit Analysis*. Cambridge, MA: Ballinger.

World Economic Forum. (2017). *The Global Risks Report*. Cologny.

Woroch, G.A. (1988). Regulatory risk, investment and welfare. *Review of Industrial Organization*, 3(3), pp. 75–99.

Wright, G. (1980). Purchasing, risk and logistics: A neglected combination? *International Journal of Operations & Production Management*, 1(1), pp. 47–58.

Wrodarczyk, J. (2011). Zarządzanie ryzykiem w przedsiębiorstwie produkcyjnym zgodnie z założeniami teorii ograniczeń. *Studia Ekonomiczne/Uniwersytet Ekonomiczny w Katowicach*, 96, pp. 215–225.

Zaleśkiewicz, T. (2012). *Psychologia ekonomiczna*. Warszawa: Wydawnictwo Naukowe PWN.

Zieleniewski, J., Szczypiorski, S. (1963). *Zasady organizacji i techniki handlu zagranicznego*. Warszawa: PWE.

Zinn, J. (2006). Risk as an interdisciplinary research area. *Risk in Social Science*, 1, pp. 20–53.

Zinn, J. (2009). *The Sociology of Risk and Uncertainty – Current State and Perspectives*. The Australian Sociological Association (TASA) Annual Conference, Canberra, Australia, December 2009.

Zinn, J. (2010). Risk as discourse: Interdisciplinary perspectives. *Critical Approaches to Discourse Analysis across Disciplines*, 4(2), pp. 106–124.

2 Concepts and standards of risk management

2.1. The place of risk management in enterprise management system

Bernstein's (1996) *Against the Gods: The Remarkable Story of Risk* was a publication that significantly contributed to distinguishing risk management as a new sub-discipline of management sciences.

Risk management constitutes now a component of overall management that often determines the viability and growth of companies in a turbulent and unpredictable economic environment (Skrzypek, 2013), which is the primary and default objective of their functioning (Christopher et al., 2011; Elahi, 2013; Bromiley et al., 2015). The statement above is justified by not only observations of what takes place in enterprises, but also the scientific literature on the subject, as risk in management has become a frequent subject of scientific research. The effectiveness of management processes under risk conditions is determined by a good understanding of risk that initiates the creation of standardized approaches to and methodologies of risk management (O'Donnell, 2005; Gjerdrum, 2015).

2.1.1. The essence and place of risk management in business enterprises

The starting point for a proper understanding and definition of risk management is a systemic approach. The systemic trend in management is based on von Bertalanffy's (1984) general systems theory, in which a system is defined as a set of elements remaining in mutual relationships. The first aspect of considering an enterprise in the category of system results from the theory of complexity in management and allows one to treat it as a complex open system participating in a constant exchange with the environment (material, financial, information flows). The second aspect concerns a relational approach according to which the proper functioning of an enterprise as a system depends on the nature of relations among its elements and between the system and the environment (Levy, 2000; Holmdahl, 2005; Sadowski and Zajdel, 2009). The systemic approach in management allows one not only to perceive an enterprise as a system functioning under risk conditions, but also to regard risk management as an integrated system

DOI: 10.4324/9781003131366-2

(the integration of management domains, hierarchical levels, processes and relations). Such a system is one of the key determinants of effective business management allowing one to react actively to the complexity of the environment, while in a process approach, it is a set of interconnected, but conceptually separate processes aimed at the following (Hilson, 2006; Fischer et al., 2010; Dionne, 2013):

- identifying the awareness of risk and taking into account its different cognitive perspectives,
- identifying the nature of risk and the scale of threats,
- properly assessing identified risks,
- developing effective ways of dealing with identified risk factors,
- monitoring responses to risk with a view to developing contingency and prevention plans.

Risk management does not function as a separate system, independent of other dimensions of an enterprise's activities. It is now a key management domain that integrates the approach to risk with the leading objectives of a strategy (Schiller and Prpich, 2012). It is also deeply embedded in many other corporate management domains. Therefore, between the risk management system and the enterprise management system there should occur feedback characterized by inextricable coexistence based on interactions (Kaczmarek, 2010) whose character can be:

- structural (merging in the form of one coherent system),
- processual (relationships in decision-making processes),
- purposive (a common catalogue of objectives resulting from a strategy).

In enterprises, the direct importance of risk management can be seen in strategic and operations management, financial management, quality management, human resources management, project management, investment management and innovation management. Risk management is also inextricably linked to crisis management and business continuity management (Figure 2.1).

2.1.1.1. Risk management vis-à-vis strategic management

An analytical approach to strategic management in an enterprise allows the identification of areas that should be considered in the context of risk in a long-term perspective. Thus, the issue of risk in the activity of enterprises itself is the subject of analysis in comprehensive strategic management determining the achievement of strategic objectives. One of the objectives of strategic management is to enable the acquisition of relevant knowledge of the specific nature of risk and to develop a methodical approach to its analysis, which in turn makes it possible to verify the scope of threats to the enterprise, to assess their potential impact on efficiency and to ensure business continuity (Urbanowska-Sojkin, 2012; Schroeder, 2014). The risk occurring in the economic environment of enterprises is also crucial

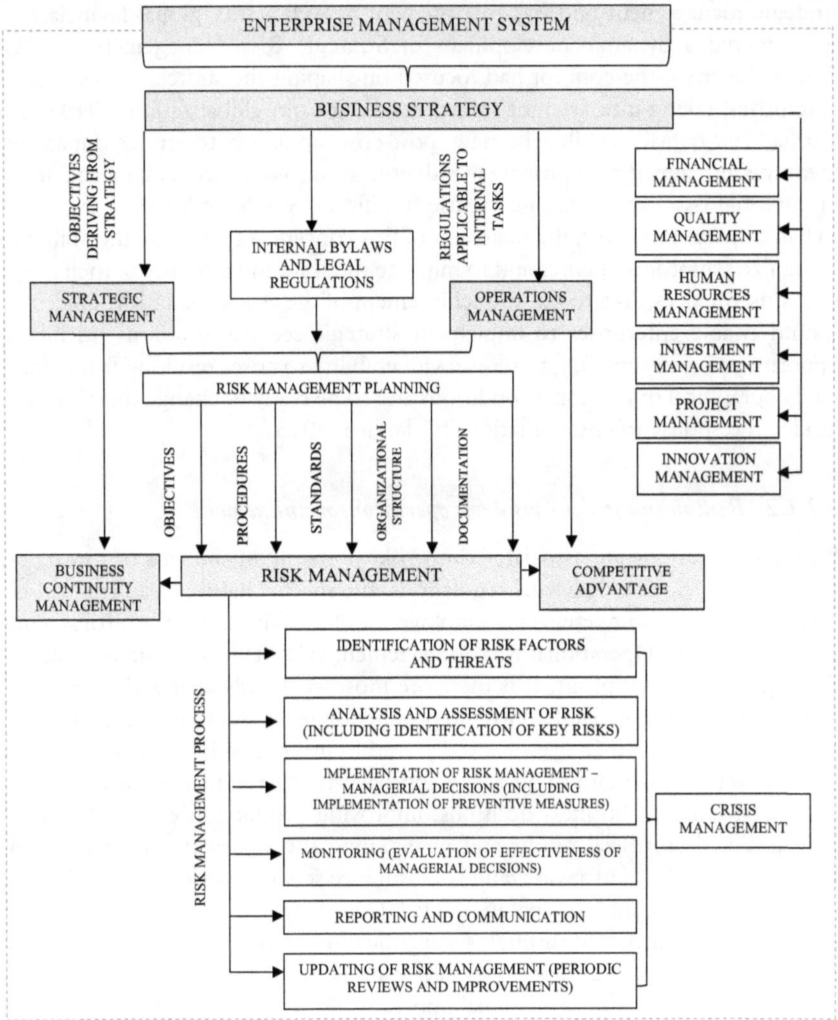

Figure 2.1 The place of risk management in enterprise management system

in selecting a development concept, i.e. at the leading stage of strategic management. In this case, a proper assessment of risk and development of methods of limiting it enables the enterprise to maintain or strengthen its competitive position, and thus determines the effectiveness of strategic management. Apart from being based on scientific theoretical foundations, the strategic approach to risk in the activities of enterprises should rely on conclusions drawn from the observation of business practices related to the stimulation of development in the face of intensifying, mainly economic and technological, threats (Goodfellow and Raynor, 2004; Urbanowska-Sojkin, 2013). The mutual relations between strategic management and risk management as well as the global financial crisis triggered a dynamic development of Strategic Risk Management (SRM). Before the crisis, the concept had focused on shaping the strategic objectives of enterprises, taking into account threats resulting from globalization (Clarke and Varma, 1999). Meanwhile, the new, post-crisis approach to strategic management was also aimed at improving the identification, assessment and management of potential risk factors that may cause significant economic losses or even lead to bankruptcy. However, the main aim of this concept is to acquire the ability to recognize symptoms of crises and to mitigate the scale and intensity of their negative consequences. As a result, the achievement of the established SRM objectives should enable enterprises to implement strategic security solutions (including opportunistic investments), to reduce vulnerability to crises resulting from sectoral, geographical or relational conditions and to be ready to change their business model in response to crisis situations (Calandro, 2015).

2.1.1.2. Risk management vis-à-vis operations management

Business operations are associated with risk, primarily in the face of threats on the micro scale, related to legal regulations, the specific nature of an enterprise's core business, the competences of employees and the efficiency of control systems and mechanisms. Operational Risk Management (ORM) is of key importance in shaping a company's profit. It is therefore most frequently analyzed in the context of threats to financial stability and production processes (e.g. decreasing productivity) (Naude and Chiweshe, 2017). In the current conditions of conducting business activity, the aim of an active approach to operational risk is improving the effectiveness of business decisions, improving production efficiency, ensuring sustainable financial results and maintaining the achieved market position. Despite the existence of a wide range of insurance services constituting traditional tools of protection against operational risk (Manning and Gurney, 2005), these aims can only be achieved through synergistic integration of the company's strategy (strategic objectives) with operational processes. Operational risk management should constitute a managerial imperative for enterprises, firstly because of the impact of small systemic failures on risk expansion in other business areas (a chain reaction) (Kleindorfer and Saad, 2005), and secondly because of the need to continuously raise the awareness of operational risk (together with indicating a degree of tolerance) in order to build resilience to risk and balance the needs of customers, suppliers, employees, shareholders and regulators (Kumar et al., 2014).

2.1.1.3. Risk management vis-à-vis other management areas

Risk in the financial management of enterprises can be considered as a key aspect in the preparation of financial plans resulting from a financial strategy, constituting a challenge to following the trends in the shaping of global or national financial policies (Li, 2003). Financial risk is therefore categorized, on the one hand, as a leading area of risk related to the occurrence of financial losses (Vaughan, 1992), but, on the other hand, as a factor that, if properly managed, can reduce the overall level of risk and thus the cost of risk, which can cause an increase in the value of the enterprise (Fairchild, 2002). Moreover, establishing their risk management objectives, companies (mainly, but not only, in the financial sector) refer to objectives related to profitability or financial reliability (Jedynak and Bąk, 2019). In view of the above arguments indicating the strength of the impact of financial risk on the overall condition of enterprises, risk is strongly methodically embedded in financial management. However, the techniques and tools for its assessment, including financial ratios (liquidity, debt, profitability) allow a diagnosis of exposure to risk that is meaningful only at the time of measurement. It is therefore necessary to implement advanced methods of early warning of a financial collapse or crisis, going beyond the statistical or mathematical calibration of financial risk models. This is particularly important given the high volatility of financial risk sources, the diversity of financial instruments and the complexity of interactions among market players. In addition, financial risk management should provide a cognitive perspective on risk at both the macro scale (in the face of globalization challenges, economic uncertainty and financial crises) (Hammoudeh and McAleer, 2015) and the micro scale (interest rate, credit, liquidity, equity, commodity, operational, market and counterparty risks) (Garcia and Javier, 2017), establishing its own transparency requirements for financial instruments, developing models of generating and processing information on threats to and opportunities for financial results and taking into account the causes and consequences of systemic risk (Mertzanis, 2014).

Risk management systems implemented by enterprises must be consistent with established quality objectives. According to the recommendations of the ISO 9001 standard (2015), modern enterprises should integrate quality management systems with business processes, taking into consideration risk-based thinking. Thus, a risk-based approach to management is the overriding intention of modern quality management. A properly conducted process of risk analysis in a quality management system should ultimately be a source of information on actions necessary to develop the enterprise without undesirable disruptions, maintain production continuity, meet customer requirements and improve the competitiveness of products on the market. Besides the area of production operations, a risk analysis of a quality management system should also address pending non-production projects, the implementation of administrative and personal changes and the improvement of relations with the environment, as risk management is a determinant of the quality of management of the entire enterprise (Lisiecka, 2012). A comprehensive approach to risk is the basis for continuous improvement of the developed quality management system (Penchansky and Macnee, 1993) and facilitates a pro-quality approach to all dimensions of enterprise management (Williams et al., 2006), which is a default objective of Total Quality Management (TQM).

A human resources policy is crucial to the functioning of enterprises. Errors in its design, implementation and maintenance can cause many risk factors, often with irreversible negative consequences. In the literature on the subject, it is possible to observe a new direction in theoretical and business research, i.e. human resource risk management (e.g. Oborilová et al., 2015; Huang et al., 2017; Mitrofanova et al., 2017). Risk in human resource management is understood as the probability of a negative event occurring as a result of personnel decisions. The causes of the occurrence of risk in human resources management can be found, among others, in insufficient qualifications of employees and managers, inappropriate decisions taken during recruitment processes, an improperly functioning system of training and improving employees' qualifications, shortcomings of an incentive and remuneration system, failures to observe ethical principles and to comply with legal regulations as well as internal bylaws and regulations (Lipka, 2002; Bochniarz and Gugała, 2005).

Operating in a turbulent environment, enterprises are obliged to adapt to market requirements and increasing volatility. To this end, they often undertake complex and multidomain tasks requiring the use of specialist project management methods. This area of activity is currently one of the determinants of building a competitive advantage for companies (Frame, 2001; Trocki, 2012). The processes of risk identification, assessment and analysis should take place at all stages of business project management, but mainly in cost management, time management, supply management, communication management, integrity management and quality management. According to international standards (PMBOK Guide ..., 2017), the primary objective of project risk management is maintaining risk within acceptable limits established for profitability, rationality and costs, which should guarantee the achievement of the expected effectiveness of a project (Cooper et al., 2005). Ward and Chapman (2003) also indicate that risk management processes in projects should focus on managing opportunities in proportion to the degree of concentration on the risk of failure in their implementation, as overestimation of threats may result in a decrease in the effectiveness of project work, which in turn may translate into a negative final result.

Investing activities undertaken by contemporary companies and above all their success understood in terms of generating profit and multiplying assets are possible thanks to hedging against their negative results (Zachorowska, 2006; Merková and Drábek, 2015). Investment decisions taken by enterprises are inextricably linked to risk that cannot be eliminated. It is only possible to properly assess such risk and develop methods for dealing with the effects of its materialization. This process is facilitated by early warning and rapid reaction systems, which are important components of integrated risk management. In investment risk management, investment controlling is an important supporting instrument. Thanks to it, it is possible to coordinate all stages of the investment process, properly adjust the budget, monitor the implementation of investment, measure its effectiveness and monitor the achievement of investment goals. Other ways of limiting investment risk include optimal allocation of investments in the capital management system, diversification of the investment portfolio as well as hedging enabling the protection of assets against losses resulting from unforeseen events and ensuring greater flexibility of investing activities (Li and Wu, 2009; Jakšić and Leković, 2015; Czyżowska, 2016).

Innovation and risk are inseparable phenomena. Innovation-oriented enterprises face the challenge of mitigating economic, technological and market risks, especially due to the heterogeneous structure of national innovation systems (mainly in developing countries) as well as economic and market instability. Threats to innovation activities should therefore be addressed in a comprehensive interpretative framework tailored to objectives established in strategies (da Silva Etges and Cortimiglia, 2019), and their assessment should be of primary importance in business decision-making processes in companies undertaking such activities (Deptuła and Knosala, 2015). The rapid development of the innovation market resulting from technological progress, and the consequent steadily increasing number of companies considered innovative, creates increasing uncertainty about the internal and external (macroeconomic) factors of the evolution of innovative business (Mortimer, 1995; Nagano et al., 2014). Such uncertainty justifies regarding risk management as a key stage in innovation management (Hauser et al., 2006; Wong and Chin, 2007). O'Connor et al. (2008) point out that the progress of innovation in enterprises should always be treated as a factor of development, but with a coexisting proactive approach to risk identification and analysis. As a result, it is possible to reconcile a high degree of uncertainty with a dynamic business environment, which in turn makes it possible to generate profits from innovation activities. The risk of innovation has intangible and global characteristics (Giugliani, 2012), and the main factors of threats are related to the failure to use or the improper use of the potential provided by invested capital and the necessity to fulfil the needs of the consumer as well as to maintain them as a recipient of an innovative product (Hauser et al., 2006).

2.1.2. The formal status of risk management

Taking into account the significance of risk in the particular management areas analyzed above, which determines the importance of risk management in the management systems, it is possible to determine its formal status (Table 2.1).

The multitude of formulations defining the formal status of risk management (Table 2.1) shows its numerous functions in the business management system. Moreover, the sources of determining the formal status of risk management should be seen in approaches to, theories and dimensions of management, the business environment (including external conditions), internal conditions (e.g. strategy, work specialization). The factors determining the status of risk management are, among others: strategic objectives, domains, processes, management concepts and systems whose implementation may be perceived as one of the elements of competitive advantage of enterprises (Bąk, 2017).

Table 2.1 The formal status of risk management

Source of status	*Determinant of status*	*The formal status of risk management*
Corporate strategy	Strategic objectives	• leading strategic objective; • determinant of ensuring business continuity; • company success factor; • managerial imperative.
Process approach	Management processes	• one of strategic management processes; • separate management process.
Systemic approach	Enterprise management system Enterprise management subsystems	• separate management system; • enterprise management subsystem; • element of enterprise management subsystems.
Management dimensions	Management domains Functional areas of enterprise	• mandatory element of all management domains and functional areas of enterprise; • specialist management domain; • enterprise management function.
Work specialization	Competencies of managers	• specialization in managerial work; • determinant of managerial competencies.
Theory of complexity Theory of integration	Complexity of management systems Integration of management systems	• reason for integration of management systems; • integrated management system; • reaction to complexity of management systems.
Globalization Sectoral circumstances Economic environment Relational approach	Management concepts	• mandatory element of management concept; • source of competitive advantage.

2.2. The embedding of risk in modern management concepts

Management concepts constitute a unique link between economic theory and practice. Thanks to methodologies and approaches recommended in particular concept guidelines, enterprises can continuously improve the effectiveness of their actions and appropriately respond to changes. Many of the current management concepts show strong links to risk, thus representing new areas of risk analysis. These include the following:

- Lean Management,
- Outsourcing,
- Corporate Social Responsibility,
- Supply Chain Management,
- Value Based Management.

The links between the above concepts and risk management can be established by identifying the significance of risk in a given concept, identifying the types of risk connected with the implementation and application of a concept, identifying key risk management principles in enterprises applying a concept.

2.2.1. Connections between Risk Management and Lean Management

Lean Management represents an approach to management whose main objectives are increasing added value and eliminating waste in the use of resources. According to the recommendations for the application of this concept, it is possible to increase added value by maximizing the use of resources and simplifying/streamlining the internal procedures and structures of the enterprise. Simplifying should also take place at the production level, where final products, while fulfilling quality requirements, should be manufactured using possibly the fewest means of production (lean manufacturing) (Womack et al., 2007; Sundar et al., 2014).

The implementation and subsequent application of the Lean Management concept at the level of individual projects results in many personal, functional and processual threats. These include, for example (Marodin and Aurin, 2015):

- a lack of managerial competencies and expertise in the implementation of the concept at the operational level,
- problems with the dynamics of improvements implementation,
- a lack of cooperation in the implementation of improvements among the operational level and middle and top managers,
- communication problems,
- resource shortages,
- employees' concerns and reluctance to implement improvements.

Responding to the identified threats to the successful implementation and application of the Lean Management concept, managers need to resort to the principles of risk management. The risk analysis process should be oriented towards the enterprise's objectives related to the implementation of Lean Management (Marodin and Aurin, 2015). Moreover, the developed methods of coping with risk should focus particularly on the enterprise's stakeholders who may have a significant impact on the achievement of objectives provided for in the principles of the concept (Sunder, 2016).

As a result of the raised awareness of threats related to Lean Management among managers implementing this concept in enterprises, the emergence of a new sub-discipline of risk management – Lean Risk Management (Bollinger, 2010) – can be observed. This approach to risk illustrates the close links among risk assessment, the results of a given undertaking and the maximum utilization of available current and historical information applicable to the undertaking. This combination of elements in risk management manifests itself in the rigorous monitoring of risk, the development of ways to respond rapidly to fortuitous events and the synergistic integration of risk management with project planning and execution (schedule, budget) using the Lean concept.

The ultimate objective of using Lean Risk Management in the implementation of projects is making the risk management process more flexible (adapting it to the variability of both the probability and impact of risk over time), which is expected to translate into improved efficiency, more reasonable management of resources and a greater focus on creating value for customers (Bollinger, 2010).

2.2.2. Connections between Risk Management and outsourcing

Outsourcing is enterprises' popular strategic behaviour used to seek more effective ways of dealing with competitiveness, reducing costs and improving profitability (Jiang and Quareshi, 2006). Separating individual functions or projects to be carried out outside the company's structure is associated with different types of risk and requires a high degree of caution and flexibility on the part of the management team. Therefore, it is necessary to ensure the management of such risk in outsourcing activities. Risk management should therefore constitute a key area for optimizing outsourcing activities, adapted to financial, information and personnel resources as well as the possibilities of implementing specialized projects. In order to effectively prevent failures arising from the application of this management concept, enterprises should treat outsourcing not as a single undertaking, but as a permanent strategic activity. In the current business environment characterized by hyper-competition, consideration should be given to moving away from the traditional approach, which prescribes the outsourcing of only non-core processes in a given business organization, towards an approach that recommends developing and improving the capacity and capability to outsource multiple processes, even key ones (Pratap, 2014). The risk factors characteristic of outsourcing activities can be divided into three categories: strategic risk, operational risk and international risk (Table 2.2).

Risk management in outsourcing processes should focus on monitoring and assessing risk over time. This process should constitute an integral part of corporate strategies. In order to respond appropriately to an emerging risk or to prevent it from occurring, companies should in particular (Lankford and Parsa, 1999):

- properly assess their individual outsourcing options (costs, resources),
- take care of the proper selection of partners (and monitor them on an ongoing basis),
- adopt a flexible approach to change.

Table 2.2 Risk in outsourcing

Category of risk	*Type of risk*
Strategic	• loss of core competencies, • loss of ability to succeed, • lack of commitment and knowledge on the part of managers, • errors in threat identification, • lack of formal outsourcing activity supervision programmes.
Operational	• quality risk – low quality of outsourced activities, • financial risk – high outsourcing costs and costs of lack of expected outsourcing effects, • time risk – failure to meet the outsourced activities schedule, • technical risk – application of inappropriate technological solutions, • supplier risk – selection of unsuitable suppliers, • reputational risk – adverse opinions about the company, • intellectual property risk – unfair practices related to communicating product information and knowledge, • flexibility risk – loss of control over outsourced projects, • communication risk – no communication plan for outsourcing, • resource risk – inappropriate planning of resources for outsourcing purposes.
International	• exchange rate volatility, • non-tariff barriers, • political risks – stability of host governments and legal systems, • social risks – social stability of host countries and socio-cultural differences.

Source: the authors' own work based on: Power et al., 2004; Leavy, 2004; Schniederjans and Zuckweiler, 2004; Gandhi et al., 2012.

2.2.3. *Connections between Risk Management and Corporate Social Responsibility (CSR)*

According to the European Commission's definition, Corporate Social Responsibility is a concept of voluntary inclusion of social and environmental aspects in the conduct of business activities and contacts with stakeholders (Green Paper for Promoting ..., 2001). In economic practice, the involvement of contemporary enterprises in CSR activities is no longer a voluntary choice, but a necessity in shaping and maintaining an organization's positive image. The reasons for strengthening the importance of this sphere of business activity are, among others, growing expectations of stakeholders regarding CSR and the downward trend in confidence in business entities (Dowling, 2006).

Therefore, the main type of risk arising from the concept of corporate social responsibility is reputational risk. Reputation is one of the results of social responsibility (Coombs and Holladay, 2015). In addition, damage to reputation caused by failing to carry out CSR activities or carrying them out in a manner inconsistent with stakeholders' expectations can often turn into an irreversible image crisis (Jedynak, 2017).

In order to properly manage risk related to CSR, enterprises should primarily focus on risk prevention in order to significantly reduce the likelihood of adverse social or economic events (resulting from a wrong approach to CSR implementation) (Ratajczak and Wołoszyn, 2011), reduce the likelihood of conflicts with stakeholders (Becchetti et al., 2015) and – at the level of multinational enterprises – reduce the risk of corruption (Krishnamurti et al., 2018).

2.2.4. Connections between Risk Management and Supply Chain Management (SCM)

Supply Chain Management is by definition a process of systematic actions aimed at ensuring the integrated management of the value of supplies in order to meet the needs and expectations of customers, from the raw materials supplier, through production processes, to the final customer (Stein and Voehl, 1998). According to Lambert et al. (1998), Supply Chain Management is the integration of business processes (services, products, information) between end users and suppliers with a view to continuously increasing value for customers. A compilation of SCM definitions prepared by Larson and Rogers (1998) is a good source for the presentation of the characteristic features of the concept. These include business process integration, flexibility, cooperation dynamics and coordination, international character, structural complexity, multiplicity of participants and control of value creation.

Given these characteristics, the risk arising from Supply Chain Management is diverse and its management should be understood as a process of cooperation among partners consisting in the joint use of risk management tools and techniques to deal with the factors affecting the existing relationships and involved resources (Norrman and Jansson, 2004). The risk factors associated with SCM are categorized in Table 2.3.

Risk management processes in the supply chain should aim at identifying and responding quickly to risks in inter-organizational business cooperation (Bowersox, 1990), mainly those arising from relations among supply chain participants (besides resources, information and benefits, they also share threats). Proper management of risk resulting from such relations is a prerequisite for the effective flow of resources in the chain (Handfield and Nichols, 2004). These activities should therefore be integrative and strategic in nature (Ajmera and Cook, 2009). The management of risk in the supply chain is a process of such importance that it has led to the emergence of another sub-discipline of risk management, i.e. Supply Chain Risk Management (e.g. Ghadge et al., 2012; Ivanov et al., 2019).

2.2.5. Connections between Risk Management and Value Based Management (VBM)

Value Based Management is a management concept whose primary objective is maximizing value for all stakeholders, from owners to consumers. This concept

Table 2.3 Risk in Supply Chain Management

Category of risk	*Type of risk*
Strategic	• market position maintenance risk, • market survival (business continuity) risk, • economic environment risk, • systemic risk, • sovereignty risk.
Operational	• quality risk, • risk of disruption of business cooperation (time, process and relationship problems), • forecasting and estimation risk, • supply risk, • demand risk, • control risk, • transport risk, • risk of disruption of production processes.
International	• risk of global change rate and frequency, • currency risk, • security risks arising from international cooperation, • cultural risk, • legal and administrative risk.

Source: the authors' own work based on: Delerue, 2005; Manuj and Mentzer, 2008; Christopher et al., 2011; Tummala and Schoenherr, 2011.

is also regarded as an element integrating the enterprise's strategy with generated profits and focused on embedding the aforementioned objective in its strategic, operational and investment decisions. The direct reason for the development of the concept was the need to compensate for differences between the potential and real values of the enterprise through adequate management processes (Dumond, 1996; Kim, 2004; Szczepankowski, 2007; Jaki, 2008).

Risk plays a significant role in the concept of value based management. It is one of the determinants of the success of its implementation, alongside growth and profitability (Black et al., 2000). The major types of risk in value based management include (Jaki, 2014):

- the risk of inappropriate measurement of the enterprise's value (inadequate measurement techniques and tools, lack of competences of the management),
- the risk of internal stakeholders (asymmetry of risk distribution among stakeholders),
- the risk related to the concept implementation process (errors in the construction of a management system focused on creating and multiplying the enterprise's value),
- global risk (the risk of failure to maintain the long-term growth of the enterprise in a situation of potential financial and economic crises).

The inseparable combination of value management and risk management has resulted in a new concept of Value Based Risk Management (Faupel and Michels, 2014) whose main objective is maintaining and increasing the value of the enterprise by investments in advanced risk analysis processes. The concept is based on an assumption resulting from observations of business practices, mainly after the global financial crisis, confirming that the implemented risk management measures and methods have a positive impact on the enterprise's value and its recovery. Furthermore, the permanent integration of risk management with value based management enables companies to maintain the stability of the already developed value as, as it were, security against its decrease or loss (Krysiak, 2011).

2.3. Professional domains of risk management

2.3.1. Business Continuity Management (BCM)

Business Continuity Management is based on maintaining the effectiveness of the business entity in undesirable situations by integrating management activities in the areas of risk management, security management and crisis management (Fischbacher-Smith, 2017). Managing the possibility of business survival should be planned and coordinated at the strategic level in a continuous management system (also in normal, non-crisis conditions). Operational continuity can be defined in normative terms as the business entity's strategic and tactical capacity (British Standards Institution BS 25999-2, 2007):

- to plan ways of responding to incidents or disruptions in its operations in order to continue its activities at the level specified in the strategy,
- to mitigate losses in the event of incidental events or disruptions.

Business Continuity Management means a continuous process of holistic management allowing the identification of threats and their impact on the functioning of the enterprise and the development of resilience and ability to respond effectively to adverse events in order to protect the interests of key stakeholders, reputation, brand and activities oriented towards increasing value (British Standards Institution BS 25999-1, 2006). Furthermore, BCM activities should be primarily aimed at ensuring that the level of risk is controlled and that the processes of primary importance for a given entity in terms of its strategic objectives are protected and continued (Randeree et al., 2012; Jedynak, 2013). The major stage of business continuity management is planning – Business Continuity Planning (BCP). It should take place at the strategic level, but with the delegation of activities also to the operational level, where early symptoms of threats can be identified as soon as possible, which serves to develop methodologies aimed at preventing, responding to and mitigating their negative consequences (Botha and Von Solms, 2004; Lindström et al., 2010). Business continuity management is strongly dependent on the pursuit of excellence and can therefore be understood as one dimension of continuous improvement (Kildow, 2011).

Although the origins of the concept of business continuity management date back to the 1970s (Herbane, 2010), a significant increase in the protection of key processes among mainly international enterprises was observed in the face of intensifying crises (Elliot et al., 2010). Global problems connected with growing threats translating themselves into internal crises of individual companies revealed their shortcomings in strategic plans to ensure business continuity. Thus, what can be observed in the current economic space is an increased emphasis on the implementation of specialist, standardized BCM solutions aimed at protecting strategic business processes and expressed in changes to management practices in order to maintain operational efficiency despite disruptions resulting from risk materialization.

Summing up the discussion of business continuity management, it is possible to identify the following distinguishing features of this specialized field of risk management (Venclova et al., 2013):

- it has the character of long-term and permanent management that cannot be limited to isolated and incidental actions,
- it should act as a safety buffer for enterprises, ensuring their survival even in the face of critical threats,
- it is one of the tools for promoting and protecting the image and reputation of the company,
- the preparation process for its implementation is time-consuming, costly and requires specialist knowledge of risk management,
- it should be one of the strategic objectives,
- compliance with its principles allows the enterprise to restore its normal functioning after a crisis,
- it constitutes a motivator for development and an area of continuous improvement.

2.3.2. Enterprise Risk Management (ERM)

Enterprise Risk Management is a modern approach to risk that dates back to the late 20th century. According to D'Arcy and Brogan (2001), it is a continuous process through which organizations, regardless of their type, can assess, control, finance and monitor risk from a variety of sources in order to improve value for stakeholders, both in the short and long term. Sobel and Reding (2004) define ERM as a structured and disciplined management approach that allows managers to understand uncertainty and risk and to manage them in an integrated and comprehensive way. Thus, ERM includes a set of processes and methods allowing enterprises to manage risk in all functional areas within a holistic and coherent system in order to ensure strategic success manifesting itself in the ability to continue business operations (Kopia et al., 2017).

As the traditional approach to risk management has become insufficient and inadequate for the increasing instability in the business world resulting from globalization and the crisis-generating environment (Quon et al., 2012), in today's business management, ERM represents a new paradigm of risk management that should have the character of strategic actions taken at all hierarchical levels and in all management areas (Beasley et al., 2005). Therefore, the (procedural and functional) integration of risk management with other management systems in the enterprise is extremely important for the successful implementation of the ERM concept. Emphasizing the importance of corporate risk management, it is possible to distinguish the following functions it fulfils in contemporary enterprises (O'Donnell, 2005; Frigo and Anderson, 2011):

- it constitutes a basis for achieving a competitive advantage,
- it provides an opportunity to prevent risk and, should risk materialize, it accelerates responses to it and improves their effectiveness,
- it focuses on risk optimization and makes it possible to take advantage of opportunities associated with its occurrence,
- it integrates the risk portfolio with strategic objectives and stakeholder expectations,
- it raises all employees' awareness of risk and risk prevention possibilities.

Bogodistov and Wohlgemuth (2017) emphasize that, in the shaping of a properly functioning ERM system, the following aspects need to be taken into account:

- the rational planning of resources related to taking risk optimization measures (allowing the setting of risk management priorities),
- the assessment of the capacity to respond to the occurrence of crises (defining tolerance levels based on past experience of dealing with unforeseeable events),
- the integration of strategic risk management activities with those at the operational level (allowing more flexibility and shorter response times to negative events).

As a result, the implementation of risk management in line with the recommendations of the ERM concept should result in the following (Fraser and Simkins, 2007):

- improving the enterprise's resistance to the occurrence of adverse events,
- decreasing risk exposure,
- integrating all business units in pursuit of risk management objectives,
- developing a strategic tool to assist managers in making decisions concerning risk prevention, incurrence and compensation.

ERM is sometimes used interchangeably with Integrated Risk Management (IRM). The scientific literature, on the other hand, provides examples where ERM and IRM are separate and different concepts. ERM is understood as above, while IRM refers to a much narrower range of activities, usually to risk management in a specific project, but with strategic support. In such cases, IRM is based

Table 2.4 A comparison of risk management domains

Domain / *Criterion*	*Business Continuity Management*	*Crisis Management*	*Enterprise Risk Management*
Objective	• ensuring ability to survive • shaping resistance	• mitigating effects of crises • shaping resistance	• optimizing risk • integrating processes • shaping resilience
Orientation	• entity as a system • reputation, brand	• functional areas affected by or exposed to crisis	• entity as a system • management functions
Hierarchical level	• strategic	• strategic • operational	• strategic with delegation to operational
Mode of operation	• permanent, continuous	• mainly incidental (crisis) • permanent (crisis prevention)	• permanent, continuous
Area of application	• critical business processes	• areas of activity susceptible to crises	• functional areas • management systems

Note: Crisis management is characterized in detail in Chapter 3.

on the integration of project objectives with project risks as well as financial and organizational aspects (Bandyopadhyay et al., 1999; Hilson, 2006; Fischer et al., 2010; Tóth and Sebestyén, 2014).

Crisis management is also a specialist domain of risk management. However, this particular area is not characterized in this chapter, as it is analyzed in detail in Chapter 3 of this work. Table 2.4 compares the currently functioning management domains representing specialist approaches to the issue of risk.

As can be seen from the comparison in Table 2.4, the common objective of all the domains of risk management under analysis is building resilience to the occurrence of undesirable situations, mainly of a crisis nature. Also, the modus operandi of a risk management system is permanent for each of the domains (also in the case of crisis management, where continuous preventive actions are necessary), which confirms the need for the permanent embedding of their specific mechanisms in organizational structures, managerial processes and all management areas.

2.4. Risk management standards

The 1990s witnessed a growing interest in opportunities to improve the ability to deal with the uncertainty of the environment and, in particular, its negative consequences for business activities. This was due to the continuous evolution and rising importance of security, uncertainty and risk management processes in the business environment. The reasons for this dynamic evolution include the following (Raz and Hillson, 2005):

- the expansion of activities by business enterprises, internationalization processes, the increasing importance of relations with stakeholders,
- a gradual transition from business models based on physical work to those based on knowledge,
- the growing role of technology and associated risk,
- the development of big-budget project management systems,
- highly competitive pressure among enterprises,
- the need to operate under conditions of limited access to information,
- the dynamic growth of complexity in the business space,
- the development of virtual business and networking,
- the intensifying influence of national and international regulations.

For these reasons, enterprises' demand for specialist, proven risk management methods and techniques was growing constantly. After some time, risk became an area of management subject to standardization processes. The result of these processes in the area of risk management was the establishment of a number of standards presenting universal patterns of conduct, comprehensive approaches and good practices. The aim of developing such standards was mainly to make the principles of risk identification, analysis and assessment uniform and to provide a set of tools and methodologies for building and improving intra-organizational risk management systems. There was also an increasing need to assess the level of progress of activities undertaken in relation to risk, which resulted in the development of a number of models for assessing the maturity of risk management, enabling enterprises to diagnose the development and effectiveness of applied risk management practices (Jedynak and Bąk, 2018).

The first published risk management standard was the Norwegian standard NS5814 Krav tilrisikoanalyser (Norges Standardiseringsforbund, 1991) that dealt with risk analysis without considering the other stages of the risk management process. Another standard from 1995 – CEI/IEC 300-3-9 Dependability Management (International Electrotechnical Commission, 1995) – also had in its structure a section devoted only to the process of risk analysis of technological systems. The first standard that systematized all stages of the risk management process was the British Standard BSI PD 6668 from 2000 (British Standards Institute, 2000), but it focused on risk management only in relation to corporate governance. Based on a scope of application, risk management standards can be divided into the following:

- holistic (focused on integrated risk management systems):
  1) FERMA Risk Management Standard (2002),
  2) COSO II Enterprise Risk Management – Integrated Framework (2004; 2017),
  3) AS/NZS 4360 The Australian and New Zealand Standard on Risk Management (2004; 2009),
  4) ISO 31000 Risk Management (2009; 2018).

- specific (focused on management areas directly related to risk management):
  1) ISO 28000 Specification for security management systems for the supply chain (2007),
  2) ISO/IEC 27005 Information technology – Security techniques – Information security risk management (2008; 2018),
  3) PMI Practice Standard for Project Risk Management (2009),
  4) ISO 22320 Societal security – Emergency management – Requirements for incident response (2011),
  5) ISO 22301 Societal security – Business continuity management systems (BCM) – Requirements (2012).

2.4.1. Holistic risk management standards

Holistic risk management standards include requirements for all stages of the risk management process. Thus, they focus on integrated management systems, providing proven, universal solutions allowing their synchronization with strategic objectives.

2.4.1.1. FERMA Risk Management Standard

FERMA Risk Management Standard (Federation of European Risk Management Associations) was developed in 2002 in consequence of the work carried out by an extensive team consisting of representatives of the following British institutions: The Institute of Risk Management (IRM), The Association of Insurance and Risk Managers (AIRMIC) and The National Forum for Risk Management in the Public Sector (ALARM). The standard can be applied in any entity, either public or private, and covers all types of risks (FERMA Risk Management Standard, 2002; Fałek, 2014). Under the FERMA standard, risk is perceived as both an opportunity and a threat (with an emphasis on the negative aspect) from the perspective of the implementing entity and its stakeholders. The standard defines risk as a combination of the probability of the occurrence of an event and its effects; it may be caused by either internal or external environmental factors. Risk management is defined as the process by means of which an organization methodically resolves its problems related to risks. It is the central element of strategic management consisting of the following stages: setting strategic objectives, assessing risk (identification, analysis, description, measurement, evaluation), reporting threats and opportunities, making decisions, dealing with risk, reporting and monitoring risk (FERMA Risk Management Standard, 2002; Koutsoukis, 2010).

The main benefits of implementing the FERMA standard are support for the pursuit of the enterprise's objectives through the following (Koutsoukis 2010; Hardy, 2015):

- improving the quality of the decision-making and planning processes,
- skilfully prioritizing extraordinary events,
- understanding business in a structured way,

- ensuring the right approach to opportunities and threats,
- allocating capital and resources more efficiently,
- reducing instability,
- protecting and improving the image of the organization,
- optimizing operational efficiency,
- improving the risk strategy at the operational level.

2.4.1.2. COSO II Enterprise Risk Management – Integrated Framework

The COSO II Enterprise Risk Management – Integrated Framework standard was published in 2004 by the Committee of Sponsoring Organizations of the Treadway Commission as the second extended version of the COSO I standard. The standard documentation formulates requirements concerning principles and concepts constituting recommendations for assessing and increasing the effectiveness of risk management at all organizational levels. COSO II can be implemented in all types of organizations. It focuses on both positive and negative aspects of risk. It analyses uncertainties and circumstances that attract risk, defining risk itself as the possibility of an event that could adversely affect the achievement of objectives. The key element of this standard is establishing the importance of corporate risk management defined as a process aimed at identifying potential threats, keeping risk within the set limits and ensuring the effective achievement of the organization's objectives. According to the recommendations of COSO II, the risk management process consists of the following stages: diagnosing the internal environment, setting goals, identifying events, assessing risk, responding to risk, as well as controlling, communicating and monitoring risk (COSO II Enterprise Risk Management Integrated Framework, 2004).

Used in an organization, COSO II can generate numerous benefits. The main advantages of its implementation include the following (COSO II Enterprise Risk Management Integrated Framework, 2004):

- more effective internal control,
- time savings (all principles, techniques and guidelines necessary to implement corporate risk management are gathered in one standard),
- the ability to effectively resolve problems at every stage of the process,
- support for risk training and communication processes at all levels of the organizational structure.

COSO updated the requirements of COSO II ERM – Integrated Framework in 2017, publishing the document titled COSO Enterprise Risk Management – Integrating with Strategy and Performance. The update was necessitated by global changes in the shaping of business risk and the resulting new challenges for enterprises. The new version of the standard indicates the need to integrate enterprise risk management with strategy and performance, which manifests itself in regarding an appropriate approach to risk as a strategic objective and a key factor determining the achievement of results (Jayantha, 2018).

2.4.1.3. AS/NZS 4360:2004 The Australian and New Zealand Standard on Risk Management

The standard was originally developed in 1995 by the technical committees of Australia and New Zealand (Joint Standards Australia/Standards New Zealand Committee OB-007). The first revision took place in 1999, and following numerous consultations with representatives of the academic, private and public sectors, further changes were introduced in the form of the second revision in 2004. The AS/NZS 4360 standard in this version became a foundation for all subsequent standardized risk management approaches. The standard is dedicated to all entities, regardless of size, business profile or industry. It applies to both the negative and positive side of risk, with emphasis on potential profits and losses. According to the provisions of the standard, risk is described as exposure to the (positive or negative) consequences of uncertainties and possible deviations from planned activities. Risk management is a process used to deal logically and systematically with the risks associated with a given activity, enabling the enterprise to minimize losses and maximize opportunities, consisting of the following stages: establishing the risk context, identifying risk, analyzing risk, assessing risk and dealing with risk. Supporting functions are also fulfilled by communication, consultation, monitoring and review activities (AS/NZS 4360 ..., 2004; Szymanek, 2014). Based on AS/NZS 4360:2004, the ISO 31000:2009 standard was developed. The implementation of AS/NZS 4360 can bring many benefits such as (AS/NZS ISO 31000 ..., 2009):

- the improved awareness of the importance of risk recognition and handling,
- the more precise identification of opportunities and threats,
- the more efficient use of resources,
- ensuring compliance with legal requirements, greater emphasis on preventive actions,
- the more effective management of extraordinary events,
- more effective internal control,
- improved resistance to crises.

2.4.1.4. ISO 31000:2018 Risk Management – Guidelines

The first version of ISO 31000 was published in November 2009 by ISO (International Organization for Standardization) as an international extension of AS/NZS 4360:2004, under the title Risk Management – Principles and Guidelines. In February 2018, ISO updated the standard by publishing its version 31000:2018 Risk Management – Guidelines. The latest document describes general guidelines (in the form of a guide or a collection of good practices) supporting enterprises in creating and implementing a risk management framework, organizing the risk management process and integrating risk management with other management systems functioning in the enterprise. The standard is dedicated to all public and private organizations, regardless of type, size, business profile or industry. It can also be applied at every stage of the organization's life cycle and to a wide range of activities, including strategies and decisions, operations, processes, functions, projects, products, services and assets. The 2018 version of the standard focuses primarily on the following (ISO 31000 Risk Management – Guidelines, 2018):

- a review of risk management principles that are considered to be key success factors,
- a greater emphasis on leadership (the management should ensure full integration of risk management with the enterprise's general management system and all actions taken),
- a stronger emphasis on the iterative nature of risk management (using new experience, knowledge and analyses of reviews of the elements, activities and controls at each stage of the process, one should monitor the impact of new data on the risks identified by the organization),
- improvements in the risk management process based on the model of an open system that constantly exchanges information with the external environment in order to adjust the process to the management context and the needs of both the enterprise itself (resulting from strategic objectives, plans, employees' needs) and its stakeholders.

The current version of the standard also aims to support better planning and decision-making in the face of new global threats (Aven and Ylönen, 2019), including terrorism, cybercrime, political risks and natural disasters. The standard covers all types of risk, regardless of its nature, i.e. either negative or positive consequences, and defines risk as the impact of uncertainty on the organization's objectives. According to the standard, risk management is coordinated activities aimed at managing and controlling the organization with regard to risk. This process can be divided into the following phases: establishing the context, criteria and scope of risk, identifying risk, analyzing risk, assessing risk, dealing with risk, as well as recording and reporting. Communication, consultation, monitoring and reviewing activities also fulfil auxiliary functions. Furthermore, ISO 31000:2018 provides for the need for the continuous integration of the risk management process with leadership as well as value creation and protection (ISO 31000 Risk Management – Guidelines, 2018).

The main benefits of implementing the guidelines and good practices presented in the ISO 31000:2018 standard include the following (Bosetti, 2015; Ahmeti and Vladi, 2017; ISO 31000 Risk Management – Guidelines, 2018):

- developing effective risk management strategies based on the guidelines of the standard,
- increasing the likelihood of achieving the organization's objectives and better protection of assets,

- improving the awareness and effectiveness of decision-making processes related to risk,
- raising the awareness of the integration, monitoring and control of risk management at all hierarchical levels,
- developing an intra-organizational risk management culture,
- improving the organization's management and efficiency,
- providing the possibility of continuous improvement of the developed risk management systems.

2.4.2. Specific risk management standards

Specific risk management standards provide tools and methods for dealing with management areas directly related to risk. Such standards can be implemented separately or together with a selected holistic standard.

2.4.2.1. ISO 28000:2007 Specification for security management systems for the supply chain

The ISO 28000 standard was developed in 2005. Its complete binding version was published in September 2007 as one of the standards belonging to the ISO 28000 series addressing potential security issues at all stages of the supply process and developed in response to the ongoing globalization processes in international trade. The standard contains requirements for the building of a system managing processes in organizations cooperating within the supply chain. It can be used in all enterprises, from small to multinational, in the areas of production, services, warehousing or transport, at any link of the production or supply chain (ISO 28000, 2007). This standard perceives risk as a security threat to the entire organization, not just its logistics department, and identifies it with such incidents as theft, smuggling, illegal cargo handling, terrorism, etc. Instead of the terms risk and risk management, the ISO 28000 standards uses such phrases as security and security management. Security management is understood as resistance to intentional and illegal incidents aimed at disrupting the functioning of supply chain processes. Security management is defined as systematic and coordinated activities and practices by means of which the enterprises optimally manage risks and related potential threats and consequences. According to the requirements of the standard, the security management process consists of the following stages: developing a security policy, conducting a risk assessment, drawing up a risk management plan, implementing the planned actions, monitoring the situation, performing preventive actions, conducting management reviews (ISO 28000, 2007; Sitkowski, 2009).

The implementation of ISO 28000 has many advantages, for example (ISO 28000, 2007; Jarysz-Kamińska, 2011; 2012):

- optimizing processes,
- improving the security management system,
- ensuring compliance with legal requirements,

- improving the security of people and cargo in the supply chain,
- facilitating international trade,
- eliminating security gaps at the strategic and operational levels,
- building business credibility,
- minimizing costs,
- reducing the time needed to resolve logistical problems.

2.4.2.2. ISO/IEC 27005:2018 Information technology – Security techniques – Information security risk management

ISO/IEC 27005 is an international standard from the ISO 27000 series applicable to information security management systems. ISO/IEC 27005 was first published in 2008. The currently applicable version of the standard was released in July 2018. The document contains guidelines for information security risk management and supplementary recommendations concerning the setting of the scope and limits of the information security risk management process, asset valuation, a catalogue of typical threats, threat vulnerability assessment methods, information security risk assessment approaches and risk modification limitations. The standard is addressed to all types of organizations (business enterprises, government agencies, non-profit organizations) intending to manage risk that may threaten information security. In this standard, the approach to risk is closely related to the security of information that is regarded as other important assets indispensable for effective business operations; hence the standard emphasizes its adequate protection (Fazlida and Said, 2015). Risk is usually perceived as a threat to the confidentiality, integrity and availability of information. According to the terminology applicable to the whole ISO/IEC 27000 series of standards, risk is defined as a potential situation in which a specific threat exploits the vulnerability of an asset or a group of assets, thus causing damage to the organization. Furthermore, risk management, according to the standard, is a coordinated activity aimed at managing and controlling risk in the system. The guidelines of ISO/IEC 27005:2018 distinguish the following stages in the information security risk management process: establishing the context of risk, estimating risk (identification, analysis, assessment), dealing with risk, accepting risk. Risk communication, consultation, monitoring and review activities also play an important role in the process (ISO/IEC 27005, 2018).

The main advantages of the information security risk management standard are the following (Everett, 2011; Dzwonkowski, 2013; ISO/IEC 27005, 2018):

- improving the image and reputation of the organization,
- ensuring better protection and improvement of information assets,
- increasing the availability of information on all possible safeguards,
- providing better synchronization of information security management with risk management,
- lowering costs,
- ensuring compliance with legal requirements,

- raising managers' and employees' awareness of the need to ensure information security,
- reducing the time necessary to investigate security breaches.

2.4.2.3. PMI Practice Standard for Project Risk Management

The Practice Standard for Project Risk Management was developed and published by the Project Management Institute in the USA in 2009. The document contains guidelines, methods and best practices for project management, with particular emphasis on project risk management. The standard is dedicated to all those participating in project management: project managers, project teams, supervisory bodies and other persons involved in business projects, regardless of their scope, reach or importance. Risk in the PMI standard is perceived as a threat or opportunity. The full definition presented in the standard recognizes risk as uncertainty as to the occurrence of an event or condition which, if it occurs, will have a materially negative or positive impact on the course and objectives of the project. Risk management is defined as a systematic process of identifying, analyzing and responding to the risk occurring in the project, in order to maximize the probability of positive events and minimize the probability and consequences of adverse events threatening the achievement of project objectives. The project risk management process according to the PMI standard comprises the following stages: risk management planning, risk identification, qualitative and quantitative risk analysis, development of ways to respond to risk and risk monitoring and tracking (Souza dos Santos and Cabral, 2008; PMI Practice Standard ..., 2009; PMBOK Guide, 2017). The implementation of the PMI risk management standard can bring benefits such as (PMI Practice Standard ..., 2009; Ridrigues-da-Silva and Crispim, 2014; PMBOK Guide, 2017):

- minimizing costs,
- improving the effectiveness of pursuing project objectives,
- improving the utilization of resources,
- reducing the probability of project disruptions,
- eliminating doubts regarding project estimations and assumptions,
- improving functioning in other areas of project management, such as budgeting, change management, time management,
- providing the possibility of constant monitoring of changes, and thus of early detection of irregularities.

2.4.2.4. ISO 22320:2011 Societal security – Emergency management – Requirements for incident response

The ISO 22320 standard was published in 2011 in response to the growing importance of crises in the functioning of enterprises. It contains guidelines on management under crisis conditions and appropriate responses to incidents. The standard is dedicated to all public, private, governmental or non-profit organizations, regardless of their profile, wishing to strengthen their resilience and prepare in a professional manner for unforeseeable events (crises, disruptions, disasters) (ISO 22320, 2011). It presents an approach to risk interpreted as incidental events that are the source of crisis situations. Consequently, instead of risk and risk management, the basic concepts in this case are incident and crisis management. The standard defines incident as an event with potentially destabilizing or disrupting effects on the proper functioning of the organization. Crisis management, according to the ISO 22320 standard, is described as an approach oriented towards preventing crisis situations and managing those that actually occur. Crisis management relies on the risk management approach to preventing and responding to potentially destabilizing or disruptive events, as well as restoring the enterprise's functionality after the occurrence of such events. The ISO 22320 standard provides for the following stages of the crisis management process: observing the situation, gathering information, assessing the situation, planning actions, taking and communicating decisions, performing actions as a result of decisions made, observing the results of actions taken, gathering feedback and exercising control (ISO 22320, 2011; Wróblewski, 2014). The main benefits of implementing ISO 22320 include the following (ISO 22320, 2011; Madu and Kuei, 2018; To and Kato, 2018):

- shaping resistance to events of an incidental character,
- improving the processes of communication and transmission of key information in crisis situations,
- minimizing the negative consequences of crises,
- shortening the time necessary to restore the functionality of the enterprise after a crisis,
- supporting the protection of key processes,
- improving the ways of responding to incidents.

2.4.2.5. ISO 22301:2012 Societal security – Business continuity management systems (BCM) – Requirements

The ISO 22301 standard was developed by the ISO/TC 223 Technical Committee and published in 2012 as the first international standard for business continuity management aiming to help companies implement appropriate processes and tools in the face of threats from terrorism, natural disasters and other catastrophes. The document provides guidance for planning, establishing, implementing, monitoring, reviewing, maintaining and continuously improving a documented business continuity management system. The standard specifies general requirements applicable to all organizations or their parts, regardless of their type, size or character of activities. The scope of application of the requirements depends on the specific nature of the activity and the complexity of the organization (ISO 22301, 2012). In the standard, risk factors are equated with incidents and crises that may disrupt the functioning of the enterprise. In the case of ISO 22301, risk is always perceived as the probability of the occurrence of a particular incident. However, with regard to business continuity, the definition of risk describes it more specifically as a situation that could lead to disruptions in operations, losses, danger or crisis. The concept of business continuity management means one of the risk management processes that identifies potential threats and the effects that such threats may have on the enterprise's operations, ensures the development of resilience to such threats and enables an effective response to protect the interests of its key stakeholders, reputation, brand and activities creating value. The standard recommends business continuity management according to the following cycle: planning BCM, implementing and using BCM, monitoring and reviewing BCM, maintaining and correcting BCM and continuously improving BCM (ISO 22301, 2012).

According to the standard, in order to ensure the effectiveness of the implemented system, the enterprise should also focus on identifying the most important values for the organization from the point of view of potential losses (Business Impact Analysis – BIA), developing ways of responding to disturbances (Business Continuity Plans – BCP), developing plans related to the recovery of critical areas of activity, services or resources (Disaster Recovery Planning – DRP). ISO 22301 allows enterprises undertaking its implementation to achieve a number of benefits, for example (ISO 22301, 2012; Baba et al., 2014):

- increasing the enterprise's resilience and stability in the face of threats,
- helping in the efficient running of the enterprise,
- reducing the frequency and negative effects of disturbances,
- effectively identifying and managing present and future risks,
- providing a proactive approach to minimizing the impact of incidents on the organization's operations,
- minimizing downtime during crises and shortening the time necessary for full operational recovery,
- improving resilience to crisis situations,
- increasing credibility.

2.4.3. A comparison of risk management standards

Table 2.5 presents the results of a comparative analysis of the risk management standards under discussion against the following criteria:

- the degree of complexity of the standard,
- the degree of universality of the standard,
- major parties interested in the implementation of the standard,
- the specific character of the standard.

The comparative analysis included in Table 2.5 shows many similarities among the analyzed risk management standards. Firstly, the holistic standards provide comprehensive guidelines for the risk management process, i.e. they formulate specific requirements for each stage, from context identification and risk

Table 2.5 A comparison of risk management standards

Criterion / *Standard*	*Degree of complexity*	*Degree of universality*	*Parties interested in implementation*	*Specific character*
ISO 31000	Comprehensive	Universal	Partners, investors, insurers	Developed based on AS/NZS 4360, concerns holistic risk management
COSO II (2004)	Focus on business structure and objectives, less attention paid to risk analysis requirements	Universal, particularly recommended for business activities	Partners, contractors, investors, insurers	Comparable to FERMA and AS/NZS 4360, concerns holistic risk management
COSO (2017)	Focus on integrating risk management with strategy and performance			
FERMA	Comprehensive	Universal	Partners, investors, insurers	Comparable to COSO II and AS/NZS 4360, concerns holistic risk management
AS/NZS 4360	Comprehensive	Universal, also suitable for newly established organizations	Partners, investors, insurers	Base for ISO 31000, comparable to COSO II and FERMA, concerns holistic risk management
ISO/IEC 27005	Comprehensive requirements for information security risk management	Universal, suitable for enterprises with priority for information protection	Partners, customers, employees, supervisory authorities	Developed based on ISO 31000, can be implemented independently or in integration with a holistic standard

ISO 22301	Focus on risk identification and methods of responding, less attention paid to requirements for risk analysis and assessment	Universal	Partners, contractors, investors, supervisory authorities, competitors	Can be implemented independently or in integration with ISO/IEC 27005 or ISO 31000
ISO 28000	Comprehensive for enterprises in a supply chain	Dedicated to enterprises cooperating within supply chains	Cooperators, partners, supervisory authorities, employees, competitors	Can be implemented independently or in integration with a holistic standard
PMI	Focus on risk identification and analysis, as well as responses to risk, less attention paid to risk assessment	Dedicated to enterprises carrying out business projects	Employees, partners, customers, cooperators, supervisory authorities	Comparable to Prince 2, CMMI, BS 6079-3 can be implemented independently or in integration with a holistic standard
ISO 22320	Comprehensive requirements for crisis management	Universal	Customers, cooperators, partners, investors	Partly replaces ISO/PAS 22399, can be implemented independently or in integration with a holistic standard

management planning, through risk identification, analysis and assessment, to risk monitoring and continuous improvement of the implemented system. Secondly, the risk management standards, mainly the holistic ones, are also highly universal, i.e. they can be applied in any enterprise, regardless of its sector, size or business profile.

Besides enterprises that decide to implement risk management standards for various reasons, there may be other parties interested in their implementation, for example employees or external stakeholders. The reasons for such interest may be determined by a business sector, relations between the enterprise and various stakeholder groups, as well as the impact of the implementation of a standard on existing activities and management processes (Jedynak and Bąk, 2017).

References

Ahmeti, R., Vladi, B. (2017). Analysis of international risk management standards (advantages and disadvantages). *European Journal of Research and Reflection in Management Sciences*, 5(3), pp. 1–5.

Ajmera, A., Cook, J. (2009). A multi-phase framework for supply chain integration. *S.A.M. Advanced Management Journal*, 74(1), pp. 37–47.

AS/NZS 4360. (2004). *The Australian and New Zealand Standard on Risk Management*. Standards Australia, Sydney; Standards New Zealand, Wellington.

AS/NZS ISO 31000. (2009). *Risk Management – Principles and Guidelines*. Standards New Zealand, Wellington.

Aven, T., Ylönen, M. (2019). The strong power of standards in the safety and risk fields: A threat to proper developments of these fields? *Reliability Engineering & System Safety*, 189, pp. 279–286.

Baba, H., Watanabe, T., Nagaishi, Matsumoto H. (2014). Area business continuity management, a new opportunity for building economic resilience. *Procedia Economics and Finance*, 18, pp. 296–303.

Bąk, S. (2017). Implementacja systemów zarządzania jako element przewagi konkurencyjnej przedsiębiorstw w świetle normalizacji i standaryzacji w gospodarce [in:] M. Bugdol, P. Jedynak (eds.), *Jakość zarządzania – refleksje, wymiary problemy*. Kraków: Wydawnictwo Uniwersytetu Jagiellońskiego, pp. 267–275.

Bandyopadhyay, K., Mykytyn, P.P., Mykytyn, K. (1999). A framework for integrated risk management in information technology. *Management Decision*, 37(5), pp. 437–445.

Beasley, M.S., Clune, R., Hermanson, D.R. (2005). Enterprise risk management: An empirical analysis of factors associated with the extent of implementation. *Journal of Accounting and Public Policy*, 24(6), pp. 521–531.

Becchetti, L., Ciciretti, R., Hasan, I. (2015). Corporate social responsibility, stakeholder risk, and idiosyncratic volatility. *Journal of Corporate Finance*, 35, pp. 297–309.

Bernstein, P.L. (1996). *Against the Gods: The Remarkable Story of Risk*. New York: John Wiley & Sons.

von Bertalanffy, L. (1984). *Ogólna teoria systemów. Podstawy, rozwój, zastosowania.*, Warszawa: Państwowe Wydawnictwo Naukowe.

Black, A., Wright, P., Bachman, J.E. (2000). *W poszukiwaniu wartości dla akcjonariuszy. Kształtowanie wyników działalności spółek*. Warszawa: Dom Wydawniczy ABC.

Bochniarz, P., Gugała, K. (2005). *Budowanie i pomiar kapitału ludzkiego w firmie*. Warszawa: Poltext.

Bogodistov, Y., Wohlgemuth, V. (2017). Enterprise risk management: A capability-based perspective. *The Journal of Risk Finance*, 18(3), pp. 234–251.

Bollinger, R. (2010). *Lean Risk Management*. Paper presented at PMI® Global Congress 2010 – North America, Washington, DC. Newtown Square, PA: Project Management Institute.

Bosetti, L. (2015). *Risk Management Standards in Global Markets. Management and Marketing*. The 3rd Virtual Multidisciplinary Conference, Slovakia.

Botha, J., Von Solms, R. (2004). A cyclic approach to business continuity planning. *Information Management & Computer Security*, 12(4), pp. 328–337.

Bowersox, D.J. (1990). The strategic benefits of logistics alliances. *Harvard Business Review*, 68(4), pp. 36–45.

British Standards Institute. (2000). *BSI PD 6668 Managing Risk for Corporate Governance*, London.

British Standards Institution BS 25999–1. (2006). *Code of Practice for Business Continuity Management*, London.

Bristish Standards Insitution BS 25999–2. (2007). *Business Continuity Management – Specification for Business Continuity Management*, London.

Bromiley, P., McShane, M., Nair, A., Rustambekov, E. (2015). Enterprise risk management: Review, critique and research directions. *Long Range Planning*, 48(4), pp. 265–276.

Calandro, J. (2015). A leader's guide to strategic risk management. *Strategy & Leadership*, 43(1), pp. 26–35.

Christopher, M., Mena, C., Khan, O., Yurt, O. (2011). Approaches to managing global sourcing risk. *Supply Chain Management: An International Journal*, 16(2), pp. 67–81.

Clarke, C.J., Varma, S. (1999). Strategic risk management: The new competitive edge. *Long Range Planning*, 32(4), pp. 414–424.

Coombs, T., Holladay, S. (2015). CSR as crisis risk: Expanding how we conceptualize the relationship. *Corporate Communications: An International Journal*, 20(2), pp. 144–162.

Cooper, D., Grey, S., Raymond, G., Walker, P. (2005). *Project Risk Management Guidelines: Managing Risk in Large Projects and Complex Procurement*. Chichester: Wiley.

COSO II Enterprise Risk Management – Integrated Framework. (2004). *The Committee of Sponsoring Organizations of the Treadway Commission*, New York.

COSO Enterprise Risk Management – Integrating with Strategy and Performance. (2017). *The Committee of Sponsoring Organizations of the Treadway Commission*, New York.

Czyżowska, J. (2016). Wybrane aspekty zarządzania ryzykiem w działalności inwestycyjnej przedsiębiorstw. *Przedsiębiorstwo i Finanse*, 1(12), pp. 19–28.

D'Arcy, S.P., Brogan, J.C. (2001). Enterprise risk management. *Journal of Risk Management of Korea*, 12(1), pp. 1–24.

Da Silva Etges, A.P.B., Cortimiglia, M.N. (2019). A systematic review of risk management in innovation-oriented firms. *Journal of Risk Research*, 22(3), pp. 364–381.

Delerue, H. (2005). Relational risk perception and alliance management in French biotechnology SMEs. *European Business Review*, 17(6), pp. 532–546.

Deptuła, A.M., Knosala, R. (2015). Risk assessment of the innovative projects implementation. *Management and Production Engineering Review*, 6(4), pp. 15–25.

Dionne, G. (2013). Risk management: History, definition and critique. *Risk Management and Insurance Review*, 16(2), pp. 147–166.

Dowling, G. (2006). Reputation risk: It is board's ultimate responsibility. *Journal of Business Strategy*, 27(2), pp. 59–68.

Dumond, E.J. (1996). Applying value-based management to procurement. *International Journal of Physical Distribution & Logistics Management*, 26(1), pp. 5–24.

Dzwonkowski, P. (2013). Wymogi norm ISO seria 27000. www.mf.gov.pl/c/document_library/get_file?uuid=e3607969-79d0-46c5-8e82-85e27331d5a3 (Access: 30.09.2020).

Elahi, E. (2013). Risk management: The next source of competitive advantage. *Emerald*, 15(2), pp. 117–131.

Elliott, D., Swartz, E., Herbane, B. (2010). *Business Continuity Management, Second Edition: A Crisis Management Approach*. New York: Routledge.

Everett, C. (2011). A risky business: ISO 31000 and 27005 unwrapped. *Computer Fraud & Security*, 2, pp. 5–7.

Fairchild, R. (2002). Financial risk management: Is it a value-adding activity? *Balance Sheet*, 10(4) pp. 22–25.

Fałek Z. (2014). Risk management standards as tools for building total corporate value of an electric power distribution company [in:] P. Urbanek (ed.), *Ekonomia i zarządzanie w teorii i praktyce. Polityka ekonomiczna i zarządzanie przedsiębiorstwem w warunkach kryzysu gospodarczego*, 3, Łódź: Wydawnictwo Uniwersytetu Łódzkiego, pp. 2–15.

Faupel, C., Michels, R. (2014). Value-based risk management: Costs and benefits [in:] M.J. Epstein, J.Y. Lee (eds.), *Advances in Management Accounting*, 24, Bingley: Emerald Group Publishing Limited, pp. 239–257.

Fazlida, M.R., Said, J. (2015). Information security: Risk, governance and implementation setback. *Procedia Economics and Finance*, 28, pp. 243–248.

FERMA . (2002). *Risk Management Standard*. Brussels: Federation of European Risk Management Associations.

Fischbacher-Smith, D. (2017). When organisational effectiveness fails: Business continuity management and the paradox of performance. *Journal of Organizational Effectiveness: People and Performance*, 4(1), pp. 89–107.

Fischer, K., Leidel, K., Riemann, A., Alfen, H.W. (2010). An integrated risk management system (IRMS) for PPP projects. *Journal of Financial Management of Property and Construction*, 15(3), pp. 260–282.

Frame, J.D. (2001). *Zarządzanie projektami w organizacjach*. Warszawa: WIG-Press.

Fraser, J.R.S., Simkins, B.J. (2007). Ten common misconceptions about enterprise risk management. *Journal of Applied Corporate Finance*, 19(4), pp. 75–81.

Frigo, M., Anderson, R.J. (2011). Strategic risk management: A foundation for enterprise risk management and governance. *Journal of Corporate Accounting & Finance*, 22(3), pp. 81–88.

Gandhi, S.J., Gorod, A., Sauser, B. (2012). Prioritization of outsourcing risks from a systemic perspective. *Strategic Outsourcing: An International Journal*, 5(1), pp. 39–71.

Garcia, P., Javier, S. (2017). *Financial Risk Management: Identification, Measurement and Management*. Cham: Palgrave Macmillan.

Ghadge A., Dani, S., Kalawsky, R. (2012). Supply chain risk management: Present and future scope. *International Journal of Logistics Management*, 23(3), pp. 313–339.

Giugliani, E.A. (2012). *Governance Model for Science and Technology Parks: What Are the STP's Evolving Into?* Tallin: International Association of Science Parks.

Gjerdrum, D. (2015). *Risk Management's Standard of Practice – An Overwiew of ISO 31000.* Gallagher ERM Practice. www.ajg.com/media/1697375/overview-of-iso-31000-2015.pdf (Access: 25.09.2020).

Goodfellow, J.L., Raynor, M.E. (2004). Managing strategic risk: A new partnership between the board and management. *Strategy & Leadership*, 32(5), pp. 45–47.

Green Paper for Promoting a European Framework for Corporate Social Responsibility. (2001). COM, 366 Final, Brussels.

Hammoudeh, S., McAleer, M. (2015). Advances in financial risk management and economic policy uncertainty: An overview. *International Review of Economics & Finance*, 40, pp. 1–7.

Handfield, R.B., Nichols, E.L. (2004). Key issues in global supply base management. *Industrial Marketing Management*, 33(1), pp. 29–35.

Hardy, K. (2015). *Enterprise Risk Management. A Guide for Government Professionals. Jossey-Bass.* San Francisco, CA: John Wiley & Sons.

Hauser, J., Tellis, G.J., Griffin, A. (2006). Research on innovation: A review and agenda for marketing science. *Marketing Science*, 25(6), pp. 687–717.

Herbane, B. (2010). The evolution of business continuity management: A historical review of practices and drivers. *Business History*, 52(6), pp. 978–1002.

Hilson, D. (2006). *Integrated Risk Management as a Framework for Organisational Success.* Paper presented at PMI® Global Congress, North America, Seattle, WA. Newtown Square, PA: Project Management Institute.

Holmdahl, L. (2005). *Complexity Theory and Strategy. A Basis for Product Development.* www.complexityforum.com/articles/complexity-strategy.pdf (Access: 25.09.2020).

Huang, W., Sun, Q., Guan, X., Peng, S. (2017). Human resource risk identification and prevention. *Control and System Engineering*, 1(1), pp. 16–21.

International Electrotechnical Commission. (1995). *CEI/IEC 300-3-9 Dependability Management*, Geneva.

ISO 22301. (2012). *Societal Security – Business Continuity Management Systems (BCM) – Requirements.*

ISO 22320. (2011). *Societal Security – Emergency Management – Requirements for Incident Response.*

ISO 28000. (2007). *Specification for Security Management Systems for the Supply Chain.*

ISO 31000. (2009). *Risk Management – Principles and Guidelines.*

ISO 31000. (2018). *Risk Management – Guidelines.*

ISO 9001. (2015). *Quality Management Systems – Requirements.*

ISO/IEC 27005. (2008). *Information Technology – Security Techniques – Information Security Risk Management.*

ISO/IEC 27005. (2018). *Information Technology – Security Techniques –Information Security Risk Management.*

Ivanov, D., Tsipoulanidis, A., Schönberger, J. (2019). Supply chain risk management and resilience. [in:] D. Ivanov, A. Tsipoulanidis, J. Schönberger (eds.), *Global Supply Chain and Operations Management: A Decision-Oriented Introduction into the Creation of Value*, 2nd ed. Cham: Springer Nature.

Jaki, A. (2008). *Wycena i kształtowanie wartości przedsiębiorstwa*. Kraków: Wolters Kluwer.

Jaki, A. (2014). Przejawy ryzyka w zarządzaniu wartością. *Zeszyty Naukowe Uniwersytetu Szczecińskiego*, 803(66), pp. 747–756.

Jakšić, M., Leković, M. (2015). Investment risk management by applying contemporary modern portfolio theory. *Megatrend revija*, 12(1), pp. 31–46.

Jarysz-Kamińska, E. (2011). Systemy zarządzania bezpieczeństwem łańcucha dostaw w Polsce. *Logistyka*, 5, pp. 656–662.

Jarysz-Kamińska, E. (2012). Wdrażanie systemu zarządzania bezpieczeństwem łańcucha dostaw – wybrane zagadnienia. *Logistyka*, 5, pp. 464–470.

Jayantha, C. (2018). COSO enterprise risk management (ERM) framework and a study of ERM in indian context. *Risk Management – ICAI*, 11, pp. 82–90.

Jedynak, P. (2013). Business continuity management – The perspective of management science. *International Journal of Contemporary Management*, 12(4), pp. 85–96.

Jedynak, P. (2017). *Znormalizowane systemy zarządzania a ryzyko działalności organizacji*. Kraków: Wydawnictwo Uniwersytetu Jagiellońskiego.

Jedynak, P., Bąk, S. (2017). Przegląd standardów zarządzania ryzykiem [in:] E. Skrzypek, A. Piasecka, S. Sagan (eds.), Nowa jakość a zadowolenie interesariuszy, Katedra Zarządzania Jakością i Wiedzą, Lublin: Wydział Ekonomiczny UMCS w Lublinie, pp. 49–68.

Jedynak, P., Bąk, S. (2018). Modele oceny dojrzałości zarządzania ryzykiem. *Problemy Jakości*, 50(10), pp. 12–18.

Jedynak, P., Bąk, S. (2019). Objectives of risk management in the financial services sector: The perspective of Polish enterprises listed on the Warsaw stock exchange. *Journal of Emerging Trends in Marketing and Management*, 1(1), pp. 231–240.

Jiang, B., Quareshi, A. (2006). Research on outsourcing results: Current literature and future opportunities. *Management Decision*, 44 (1), pp. 44–55.

Kaczmarek, T.T. (2010). *Zarządzanie ryzykiem ujęcie interdyscyplinarne*. Warszawa: Difin.

Kildow, B.A. (2011). *A Supply Chain Management Guide to Business Continuity*. New York: Amacom.

Kim, K.S. (2004). Strategic planning for value-based management: An empirical examination. *Management Decision*, 42(8), pp. 938–948.

Kleindorfer, P.R., Saad, G.H. (2005). Managing disruption risks in supply chain. *Production and Operations Management*, 14(1), pp. 53–68.

Kopia, J., Just, V., Geldmacher, W., Bubian, A. (2017). Meaning and usage of a conceptual enterprise risk management framework – A case study. *EcoForum*, 6(2), pp. 1–10.

Koutsoukis N.S. (2010). Risk management standards: Towards a contemporary, organisation – Wide management approach. *International Journal of Business Policy and Economics*, 3(1), pp. 47–64.

Krishnamurti, C., Shams, S., Velayutham, E. (2018). Corporate social responsibility and corruption risk: A global perspective. *Journal of Contemporary Accounting & Economics*, 14(1), pp. 1–21.

Krysiak, Z. (2011). Wartość ryzyka. *Kwartalnik Nauk o Przedsiębiorstwie*, 2, pp. 32–40.

Kumar, S., Himes, K.J., Kritzer, C.P. (2014). Risk assessment and operational approaches to managing risk in global supply chains. *Journal of Manufacturing Technology Management*, 25(6), pp. 873–890.

Lambert, D.M., Stock, J.R., Ellram, L.M. (1998). *Fundamentals of Logistics Management*. Boston, MA: Irwin/McGraw-Hill.

Lankford, W.M., Parsa, F. (1999). Outsourcing: Aprimer. *Management Decision*, 37(4), pp. 310–316.

Larson, P.D., Rogers, D.S. (1998). Supply chain management: Definition, growth and approaches. *Journal of Marketing Theory and Practice*, 6(4), pp. 1–5.

Leavy, B. (2004). Outsourcing strategies: Opportunities and risks. *Strategy & Leadership*, 32(6), pp. 20–25.

Levy, D.L. (2000). Applications and limitations of complexity theory in organizational theory and strategy. http://citeseerx.ist.psu.edu/viewdoc/download?doi=10.1.1.725.7357&rep=rep1&type=pdf (Access: 25.09.2020).

Li, S. (2003). Future trends and challenges of financial risk management in the digital economy. *Managerial Finance*, 29(5/6), pp. 111–125.

Li, X., Wu, Z. (2009). Corporate risk management and investment decisions. *The Journal of Risk Finance*, 10(2), pp. 155–168.

Lindström, J., Samuelsson, S., Hägerfors, A. (2010). Business continuity planning methodology. *Disaster Prevention and Management: An International Journal*, 19(2), pp. 243–255.

Lipka, A. (2002). *Ryzyko personalne. Szanse i zagrożenia zarządzania zasobami ludzkimi*. Warszawa: Poltext.

Lisiecka, K. (2012). Zarządzanie ryzykiem – determinanta jakości zarządzania przedsiębiorstwem. *Zarządzanie i Finanse*, 3(1), pp. 557–573.

Madu, C.N., Kuei, C. (ed.). (2018). *Handbook of Disaster Risk Reduction & Management*. Singapore: World Scientific Publishing Co.

Manning, S., Gurney, A. (2005). Operational risk within an insurance market. *Journal of Financial Regulation and Compliance*, 13(4), pp. 293–300.

Manuj, I., Mentzer, J.T. (2008). Global supply chain risk management strategies. *International Journal of Physical Distribution & Logistics Management*, 38(3), pp. 192–223.

Marodin, G.A., Aurin, T.A. (2015). Classification and relationships between risks thataffect lean production implementation. A study in southern Brazil. *Journal of ManufacturingTechnology Management*, 26(1), pp. 57–79.

Merková, M., Drábek, J. (2015). Use of risk analysis in investment measurement and management. *Procedia Economics and Finance*, 34, pp. 656–662.

Mertzanis, C. (2014). Complexity analysis and risk management in finance [in:] J.A. Batten, N.F. Wagner (eds.), *Risk Management Post Financial Crisis: A Period of Monetary Easing. Contemporary Studies in Economic and Financial Analysis*, 96, Bingley: Emerald Group Publishing Limited, pp. 15–40.

Mitrofanova, A., Mitrofanova, E., Konovalova, V., Ashurbekov, R. (2017). Human resource risk management in organization: Methodological aspect. *Advances in Economics, Business and Management Research*, 38, pp. 699–705.

Mortimer, A.L. (1995). Managing innovation and risk. *World Class Design to Manufacture*, 2(5), pp. 38–42.

Nagano, M.S., Stefanovitz, J.P., Vick, T.L. (2014). Innovation management processes, their internal organizational elements and contextual factors: An investigation in Brazil. *Journal of Engineering and Technology Management*, 33, pp. 63–92.

Naude, M.J., Chiweshe, N. (2017). A proposed operational risk management framework for small and medium enterprises. *South African Journal of Economic and Management Sciences*, 20(1), pp. e1–e10.

Norges Standardiseringsforbund. (1991). *NS5814 Norsk Standard Krav til risikoanalyser*, Norway.

Norrman, A., Jansson, U. (2004). Ericsson's proactive supply chain risk management approach after a serious sub-supplier accident. *International Journal of Physical Distribution & Logistics*, 34(5), pp. 434–456.

O'Connor, G.C., Ravichandran, T., Robeson, D. (2008). Risk management through learning: Management practices for radical innovation success. *The Journal of High Technology Management Research*, 19(1), pp. 70–82.

O'Donnell, E. (2005). Enterprise risk management: A system-thinking framework for the event identification phase. *International Journal of Accounting Information Systems*, 6, pp. 177–195.

Oborilová, I., Myšková, R., Melichar, V. (2015). Risks associated with the human resources management in transport companie. *Procedia Economics and Finance*, 34, pp. 352–359.

O'Donnell, E. (2005). Enterprise risk management: A system-thinking framework for the event identification phase. *International Journal of Accounting Information Systems*, 6, pp. 177–195.

Penchansky, R., Macnee, C.L. (1993). Ensuring excellence: Reconceptualizing quality assurance, risk management, and utilization review. *QRB – Quality Review Bulletin*, 19(6), pp. 182–189.

PMI . (2009). *Practice Standard for Project Risk Management.* Newtown Square, PA: Project Management Institute.

PMBOK . (2017). *Guide to the Project Management Body of Knowledge.* 6 edition. Newtown Square, PA: Project Management Institute.

Power, M., Bonifazi, C., Desouza, K.C. (2004). The ten outsourcing traps to avoid. *Journal of Business Strategy*, 25(2), pp. 37–42.

Pratap, S. (2014). Towards a framework for performing outsourcing capability. *Strategic Outsourcing: An International Journal*, 7(3), pp. 226–252.

Quon, T.K., Zeghal, D., Maingot, M. (2012). Enterprise risk management and firm performance. *Procedia – Social and Behavioral Sciences*, 62, pp. 263–267.

Randeree, K., Mahal, K.A., Narwani, A. (2012). A business continuity management maturity model for the UAE banking sector. *Business Process Management Journal*, 18(3), pp. 472–492.

Ratajczak, M., Wołoszyn, J. (2011). Innowacyjność i ryzyko w obszarze społecznej odpowiedzialności biznesu. *Prace Naukowe Uniwersytetu Ekonomicznego we Wrocławiu*, 220, pp. 84–90.

Raz, T., Hillson, D. (2005). A comparative review of risk management standards. *Risk Management: An International Journal*, 7(4), pp. 53–66.

Ridrigues-da-Silva, L.H., Crispim, J.A. (2014). The project risk management process, a preliminary study. *Procedia Technology*, 16, pp. 943–949.

Sadowski, A., Zajdel, M. (2009). Podejście systemowe w naukach o zarządzaniu. *Studia Prawno-Ekonomiczne*, LXXX, pp. 271–278.

Schiller, F., Prpich, G. (2012). Learning to organise risk management in organisations: What future for enterprise risk management? *Journal of Risk Research*, 17(8), pp. 999–1017.

Schniederjans, M.J., Zuckweiler, K.M. (2004). A quantitative approach to the outsourcing-insourcing decision in an international context. *Management Decision*, 42(8), pp. 974–986.

Schroeder, H. (2014). An art and science approach to strategic risk management. *Strategic Direction*, 30(4), pp. 28–30.

Sitkowski, L. (2009). Zarządzanie bezpieczeństwem dla łańcucha dostaw – ISO 28000. *Przemysł i Środowisko. Jakość – Zarządzanie*, 4(13), pp. 28–29.

Skrzypek, E. (2013). Uwarunkowania efektywności organizacyjnej w nowej ekonomii. *Annales Universitatis Mariae Curie-Skłodowska. Sectio H, Oeconomia*, 47(1), pp. 167–178.

Sobel, P.J., Reding, K.F. (2004). Aligning corporate governance with enterprise risk management. *Management Accounting Quarterly*, 5(2), pp. 1–9.

Souza dos Santos, F.R., Cabral, S. (2008). FMEA and PMBOK applied to project risk management. *Journal of Information Systems and Technology Management*, 5(2), pp. 347–364.

Stein, M., Voehl, F. (1998). *Macrologistics Management: A Catalyst for Organizational Change*. Boca Raton, FL: St. Lucie Press.

Sundar, R., Balaji, A.N., Satheesh Kumar, R.M. (2014). A review on lean manufacturing implementation techniques. *Procedia Engineering*, 97, pp. 1875–1885.

Sunder, V. (2016). Lean six sigma project management – A stakeholder management perspective. *The TQM Journal*, 28(1), pp. 132–150.

Szczepankowski, P. (2007). *Wycena i zarządzanie wartością przedsiębiorstwa*. Warszawa: Wydawnictwo Naukowe PWN.

Szymanek, A. (2014). Rozwój standardów zarządzania ryzykiem w transporcie drogowym. *Logistyka*, 3, pp. 6185–6191.

To, N.T., Kato, T. (2018). Characteristics and development of policy and institutional structures of emergency response in Vietnam. *International Journal of Disaster Risk Reduction*, 31, pp. 729–741.

Tóth, T., Sebestyén, Z. (2014). Integrated risk management process for building projects. *Procedia Engineering*, 85, pp. 510–519.

Trocki, M. (2012). *Nowoczesne zarządzanie projektami*. Warszawa: PWE.

Tummala, R., Schoenherr, T. (2011). Assessing and managing risks using the supply chain risk management proces (SCRMP). *Supply Chain Management: In International Journal*, 16(6), pp. 474–483.

Urbanowska-Sojkin, E. (2012). Ryzyko w zarządzaniu strategicznym przedsiębiorstwem: Teoria i praktyka. *Zeszyty Naukowe Uniwersytetu Ekonomicznego w Poznaniu*, 235, pp. 35–53.

Urbanowska-Sojkin, E. (2013). *Ryzyko w wyborach strategicznych w przedsiębiorstwach*. Warszawa: PWE.

Vaughan, E.J. (1992). *Fundamentals of Risk and Insurance*. 6th edition. New York: John Wiley & Sons.

Venclova, K., Urbancova, H, Vydrova, H.V. (2013). Advantages and disadvantages of business continuity management. *Social, Behavioral, Educational, Economic, Business and Industrial Engineering*, 7(4), pp. 895–899.

Ward, S., Chapman, C. (2003). Transforming project risk management into project uncertainty management. *International Journal of Project Management*, 21(2), pp. 97–105.

Williams, R., Bertsch, B., Dale, B., van der Viele, T., van Iwaarden, J., Smith, M., Visser, R. (2006). Quality and risk management: What are the key issues? *The TQM Magazine*, 18(1), pp. 67–86.

Womack, J.P., Jones, D.T., Ross, D. (2007). *The Machine that Changed the World: The Story of Lean Production*. New York: Free Press.

Wong, S., Chin, K. (2007). Organizational innovation management. *Industrial Management & Data Systems*, 107(9), pp. 1290–1315.

Wróblewski, D. (ed.). (2014). *Przegląd wybranych dokumentów normatywnych z zakresu zarządzania kryzysowego i zarządzania ryzykiem wraz z leksykonem*. Józefów: Centrum Naukowo-Badawcze Ochrony Przeciwpożarowej.

Zachorowska, A. (2006). *Ryzyko działalności inwestycyjnej przedsiębiorstw*. Warszawa: Polskie Wydawnictwo Ekonomiczne.

3 Challenges of risk management during crisis situations

3.1. Crisis as a specific management situation

The dynamic and continuous changes in the business environment have increasingly negative consequences, especially in the case of smaller companies with a short market history. The observed changes generate higher and higher requirements that have to be met in order to ensure continuity of business activities (Mikušová and Horváthová, 2019). If such requirements are not fulfilled, enterprises may find themselves in circumstances indicating an impending crisis. Enterprises are also exposed to external crises whose occurrence is beyond their control.

3.1.1. The essence of a crisis situation

In a business context, crisis can be defined as an unnatural, complex and unstable situation that threatens the achievement of an enterprise's strategic objectives, its reputation or even survival (British Standards Institution, 2011). Crisis is a dynamic and progressive process that is never limited to one functional area of an enterprise, and its boundaries are blurred. The symptoms of crisis tend to be easily dispersed throughout an enterprise and beyond (Hart et al., 2001). According to Perrow (1999), increased susceptibility to such states results from environmental influences or technological changes, while Reason (1990) points at human errors as the main causal factor. Crisis in enterprises is characterized by the following three features: threat, surprise and relatively short response times. A few major definitions of crisis in the context of management are presented in Table 3.1.

A crisis appearing in an enterprise, regardless of its size or business profile, is a specific management situation requiring reorganization of business processes, implementation of adjustment mechanisms and extensive corrective and remedial actions or actions limiting the scale of negative and irreversible consequences of a crisis. The course of a crisis cycle can be divided into the following successive phases (Sienkiewicz-Małyjurek, 2015):

- the potential phase that applies to all enterprises and is difficult to notice – the degree of exposure to crisis can be determined by means of early warning systems,

DOI: 10.4324/9781003131366-3

Table 3.1 An overview of major definitions of crisis

Author	*Definition of crisis*
Hermann (1972)	A situation that threatens the priority objectives of the decision-making unit, limits the amount of time available to respond before a decision is made and takes members of the decision-making unit by surprise
Selbst (1978)	Any act or omission that collides with the organization's current functions, the acceptable achievement of the organization's objectives, its longevity or survival, or that has harmful personal effects in the opinion of the majority of its employees, customers, or constituent parts
Pauchant and Mitroff (1992)	A disruption that physically influences the system as a whole and jeopardizes its fundamental principles
Rosenthal and Kouzmin (1997)	A serious threat to the basic structures or basic values and norms of the system that, under the pressure of time and highly uncertain circumstances, forces critical decisions to be taken
Hart et al. (2001)	A progressive process that is not confined to just one area of the enterprise and tends to spread rapidly
Venette (2003)	A process of transformation after which it is impossible to return to the previous system
Boin et al. (2005)	A situation characterized by threat, uncertainty and a sense of urgency
Leidner et al. (2009)	A situation that constitutes a high priority threat. Crises are characterized by non-trivial threats to important assets and values, unpredictability and urgency.
Herbane (2010)	An emergency, disaster, disruption of business continuity
Bundy et al. (2017)	An event that is perceived by managers and stakeholders as very significant, unexpected and potentially destructive; an event that may jeopardize the organization's objectives and have serious consequences for its relations with stakeholders
Mikušová and Horváthová (2019)	A situation that is regarded as undesirable or harmful, requiring to be resolved and overcome. Its severity depends on the intensity of its effects and the time needed to resolve the problem.

- the hidden phase – contrary to its name, it is visible and heralds the possibility of a crisis, which allows the identification of the first symptoms of a crisis,
- the open phase in which a crisis escalates.

Crises are an indispensable element of the dynamic business world. Unexpected and violent organizational changes, personnel problems, technological and political transformations as well as changes in economic conditions cause instability in business activities. If a crisis that may appear in an enterprise as a result of such changes is not properly managed and brought under control in due time, it may trigger a chain reaction in which the crisis will spread throughout the enterprise and even among its stakeholders (Fener and Cevik, 2015).

3.1.2. The need for crisis leadership

The specific managerial situation triggered in enterprises by a crisis requires a special attitude on the part of the top management, which, in cooperation with lower-level managers, may influence the enterprise's ability to minimize the severity of the negative effects of crisis events (Crandall et al., 2014). This attitude can be referred to as crisis leadership (Wang and Belardo, 2005). Crisis leadership is considered to be the optimal process for assessing the impact of adverse changes, regardless of their cause. What can be observed nowadays is a clear shift from authoritarian leadership to a participatory leadership model, with employees at different hierarchical levels participating in the crisis management process (Fener and Cevik, 2015). A leadership style adopted during a crisis has an impact on the effectiveness of the management process, especially when actions need to be taken that require a rapid response to changes resulting from the crisis (Lester and Krejci, 2007). Therefore, crisis leadership is treated as one of the responsibilities of the management of an enterprise affected by a crisis. It is also one of the key determinants of the effectiveness of anti-crisis measures taken. The core of the leader's responsibility during a crisis is to look for new, surprising actions aimed at protection against the effects of the crisis when other managers accept the impossibility of counteracting threats, representing a passive attitude. Managers become leaders during a crisis when they are able to manage risk in extraordinary and exceptional situations (Tutar, 2004). Thus, crisis leadership can be described as initiatives and activities undertaken in the face of a crisis and aimed at looking for new solutions.

In response to increasing requirements imposed on managers in the face of a crisis, the literature on the subject proposes a number of concepts of crisis. Karim (2016) developed a model that indicates the features and skills of a leader who is capable of effectively dealing with an identified crisis. Fragouli and Ibidapo (2015) emphasize that crisis management requires that leaders adopt an attitude that will enable them to transform the crisis into a state predisposing the organization to continue its development and initiate changes that could not be effectively implemented under normal conditions. Civelek et al. (2016) also perceive crisis as an opportunity for development.

The situation in which enterprises find themselves during a crisis requires that managers first of all identify the problem when its first symptoms or early signals appear. Once the threats have been identified, the top management faces the challenge of assessing to what extent the possible effects of the crisis will affect the strategic objectives of their enterprise (whether the possibilities of achieving such objectives will be reduced). Another task is to develop a methodology for dealing with crises, and then to implement it gradually in combination with ongoing monitoring of effectiveness (Tutar, 2007).

3.1.3. Tasks of leaders in a crisis situation

To some extent, every crisis disrupts intra-organizational relations and organizational culture. It is therefore the task of leaders to overcome the chaos that is often the first reaction to a crisis, to adapt the enterprise to the changes forced by the crisis and to motivate all employees to fight the crisis together. Cener (2007) drew up a list of obligatory tasks of leaders managing enterprises in situations of crisis. Such tasks include the following:

- identifying the first signs of threats,
- getting ready for potential crises and ensuring maximum protection against their negative effects,
- making decisions dynamically and effectively in all phases of crisis management,
- delegating powers and responsibilities skilfully in the crisis management process,
- exercising planning, forecasting and organizational skills,
- ensuring an efficient communication system for anti-crisis measures within the organizational structure,
- coordinating all phases of crisis management,
- exercising continuous supervision of the crisis management process,
- drawing conclusions as well as assessing events and changes,
- developing ways of returning to the pre-crisis state and using changes caused by the crisis to improve the organization.

The experience gained from past crises should be momentum for organizations to revise and make necessary changes in their strategies (Bayazıt et al., 2003) and established strategic objectives should influence the shape and scope of actions aimed at preventing potential crises. Therefore, crisis management and strategic management should be areas of continuous cooperation generating valuable mutual feedback.

A managerial situation created by a crisis emerging in the enterprise also requires the development of effective change management mechanisms. Each crisis gives rise to organizational changes, regardless of the scope and severity of its effects. Due to the turbulent character of the environment, far-reaching technological changes, dynamic globalization processes and a continuous increase in the competitiveness of enterprises, organizational crises (regardless of their sources) have become a common phenomenon. The management of changes resulting from them has become a standard corporate process. Chosen by the management team, the methods and tools of conducting the change management process determine the effectiveness of crisis management. In order to achieve this goal, enterprises are obliged to combine activities in the area of crisis management and organizational change management, which is currently one of the most important areas of managers' activities (Kuzmanova and Ivanov, 2019). In the process of harmonizing decisions in the area of change management and crisis management, managers should pay particular attention to the objectives of these two processes (Jarrett, 2003). Introducing organizational change in normal business conditions is a long and complicated process, while in a crisis environment it is often a challenge that some enterprises may fail to rise to. The common stage of both change management and crisis management is adaptation. Each crisis requires the enterprise to adapt to the new operating conditions changed as a result of its consequences. Implemented organizational changes also need to be adapted to the enterprise's individual capabilities and conditions (Greiner 1972; 1998). Therefore, it should be concluded that change management and crisis management measures interact with each other and thus make it possible for enterprises to look for opportunities to overcome crises and maintain their growth potential (Kuzmanova and Ivanov, 2019).

3.1.4. The occurrence of a crisis and the improvement of enterprises

Any crisis, regardless of its consequences for the enterprise, should provide impetus for drawing conclusions and subsequently using them to improve the enterprise. In the natural course of events, such impetus triggers a series of organizational changes whose alleged aim is to restore the enterprise to the state of equilibrium from before the crisis (if its consequences are exclusively negative) or to continue the enterprise's development (if the core activities are maintained during the crisis). However, it is worth remembering that there is no ideal and uniform standard of coordinating change management in enterprises during and after a crisis, as well as adapting enterprises to occurring changes. The development of an individual system in this area, adapted to a particular company, is a long-term and methodologically advanced process requiring close integration with strategic management, because crisis itself is treated as a change of strategic character. Searching for a post-crisis intra-organizational balance by means of consistently implemented organizational changes requires that the management system model the environment of change in order to achieve the highest possible degree of adaptation, which in the long term may also contribute to increasing resistance to subsequent crisis events (Rochet et al., 2008).

Crises appearing as indispensable moments in conducting business activities have a number of managerial implications. In addition to the aforementioned impact of crises on the processes of strategic management and organizational change management, as well as managers' attitudes and actions within the scope of crisis leadership, attention should be paid to other areas of the enterprise that also undergo transformations in the wake of a crisis (regardless of whether a crisis is caused by external factors or is an internal problem of a particular enterprise). Thus, it becomes possible to formulate the following guidelines whose implementation can support managers in combating crises effectively:

- modelling the course of a crisis, with particular emphasis on post-crisis measures, aimed at not only restoring the normal functioning from before the crisis, but also preventing future crises (Pedersen and Ritter, 2020),

- examining relationships among enterprises within business networks, mainly to assess such networks' resilience to crises (Håkansson and Ford, 2002),
- increasing employees' autonomy, which can translate into shorter response times and greater creativity in dealing with dynamic and unexpected changes (Pedersen, 2019),
- digitizing the communication channels used throughout the crisis management process, which may result in increased resilience of business models in comparison to those used by competitors (Ritter and Pedersen, 2020).

3.2. Types of management crises

A typology of crises is a structured approach that forms the basis for analyzing crisis situations and implementing measures to prevent and contain crises (Mikušová and Horváthová, 2019).

The basis for developing a typology of crises or crisis situations is a group of features which, when combined, allow an in-depth description of a crisis. These features include (Ziarko and Walas-Trębacz, 2010) the occurrence of a critical event, the perception of the critical event by the enterprise, its stakeholders and society at large, and the degree of control over critical events.

The first step in developing a typology of management crises is to classify their causes and sources. According to one of the basic approaches, the sources of crises can be divided as follows (Sienkiewicz-Małyjurek, 2015):

- natural sources – sudden, one-off and socially destructive events resulting from natural causes and happening at a particular place and time,
- sources related to human activity – sudden events resulting from complex technological, organizational and social processes or human errors; their impact may be unlimited geographically, and the consequences may appear with a delay,
- hybrid sources – they result from the coexistence of the two other types; they are events resulting from both human activity and the natural forces.

According to Mitroff et al. (1987), the causes of crises can be divided into internal and external. In both groups, techno-economic and socio-organizational causes are distinguished.

Internal causes include the following:

- within the range of techno-economic causes, for example: defects in products/services, technical and infrastructural problems, industrial failures, IT failures, lack of access to information, bankruptcy,
- within the range of socio-organizational causes, for example: lack of adaptation to changes in the environment, organizational and personal problems, faulty communication systems, dishonesty of employees, loss of reputation, accidents at work.

External causes include the following:

- within the range of techno-economic causes, for example: environmental degradation, large-scale industrial accidents, large-scale system failures, natural disasters, political crises, international and global crises,
- within the range of socio-organizational causes, for example: terrorism, industrial actions, boycotts, fraud.

Crises can vary in nature and either affect individual areas of enterprise management or be systemic in character. According to Mitroff (2004), the main types of management crises can be categorized according to their sources as follows:

- economic crises (market, financial, growth, employment crises; crises resulting from changes in legislation),
- information crises (problems with communication or access to market information; loss of confidential data or information),
- physical crises (production disruptions, product quality problems),
- crises related to human resources (loss of employees, employees' fraudulent activities),
- crises related to reputation (negative opinions),
- crises related to natural disasters and terrorism.

Crises can also be categorized on the basis of a number of other criteria, for example (Zelek, 2003): the place where the crisis occurs in the company, the ability to adapt to changes caused by the crisis, the processual nature of crisis management, the life cycle phase of the organization, the warning time (the time between the first symptoms of a possible danger and the occurrence of the crisis), the pace of the crisis, the nature of the course of the crisis. A detailed typology of crises in management is presented in Table 3.2.

Prepared on the basis of a number of division criteria, the classification of management crises presented in Table 3.2 indicates a wide diversity of crises that can potentially occur in an enterprise. Such an extensive division also proves the complexity of a crisis as a phenomenon interfering with the enterprise's activities (irrespective of its sources). Inherent in conducting business activities, crises are phenomena that, with greater or lesser intensity, restrict basic functions or require managerial changes. From the managerial point of view, the most dangerous type of crisis is a strategic crisis. It usually occurs as a cumulative form of serious problems in various functional areas of an enterprise whose consequences may significantly disrupt the pursuit of the enterprise's basic strategic objectives and even threaten the continuation of its activities.

A crisis spreading in the enterprise and recognized as a problem transforming into a strategic crisis has several characteristic features. These include, for example the loss of the capacity to self-regulate by the enterprise management system. Another symptom of the strategic dimension of a crisis is a sudden slowdown

Table 3.2 A typology of crises in management

Division criterion	*Types of crises*
The place where the crisis originates in the organization	• crises arising in the area of management, • crises arising in the area of people management, • crises arising in the area of sales, • crises arising in the area of organization, • crises arising in production, • crises arising in logistics and procurement, • crises arising in the area of research and development, • crises arising in the area of investments, • crises arising in the areas of finance, controlling and planning.
The ability to adapt to changes brought about by the crisis	• a crisis of adaptation manifesting itself in problems with adapting to threats. The most common cause is the petrification of organizational structures and management procedures, • a crisis of continuity – it consists in the lack of inertia and is caused by the deregulation of the management process due to constant changes.
The processual nature of crisis management	• a potential crisis – a threat to the enterprise's operations and pursuit of objectives resulting from the adverse influence of various external and internal phenomena, • a latent crisis – difficulties in achieving the enterprise's objectives and managing its resources, often equated with so-called "temporary difficulties", • an overt crisis – the emergence of difficulties in the functioning of the enterprise that seriously threaten its economic existence.
The life cycle phase of the organization	• a crisis of leadership – such an increase in the size of the enterprise that it can no longer be controlled by its founder. It most often results in the loss of control over the growing scale of operations and size of the enterprise, • a crisis of autonomy – the emergence of chaos in a well-established organizational structure, the loss of control over the supervised areas of the enterprise's operations at individual hierarchical levels, • a crisis of decentralization – it forces the enterprise to better coordinate its decentralized activities and may indicate another phase of growth for the enterprise, • a crisis of bureaucratization – a reduction in the efficiency of large enterprises due to their natural tendency to increase bureaucracy and thus, fixed costs, • a crisis of maturity – it is related to the lack of further development of the enterprise.

(*Continued*)

Table 3.2 (Continued) A typology of crises in management

Division criterion	*Types of crises*
The warning time	• a sudden crisis – it is defined as disruptions to activities that occur without warning, • a smouldering crisis – it is defined as any business problem that intensifies over time, regardless of its origin.
The nature of a crisis	• an internal crisis – it constitutes a subsystem of management and is caused by internal factors such as the enterprise's improper management or wrong financial policy, • an external crisis – it is caused primarily by macroeconomic processes, new social phenomena, technological progress, market globalization, etc.
The pace of the crisis	• a sudden/immediate crisis – it is characterized by the lack of time for the examination of causes and further planning. Decisions have to be taken at once, • a chronic crisis – it can last for months or even years. Its long duration is not conducive to taking effective actions aimed at its containment.
The reality of the crisis	• a real crisis – it is caused by various factors and usually leads to many problems within the enterprise, • a virtual crisis – it is artificially created in order to bring about change and, consequently, to develop the enterprise and increase its revenues.
The course of the crisis	• type I crisis – it is characterized by a gradual intensification of negative effects and a long-term growth of crisis phenomena, • type II crisis – it is characterized by average duration, rapid spread and varying intensity of destructive effects, • type III crisis – it is characterized by a short duration, a violent course and a very rapid increase of destructive effects.

Source: the authors' own work based on: Krystek, 1987; Sienkiewicz-Małyjurek, 2015; Zelek, 2003; Ziarko and Walas-Trębacz, 2010.

in or complete halt to the enterprise's continued development under given circumstances. The third, extremely important manifestation of the achievement of strategic potential by a crisis is the malfunctioning of basic business mechanisms (Shiller, 2012; Groh, 2014).

3.3. Approaches and strategies used in crisis management

3.3.1. The concept of crisis management

There are many definitions of crisis management. The most appropriate seems to be the proposal of Bundy et al. (2017), who refer to crisis management as a process in which an organization copes with a destructive and unexpected event that threatens to harm the organization, its stakeholders or the general public. Furthermore, crisis management comprises both leaders' actions and communication activities aimed at minimizing the likelihood of crisis occurrence (before a crisis), minimizing the scale and extent of damage that a crisis has caused (during a crisis) and restoring the organization's normal functioning (after a crisis) (Pearson and Clair, 1998; Kahn et. al., 2013; Bundy and Pfarrer, 2015).

Crisis management can be described as a holistic and integrated management process consisting of the following (Jaques, 2007): the phase of preparation for a crisis (forecasting, risk estimation, prevention), the decision-making phase (if a crisis actually occurs), the post-crisis phase (containing the negative effects of a crisis, restoring the functionality of the enterprise). The approach represented by Coombs and Hollady (2012) is also consistent with this understanding of crisis management. These authors equate crisis management with three inextricably linked processes: the pre-crisis process (preventing and getting ready for a potential crisis), the crisis process (ensuring adequate responses to crisis events) and the post-crisis process (verifying implemented anti-crisis strategies and initiating improvement activities).

According to Mitroff and Pearson (1993), the crisis management process is formally divided into the following stages: identifying early warning signals, preparing preventive actions, controlling a crisis in the case of its occurrence (anti-crisis actions), restoring normal functioning after a crisis, maintaining continuous improvement on the basis of experience gained and reviewing the crisis management system.

Crandall et al. (2014) also developed a cycle describing the process of building an effective crisis management system that should provide for the following implementation stages: identifying the real causes of a crisis, establishing a crisis management team, developing and implementing corrective strategies (planning corrective actions, implementing corrective actions), monitoring the effects of adopted corrective strategies.

Other definitions of crisis management based on a processual approach were proposed, among other researchers, by Pearson and Clair (1998), Starbuck and Milliken (1988), Bigley and Roberts (2001), Gephart et al. (2009). According to these authors, crisis management can be generally defined as coordination of complex systems and designing the organizational structure in such a way that the process serves to prevent the occurrence of a crisis, reduce the scale and scope of negative effects of a crisis and improve the enterprise based on the experience gained during a crisis. Therefore, the ideal form of management under crisis conditions is integrated crisis management that propagates preventive and reactive actions before, during and after a crisis (Mitroff et al., 1996). The domain of crisis management is the integration of prevention and confrontation (Glaesser, 2006).

The objectives of crisis management are the following (British Standards Institution, 2011): to identify and understand the risks and challenges resulting from external threats from a strategic perspective, to assess the consequences of potentially possible crises, to build resilience to crises and to adapt the management model to appropriate responses in the event of crisis occurrence.

3.3.2. Crisis strategies and crisis management tools

Since crises can threaten the continued existence of an enterprise in an uncertain business environment, crisis management should constitute one of the leading stages of strategic management. The proper integration of the orientation towards crises with the strategic objectives of the enterprise at the decision-making level may result in the development of effective crisis prevention measures (Chong, 2004). Therefore, the preparation and implementation of crisis strategies becomes extremely important. The choice of an appropriate crisis strategy is determined by the internal and external environment of the enterprise (Litovchenko, 2012), the time, as well as the needs and requirements of all its stakeholders. After all these factors have been taken into account, a defence strategy is selected (Tănase, 2012).

The main division of crisis management strategies makes it possible to distinguish the following (Mikušová and Horváthová, 2019): a passive strategy (no response to a crisis), a defence strategy (a fight for the survival of the organization), a challenge strategy (adapting to crisis conditions and using post-crisis changes to develop the organization), termination of business (winding up the organization).

Meanwhile, Zelek (2003) divides crisis management strategies as follows:

- a reform strategy – it is oriented primarily towards stabilizing the crisis and, in the long term, achieving permanent improvement in the enterprise's financial and competitive position,
- a liquidation strategy – it includes sales and liquidation strategies providing for the maintenance of liquidity. The aim of this strategy is not so much to liquidate the company as a separate entity as to generate positive liquidation capital. Therefore, it can only be implemented in the case of enterprises with positive equity,
- a growth strategy – it manifests itself in aggressive strategic actions aimed at strengthening the enterprise. Such actions take the form of investment and integration (mergers, acquisitions, strategic alliances),
- a bankruptcy strategy – consists in the liquidation of the enterprise without regard to solvency, which always results from the enterprise's poor economic condition. This strategy means the final liquidation of the enterprise preceded by the settlement of liabilities to creditors.

Another catalogue of management strategies in crisis situations was proposed by Wawrzyniak (1999). According to this author, these strategies can be divided according to the identified causes of a crisis (e.g. causes related to management or types of business activities) as follows: subordination strategies, withdrawal strategies, investment strategies and consolidation strategies. If the criterion of the nature of anti-crisis measures is taken into account, Wawrzyniak (1999) divides crisis management strategies into reactive strategies (eliminating the consequences of past events) and proactive strategies (anticipating the future).

Crisis management strategies also include recovery strategies diversified according to the source of a crisis, for example (Slatter and Lovett, 2001): crisis stabilization, leadership, interest group support, focus on strategic issues, organizational changes, reorganization of key processes and financial restructuring.

Crisis response strategies (crisis communication) also play a special role in crisis management (Noratikah et al., 2017). They aim at influencing the course of the crisis in the enterprise, reducing the negative consequences of the crisis and changing the perception of the enterprise affected by the crisis (Coombs and Hollady, 2012).

Strategic crises require a specific management approach. Crises of this type that threaten the fulfilment of the enterprise's core functions require precise adjustment of the existing strategy, vision and mission to the changes necessitated by the occurrence of the crisis. Such adjustment creates opportunities for transition to a new sustainable system after the crisis has been overcome. The strategic nature of a crisis also requires strategic responses. Such strategic responses to a crisis include (Wenzel et al., 2020): retrenchment, persevering, innovating and exit.

One of the strategic tools for crisis management is the creation of crisis portfolios as a means of rationalizing crisis management. It consists in identifying the enterprise's weaknesses and using them as criteria in the assessment of its vulnerability to crisis. On this basis, it is possible to define possible crisis scenarios. The adoption of this strategy may significantly improve the process of crisis management, without, however, guaranteeing the prevention of future crises (Zapletalová, 2012).

Simulations of the crisis management process based on the identification of its sources and the design of possible responses are also extremely important in crisis management (Papalová, 2015). The creation of simulations of the course of a crisis and responses to it is aimed at enabling the development of effective tools and methods for neutralizing its negative consequences (Hrdina and Maléřová, 2012). The training of teams responsible for crisis management in the enterprise should also be based on the knowledge and experience acquired from such simulations (Waller et al., 2014).

Early warning systems are also of strategic importance for effective crisis management as they provide effective support to managers in quickly identifying the symptoms of crises (Xu, 2010). They should be built in such a way as to allow them to anticipate a crisis when there is only a risk of its occurrence (Zhang and Wang, 2016). If early warning systems are to fulfil their intended function, they have to (Dimitrov and Yangyozov, 2013): identify the symptoms of a crisis on the basis of information from external and internal sources, allow the classification and assessment of the identified symptoms in order to clarify which ones require immediate action and continuously collect information from the environment in order to refine and improve the methods for diagnosing changes that could be a source of a crisis.

3.3.3. Crisis management approaches and concepts

On the basis of the different types of strategies outlined above, it is possible to distinguish the following approaches to crisis management (Sahin et al., 2015):

- an escaping approach,
- a solving approach,
- a proactive approach,
- a reactive approach,
- an interactive approach.

The escaping approach requires constant monitoring of both internal and external environment and continuous improvement of the methodology for predicting and estimating the possibility of occurrence of crisis events. It is also essential for enterprises adopting this approach to identify and clarify their key values and needs in order to orient their basic risk management processes towards them, thus increasing the likelihood of preventing or minimizing the negative effects of a crisis. The intra-organizational communication process is also an important element. The identified key values and actions aimed at their protection should be known to all employees, at all levels of the organizational structure. Together with an adequate diagnosis of early signs of danger, this is the basis for implementing effective solutions during a crisis and increasing flexibility for organizational changes forced by it (Milburn et al., 1983).

The implementation of the solving approach requires both structured pre-crisis risk management in order to anticipate possible adverse events and effective responses when a crisis occurs. Enterprises that decide to follow this approach should – before, during and after the crisis – take into account the criteria that will determine the shape of actions to be taken. These include, for example (Sahin et al., 2015):

- besides bringing negative consequences, a crisis may become an opportunity for beneficial organizational changes and development,
- crisis management strategies should be precisely defined and methodically embedded in the functioning business management system,
- the reasonable use of financial and non-financial resources is particularly important,
- all employees should be informed and motivated to take joint action to combat the crisis,
- if the crisis is external and affects many enterprises, it is important to follow the behaviour and changes of competitors,
- during the crisis, the enterprise's core objectives (such as customer satisfaction) should be pursued to the maximum possible extent,
- the planning of crisis strategies should be carried out by qualified and experienced personnel,

- defence strategies not only increase the opportunities for exiting the crisis, but also allow the enterprise to minimize the effects of its negative consequences.

The proactive approach provides for the development of solutions and actions to be implemented in the event of crises that hypothetically could occur in the enterprise. Such an approach is based on the maximum utilization of measures allowing the prevention of foreseeable crises. This translates into faster and more effective actions taken against crisis events when they factually take place. Enterprises that are well prepared in advance are better able to cope with time pressure and chaos, which is often the first reaction to a rapid escalation of a crisis. If such a proactive approach to crisis management is to be feasible, the following are necessary: an efficient communication system, the proper identification and assessment of risks, the development and implementation of early warning systems, the building of crisis prevention plans, the establishment of a permanent organizational unit responsible for the crisis management process (Sahin et al., 2015).

The reactive approach is chosen most often in the event of unexpected crises. Actions taken at such circumstances are spontaneous, dynamic and immediate. They often take the form of aggressive decisions involving significant losses to the enterprise – for example: shutting down certain parts of the enterprises, reducing salaries, narrowing the range of production or service provision operations. Thus, the reactive approach is the most risky and exposes the enterprise to dissatisfaction and the loss of trust on the part of both employees and customers (Sahin et al., 2015).

On the other hand, the interactive approach provides for the development of integrated actions that need to be taken before, during and after a crisis. A characteristic feature of this approach is an efficiently functioning mechanism of self-control and continuous improvement of the system developed on the basis of gained experience. However, it requires a highly efficient system of communication with all groups of stakeholders, because only broad cooperation on improving the crisis management policy can, on the one hand, eliminate the enterprise's problems during and after a crisis, and on the other hand, ensure the achievement of leading strategic objectives despite the occurrence of a crisis (Sahin et al., 2015).

Besides approaches, there are also concepts associated with crisis management. The three basic concepts of crisis management are the concept of vulnerability, the concept of resilience and the concept of adaptation. Vulnerability to crisis refers to a situation in which a system fails to cope with increasing threats and becomes vulnerable to negative changes that earlier have been successfully absorbed. The concept of vulnerability defines the types of threats/risks to which a given crisis management system is exposed. It ultimately focuses on three elements: the degree of damage caused by a specific threat, the degree of exposure to a threat and the degree of resilience to a threat. Resilience is associated with sudden and unforeseeable changes, and the main objective of the concept of resilience is to restore the enterprise as quickly as possible to the state before the occurrence of such changes. This concept is based on the premise that any unforeseeable changes or threats provide opportunities for an analysis and assessment of the current situation as well as new applications of existing knowledge and experience, so that crises can sometimes turn into opportunities for change and development. Resilience primarily focuses on maximum adaptation to occurring changes, difficulties related to such adaptation and the critical threshold, i.e. a situation in which the enterprise is unable to resist the negative consequences of a crisis and ceases to be resilient. Adaptation, on the other hand, manifests itself through adaptability, which is the foundation for reducing vulnerability to crises and increasing resilience. The concept of adaptation is therefore an inclusive concept. The enterprise's adaptive capacity is the abilities to surrender to changes in its environment and to implement changes constituting natural consequences of crises in management systems. These abilities relate to the long-term mobilization of the system to implement changes resulting from the specificity of a particular crisis. They are the opposite of short-term response capabilities. The development of adaptive abilities is determined by economic, technological, infrastructural, information, administrative and personnel factors (Sienkiewicz-Małyjurek, 2015).

3.3.4. Crisis management models

Crisis management is a process of coordinated actions based on the ability to deal with what is unexpected and to gather and process the mass of incoming information in order to make optimal decisions (Bénaben, 2016). For the purpose of standardizing and formalizing guidelines for the building and implementation of effective crisis management systems, models of the crisis management process have been developed. The frameworks of the selected models are presented in Table 3.3.

In order to survive a crisis, enterprises strive to minimize the negative effects of crisis events or adapt to the changed business environment resulting from the crisis. In order to achieve these goals, they may, among other things (Mikušová and Horváthová, 2019):

- sell assets to obtain additional funds that will be used to finance crisis-related losses,
- increase or decrease the amount of equity,
- capitalize debts,
- change the structure of the assortment or range of services offered,
- reorganize the key business processes,
- implement changes in the ownership structure (e.g. mergers, strategic alliances),
- review the strategy and correct strategic plans (new strategic planning systems),
- rationalize the management of financial and non-financial resources,
- restructure employment,

Table 3.3 Selected crisis management models

Author of the model	*Framework of the crisis management model*
Burnett (1998)	• identification (goal formation and environmental analysis – the preparation for the crisis), • confrontation (encompasses strategy formulation and strategy evaluation – the point when an organization is involved in the crisis), • reconfiguration (strategy implementation and strategic control – how the organization adapts to crisis intervention).
Elsubbaugh et al. (2004)	• general preparation phase (cultural preparedness, strategic preparedness), • detection of early warning signals, • specific preparation or crisis management stage (quick decision response, resource mobilization, information flow), • crisis outcome.
Valackiene (2011)	• strategy of crisis management in organization, • preparation of crisis situation prevention programme, • identification of crisis nature, • operative actions when crisis appears, • liquidation of crisis consequences, rehabilitating the organizational performance, • preparation of new crisis situation management programmes.
Sahin et al. (2015)	• prediction, • prevention and preparation, • control, • recovery, • learning and evaluation.
Bénaben (2016)	• crisis definition: function, intrinsic risk, stake, • crisis analysis: objective, • crisis management: define, realize, maintain.

- effect marketing changes,
- improve communication processes within the enterprise and with the environment.

The diversity of strategies and approaches to management in crisis situations proves that there is no single best way to overcome a crisis in an enterprise. In economic practice, the most effective solution is hybrid programmes combining elements of different strategies. However, it should be remembered that, besides designing a sound strategy, overcoming a crisis also depends on linking such a strategy to an appropriate organizational culture and structure, using the enterprise's skills and resources as well as exercising strong leadership. Thus, what the enterprise needs in a crisis situation is holistic and integrated management.

3.3.5. Crisis management versus risk management

Risk management plays a special role in crisis management. Although risk management is generally considered to be a process of a preventive nature and designed to minimize as far as possible the possibility of the occurrence of negative events (constituting the best way to anticipate and prevent a crisis), one of its implied aims is also to minimize the scale of negative effects of such events. Therefore, the risk management process, and especially the phases of risk identification and analysis, may prove to be effective tools for improving the efficiency of management when a crisis actually occurs. If it happens, management does not concern the risk of a potential crisis, but takes the form of actions oriented towards the risk of its negative consequences. Risk management during a crisis can also influence the scale of such consequences. A diagram showing the relationships between risk management and crisis management is shown in Figure 3.1.

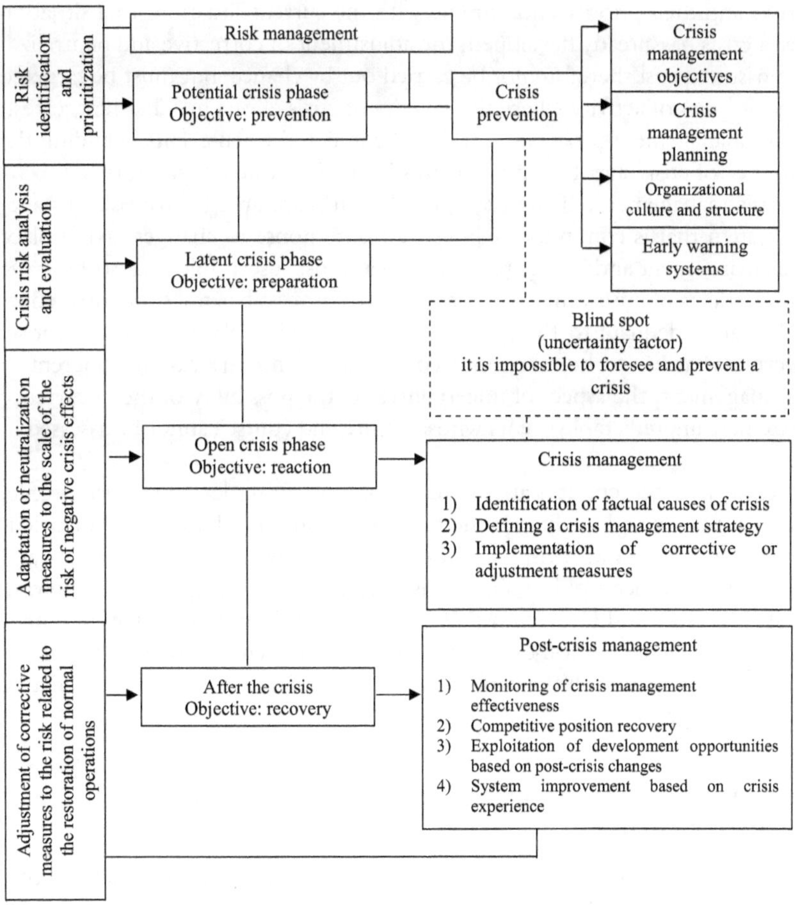

Figure 3.1 Relationships between risk management and crisis management

Presented in Figure 3.1, the relationships and connections between risk management and crisis management indicate that both processes should function on a feedback loop basis. Moreover, crisis management is an indispensable element of a risk management system, i.e. a holistic approach to risk in business activities. Thus, it should be borne in mind that crisis management must not be limited to active anti-crisis measures alone. One of its objectives should also be anticipating and preventing the occurrence of crises or preparing the enterprise for their arrival. Furthermore, as one of the domains of management, crisis management must not be reduced to episodic interventions. It should be a continuous process permanently integrated into the enterprise management system, compatible with risk management at the prevention stage and with business continuity management at the counteraction stage (e.g. as part of the development of business continuity plans in the event of a crisis).

The sources of threats to enterprises are very diverse. Consequently, the process of preventing and managing a crisis should start with the identification of key risks and their prioritization in line with the current situation. In a situation where a crisis has already developed, the adjustment of corrective and neutralization measures must therefore not be carried out by chance, but must be targeted at specific areas of activity where the severity of crisis effects may be the greatest. The risk management process should not be initiated when events heralding the occurrence of crisis start to unfold, as this is the time when it transforms directly into crisis management. If the enterprise has in place an effective risk management system that is continuously improved in response to changes taking place in the environment and is targeted at the areas most susceptible to absorbing the negative effects of crises, the crisis management process becomes the most effective, fast and adequate to the nature of changes taking place in the enterprise. However, what has to be taken into consideration in every case is, inherent in risk management, the aspect of uncertainty, i.e. the possibility of the occurrence of extremely unpredictable events whose nature and course cannot be assessed in advance.

In crisis management, it is also extremely important to develop a crisis profile, using quantitative and qualitative methods based on the risk profile of a particular enterprise. Aimed at identifying the enterprise's possible vulnerabilities and weaknesses, the process of building a crisis profile should comprise the following actions (Mikušová and Horváthová, 2019): the identification of sources of potential crises, the categorization of the crises to which the enterprise may be vulnerable, the determination of the probability, impact, and time of the occurrence of the selected types of crises.

3.4. Experiences from selected crises for enterprise management

Regardless of their origin, crises lead to numerous economic consequences that translate into problems for enterprises, regardless of their size or economic sector (although the nature of a crisis may cause certain sectors of the economy to be more susceptible to absorbing the negative effects of specific crises). The history of the world has witnessed a number of different types of crises that, to various degrees, have disrupted the functioning of business enterprises, in each case forcing them to introduce a certain range of changes in the area of management and making them aware of the importance of implementing crisis prevention measures, becoming prepared for a crisis, as well as developing techniques and methods of neutralizing the negative consequences of crisis events. Post-crisis experience has also significantly influenced the development of the discipline of risk management, i.e. the invention of methods and tools for dealing with risks, and has highlighted strong relationships between effective risk management and crisis management. The following part of the chapter discusses the impact of selected crises of the 21st century on enterprise management. The analysis includes crises representing the following three categories:

- a financial crisis (the global financial crisis in the beginning of 2007),
- a crisis caused by a natural disaster (the tsunami in Japan in 2011),
- a political crisis (the destabilization of North Africa and the Middle East in the years 2009–2017).

3.4.1. The global financial crisis

The global financial crisis of 2007 was one of the greatest ever to hit the world economy. The extent and severity of the negative consequences of the crisis for businesses was mainly due to its scale. The crisis quickly spread to almost all countries around the world. The factors facilitating such a rapid transmission of the crisis included globalization, the liberalization of trade, the internationalization of enterprises, supranational transactions, international and global cooperation within supply chains and international competitiveness. Rose and Spiegel (2012) emphasize, however, that the severity of the global financial crisis for enterprises differed from country to country.

The crisis affected the economies of both developed and developing countries, resulting in numerous problems for individual enterprises. The main challenges faced by enterprises were as follows: shocks in financial and currency exchange markets, a drop in demand translating into problems with global exports, a plunge in consumption, a drop in production, a slowdown in investment activity and rising foreign trade deficits (Czekaj, 2010). These and other factors caused dramatic financial, managerial and organizational problems in many enterprises, quite a few of which failed to cope with them and were forced into bankruptcy. Some organizations had to introduce various changes, for example in their ownership structure, range of operations, product or service offers, financing structure, relations with the environment, etc. The enterprises that had survived the crisis were obliged to implement different adaptation measures. Sometimes they were forced to make dynamic and previously unplanned managerial decisions to ensure the continuity of their business operations. This was a particularly difficult task for those enterprises that, before the onset of the crisis, had not had an effective risk management system (based on the identification and prioritization of the leading risk factors) or a business continuity management system (mainly in terms of business continuity plans in the event of crises), and had not implemented crisis management procedures in the first stage of the crisis when symptoms noticeable in the environment indicated upcoming complications. Delayed responses to the crisis manifesting themselves in employing anti-crisis measures only when the crisis had already been transmitted to the enterprise significantly reduced the chance to maintaining business continuity.

For obvious reasons, smaller companies with a poor competitive position, lower development potential and lack of financial and non-financial resources to deal with the aftermath of the global financial crisis were less successful in their attempts at survival. The main types of problems that emerged during the crisis in small and medium-sized enterprises (SMEs) include the following (Soininen et al., 2012):

- a decrease in sales revenue translating negatively into profit generation opportunities,
- liquidity and solvency problems,
- deteriorating profitability ratios,
- the falling value of assets,
- problems with access to external sources of funding,
- personnel problems (the need to reduce employment).

A slowdown in enterprises' economic growth was another serious consequence of the global financial crisis. The degree to which individual enterprises suffered from negative development trends and the lack of conditions for implementing innovation was largely dependent on the previously achieved resistance to crises (Peric and Vitezic, 2016). Bartram and Bodnar (2009) also emphasize that the global financial crisis exerted a negative impact on enterprises, exposing their shortcomings in many areas and weakening their position. The serious problems faced by enterprises at large in the wake of the crisis have triggered a feedback loop, thus exposing the whole economy to an increased risk of destabilization.

Therefore, the global financial crisis required a reorganization of business management systems. This reorganization manifested itself mainly in the development and implementation of a crisis management strategy commensurate with changes observable in the environment (Lee et al., 2017). Sometimes management teams had to redefine the leading strategy and establish new strategic objectives because the activities of the enterprises that survived the crisis differed significantly from those pursued in the period before its onset. The enterprises that survived the crisis are expected to use their newly gained experience and knowledge firstly, to make more conscious managerial decisions concerning the areas that the crisis allowed them to diagnose as critical and secondly, to develop emergency strategies in the event of a crisis occurring in the future (Robertson and Chetty, 2000). This type of approach is currently widely utilized in risk management, crisis management and business continuity management.

After the global financial crisis, significant changes could be observed in the area of risk management as effective risk management was becoming a priority for many enterprises. The enterprises that were forced by the crisis to focus on both post-crisis recovery and preventive measures had to develop new, or improve previously functioning, risk management systems. First of all, the way of building a risk profile was changed (Maingot et al., 2012). The catalogue of risks identified as those to which a particular enterprise is most exposed was expanded to include those risks that had materialized during the global crisis and whose gravity had not been recognized before. In addition, enterprises intensified the use of professional methods and techniques to assess the likelihood of, and exposure to, particular risks. Such changes and ex-post experience formed the basis for the development of contingency plans, early warning systems and business continuity plans.

Another lesson learned from the experience gained by enterprises during the global financial crisis is the need for greater integration of risk management into corporate governance. This means that managers at all levels of the organizational structure have to cooperate with internal auditors, persons responsible for internal controlling and risk owners (Sobel and Reding, 2004). The range and intensity of internal controlling also increased, with the aim of developing risk mitigation mechanisms and thus increasing the likelihood of achieving the enterprise's basic objectives, even under crisis conditions. According to Fabozzi and Drake (2009), the development of Enterprise Risk Management (ERM) requires the following: defining precisely the level of risk that the enterprise is able to accept without disrupting the performance of its basic functions (defining the appetite for risk and the degree of tolerance) and adapting decisions on the building and improvement of a risk management system to the existing risk management policy (which can be redefined on the basis of post-crisis experience).

The global financial crisis also revealed that the risks facing enterprises were more complex than it had been previously assumed and that, despite their different sources, they showed close interdependencies. Therefore, the way they are managed requires innovative methods as well as extensive preventive and corrective measures. Furthermore, one of the biggest challenges for enterprises is to strike the right balance between generating profit and taking risk. This task proves to be particularly complicated in view of the uncertainty in the world economy following the global financial crisis (Maingot et al., 2012).

3.4.2. Crisis following a natural disaster

The tsunami that hit north-eastern Japan on 11 March 2011 was one of the most devastating natural disasters in world history. It caused the death of several tens of thousands of people and destruction estimated at around USD 210 billion. The earthquake that triggered the tsunami also caused the failure of the Fukushima nuclear power plant, whose dramatic consequences were to be suffered for a long period of time (Ranghieri and Ishiwatari, 2014).

This event precipitated a crisis that was a combination of a number of negative environmental, political, technological and, above all, economic and business consequences. The crisis struck particularly hard business enterprises, physically destroying their premises, causing widespread losses and irreversible changes in conducted business activities, strongly weakening the dynamics of production and limiting opportunities for international trade. One of the key problems was also the severance or strong disruption of supply chain flows because even if enterprises had not been directly destroyed, they were not able to trade with other supply chain links that had been affected by the disaster (Saito, 2015). Moreover, disruptions were also experienced by enterprises in other parts of the world that were links in the same supply chains together with Japanese business struck by the tsunami. Also, within one year of the disaster, 656 mainly small and medium-sized enterprises from various regions of Japan went bankrupt, citing a break in a supply chain or a lack of financial resources to overcome the crisis as the cause of bankruptcy (Ono and Watanabe, 2015). One of the main reasons for these problems was the failure of some of such enterprises to develop formal Business Continuity Plans (BCPs), which significantly increases an organization's vulnerability to the negative effects of natural disasters and creates real barriers to recovery (Li, 2015). For managers, it is a significant challenge requiring the implementation of appropriate actions in the areas of both operational management – mainly with respect to diagnosing the main effects of interruptions in the performance of specific operational activities – and strategic management – mainly with respect to developing ways and methods of responding to crisis events and regaining the ability to perform basic functions (Krawczyk, 2013). A few years after the dramatic events of 2011, it turned out that Japanese companies had not introduced any dramatic changes in their supply chain risk management strategies. Supplier diversification and sub-supplier identification remained the leading strategies in this regard (Grabowiecki and Dąbrowski, 2016). However, the methodical approach to improving these strategies using proactive risk management tools was strengthened.

Another experience gained by enterprises from the 2011 tsunami is the awareness of the need for a strong diversification of disaster-related risks, and therefore for improvement of the processual approach to risk, mainly in its first phase, namely, the identification of risks. Compared with the situation before the disaster, it turned out that enterprises began to diversify their risks to a wider extent by, for example, increasing the number of suppliers, identifying their supply chains from a broader perspective, or demanding that their suppliers undertake risk diversification. Moreover, many enterprises changed their major strategic orientation. In order to protect themselves against the large scale and severity of negative effects of potential future natural disasters, they started to implement strong management measures such as (Grabowiecki and Dąbrowski, 2016):

- building distribution facilities in several locations so as to diversify the risk of suspended operations in the event of another disaster,
- adequately securing the existing infrastructure,

- redefining the application of the just-in-time concept to production systems, mainly in terms of developing methods for dealing with potential production interruptions,
- considering changes in the strategy for maintaining additional stocks of manufacturing materials.

The crisis triggered by the tsunami also verified the validity of crisis management systems functioning in Japanese enterprises. It was found that, despite their good preparation for natural disasters, their crisis management systems required improvement so that they could (Krausmann and Cruz, 2013):

- precisely predict natural disasters on the basis of relevant forecasting and estimation methods,
- identify ways to prevent or limit the negative consequences of such disasters,
- define early warning systems as a mandatory element,
- take into account the extensive ways (strategies) of responding in the event of different possible courses of a crisis resulting from a natural disaster.

3.4.3. *Political crisis*

Following a series of political conflicts, the years 2009–2017 witnessed the crisis related to the destabilization of the Middle East and North Africa (MENA). The accumulation of various factors made this area an arena of escalating conflicts and crises whose negative consequences struck enterprises not only there, but also in other distant parts of the world. Besides economic and political crises, the countries of the region had to cope with numerous problems associated with refugee migration and terrorist attacks (Zając, 2018).

The major lessons that managers could learn from the MENA crisis are related to risk management. Conducting research on the risk landscape assessment from both a global and local point of view, the World Economic Forum published a document entitled *The Middle East and North Africa Risks Landscape*. Using data from the Global Risks Perception Survey conducted among the stakeholders of various MENA enterprises and the Executive Opinion Survey targeted at business leaders from the MENA region, the Forum presented its assessment of global, national and market risks with a view to developing a comprehensive description of threats faced by enterprises there. The published report indicates that, from the series of political crises, businesses in the region have drawn the following conclusions that should be used in introducing various risk management and crisis management measures (World Economic Forum, 2019):

- business executives continue to be concerned about the condition of the world economy,
- enterprises and their stakeholders expect increasing risks related to economic confrontations and international agreements,

- enterprises continue to suffer from tensions in international trade, mainly in terms of costs incurred,
- enterprises experience market repercussions related to the extraction of, and trade in, fossil fuels,
- enterprises feel the need to take action aimed at curbing corruption and improving access to sources of financing,
- enterprises have to cope with very high rates of unemployment,
- enterprises feel uncertain about the continuity of their business activities, for example because of terrorist attacks.

Furthermore, the results of the research conducted by the World Economic Forum also indicate that companies in the MENA region are fully aware of the importance of improving management systems in gradually recovering from post-crisis destabilization. They also show that the way to restore stability is through the integration of management systems with a productive economy. On the basis of experience gained from previous crisis years, the business leaders and stakeholders of enterprises in the region have proposed a catalogue of key risk towards which effective management systems should be oriented. The top ten risks identified as the most important in terms of impact and likelihood of occurrence are as follows (World Economic Forum, 2019):

- energy price shock,
- unemployment and underemployment,
- terrorist attacks,
- failure of regional and global governance,
- fiscal crises,
- cyber-attacks,
- unmanageable inflation,
- water-crises,
- illicit trade,
- failure of financial mechanism or institution.

An important issue relating to the management of the MENA region's enterprises in the wake of a series of political crises in the years 2009–2017 is their entrepreneurship, which was severely hampered and reduced during prolonged conflicts. The challenge for their managers is to implement management measures that will revive their entrepreneurship as well as re-establish and strengthen their international business contacts. Conducted by Aljuwaiber (2020), a review of research papers on entrepreneurship in the MENA region published between 2009 and 2019 shows that what its enterprises need is a balanced stimulation of entrepreneurship (Aljuwaiber, 2020) at the microeconomic level, which should ultimately strengthen the region's development and economic growth, for the benefit of enterprises as well as their stakeholders, business partners, customers, suppliers, etc., i.e. other businesses located all over the world. This is currently one of the major post-crisis challenges for the management community (mainly at the strategic level) in the MENA region.

References

Aljuwaiber, A. (2020). Entrepreneurship research in the Middle East and North Africa: Trends, challenges, and sustainability issues. *Journal of Entrepreneurship in Emerging Economies*, ahead-of-print, https://doi.org/10.1108/JEEE-08-2019-0123.

Bartram, S.M., Bodnar, G.M. (2009). No place to hide: The global crisis in equity markets in 2008/2009. *Journal of International Money and Finance*, 28, pp. 1246–1292.

Bayazıt, Z.D., Cengel, O., Tepe, F.F. (2003). Crisis management in organizations and a case study. *11th National Management and Organization Congress Leaflet of Notices.* Afyon, pp. 366–377.

Bénaben, F. (2016). A formal framework for crisis management describing information flows and functional structure. *Procedia Engineering*, 159, pp. 353–356.

Bigley, G.A., Roberts, K.H. (2001). The incident command system: High-reliability organizing for complex and volatile task environments. *Academy of Management Journal*, 44, pp. 1281–1299.

Boin, A., Paul's, H., Stern, E., Sundelius, B. (2005). *The Politics of Crisis Management, Public Leadership under Pressure.* Cambridge: Cambridge University Press.

British Standards Institution (2011). *PAS 200 Crisis Management – Guidance and Good Practice.* London.

Bundy, J., Pfarrer, M.D. (2015). A burden of responsibility: The role of social approval at the onset of a crisis. *Academy of Management Review*, 40, pp. 345–369.

Bundy, J., Pfarrer, M.D., Short, C.E., Coombs, W.T. (2017). Crises and crisis management: Integration, interpretation, and research development. *Journal of Management* 43(6), pp. 1661–1692.

Burnett, J.J. (1998). A strategic approach to managing crises. *Public Relations Review*, 24(4), pp. 475–488.

Cener, P. (2007). Crisis management. www.danismend.com/ (Access: 1.11.2020).

Chong, J.K.S. (2004). Six steps to better crisis management. *Journal of Business Strategy*, 25(2), pp. 43–46.

Civelek, M.E., Çemberci, M., Eralp, N.E. (2016). The role of social media in crisis communication and crisis management. *International Journal of Research in Business and Social Science*, 5(3), pp. 111–120.

Coombs, T., Hollady, S.J. (2012). *The Handbook of Crisis Communication.* New York: Wiley.

Crandall, W.R., Parnell, J.A., Spillan, J.E. (2014). *Crisis Management. Leading in the New Strategy Landscape* (2nd ed.). Los Angeles, CA: Sage.

Czekaj, J. (2010). Wpływ światowego kryzysu gospodarczego na polską gospodarkę [in:] Kołodko, G. (ed.), *Globalizacja, kryzys i co dalej?* Warszawa: Wydawnictwo Poltext, pp. 189–209.

Dimitrov, I., Yangyozov, P. (2013). Application of an early warning system in the dynamic model for business processes improvement. *Central European Review of Economics and Finance*, 3(1), pp. 27–38.

Elsubbaugh, S., Fildes, R., Rose, M.B. (2004). Preparation for crisis management: A proposed model and empirical evidence. *Journal of Contingencies and Crisis Management*, 12(3), pp. 112–127.

Fabozzi, F.J., Drake, P.P. (2009). *Finance, Capital Markets, Financial Management and Investment Management.* Hoboken, NJ: John Wiley & Sons.

Fener, T., Cevik, T. (2015). Leadership in crisis management: Separation of leadership and executive concepts. *Procedia Economics and Finance*, 26, pp. 695–701.

Fragouli, E., Ibidapo, B. (2015). Leading in crisis: Leading organizational change and business development. *International Journal of Information, Business, and Management*, 7(3), pp. 71–90.

Gephart, R.P., Van Maanen, J., Oberlechner, T. (2009). Organizations and risk in late modernity. *Organization Studies*, 30, pp. 141–155.

Glaesser, D. (2006). *Crisis Management in the Tourism Industry*. Burlington, MA: Elsevier.

Grabowiecki, J., Dąbrowski, M. (2016). Wpływ katastrof naturalnych na międzynarodowe łańcuchy dostaw japońskich grup Keiretsu. *Studia i Materiały. Miscellanea Oeconomicae. Uniwersytetu Jana Kochanowskiego w Kielcach*, 3(3), pp. 97–103.

Greiner, L.E. (1972). Evolution and Revolution as Organizations Grow. *Harvard Business Review*, 50(4), pp. 37–46.

Greiner, L.E. (1998). Evolution and revolution as organizations grow, with an updated commentary: Revolution is still inevitable, *Harvard Business Review*, 76, pp. 55–67.

Groh, M. (2014). Stategic management in times of crisis. *American Journal of Economics and Business Administration*, 6(2), pp. 49–57.

Håkansson, H., Ford, D. (2002). How should companies interact in business networks? *Journal of Business Research*, 55(2), pp. 133–139.

Hart, P., Heyse, L., Boin, A. (2001). New trends in crisis management practice and crisis management research: Setting the Agenda. *Journal of Contingencies and Crisis Management*, 9(4), pp. 181–199.

Herbane, B. (2010). Small business research – Time for a crisis-based view. *International Small Business Journal: Researching Entrepreneurship*, 28(1), pp. 43–64.

Hermann, C.F. (1972). *Some Issues in the Study of International Crisis. International Crises: Insights from Behavioral Research*. New York: The Free Press.

Hrdina, P., Maléřová, L. (2012). *Simulation of Crisis Management Processes as a Means of Education*. Paper presented at the Sborník vědeckých prací Vysoké školy báňské – Technické univerzity Ostrava. Řada bezpečnostní inženýrství, [*Proceedings of Scientific Papers Technical University of Ostrava. Series of Safety Engineering*.] 7(1), pp. 73–76.

Jaques, T. (2007). Issue management and crisis management: An integrated, non-linear, relational construct. *Public Relations Review*, 33(2), pp. 147–157.

Jarrett, M. (2003). The seven myths of change management. *Business Strategy Review*, 14(4), pp. 22–29.

Kahn, W.A., Barton, M.A., Fellows, S. (2013). Organizational crises and the disturbance of relational systems. *Academy of Management Review*, 38, pp. 377–396.

Karim, A.J. (2016). The Indispensable styles, characteristics and skills for charismatic leadership in times of crisis. *International Journal of Advanced Engineering, Management and Science*, 2(5), pp. 363–372.

Krausmann, E., Cruz, A. (2013). Impact of the 11 March 2011, Great East Japan earthquake and tsunami on the chemical industry. *Natural Hazards*, 67(2), pp. 811–828.

Krawczyk, I. (2013). Kataklizm w Japonii: kumulacja zagrożeń a systemowe rozwiązania. *Bezpieczeństwo Narodowe*, 1(25), pp. 169–198.

Krystek, U. (1987). *Unternehmungskrisen. Beschriebung, Vermeidung und Bewältigung Überlebenskrisischer Prozesse in Unternehmungen*. Wiesbaden: Gabler.

Kuzmanova, M., Ivanov, I. (2019). Relation between change management and crisis management: Survey Evidence. *International Conference Knowledge-Based Organization*, XXV(1), pp. 255–260.

Leidner, D., Pan, G., Pan, S. (2009). The role of IT in crisis response: Lessons from the SARS and Asian Tsunami disasters. *Journal of Strategic Information Systems*, 18, p. 80.

Lee, C., Chen, M., Ning, S. (2017). Why did some firms perform better in the global financial crisis? *Economic Research-Ekonomska Istraživanja*, 30(1), pp. 1339–1366.

Lester, W., Krejci, D. (2007). Business "not" as usual: The national incident management system, federalism, and leadership. *Public Administration Review*, 67(1), pp. 84–93.

Li, W.S. (2015). Experience of APEC in disaster management: importance of BCP [in:], T. Izumi, R. Shaw (eds.), *Disaster Management and Private Sectors: Challenges and Potentials.* Tokyo: Springer, pp. 31–45.

Litovchenko, Y. (2012). The choice and justification the strategy of enterprise crisis management. *Bìznes Inform*, 12, pp. 308–312.

Maingot, M., Quon, T.K., Zeghal, D. (2012). The effect of the financial crisis on enterprise risk management disclosures. *International Journal of Risk Assessment and Management*, 16(4), pp. 227–247.

Mikušová, M., Horváthová, P. (2019). Prepared for a crisis? Basic elements of crisis management in an organisation. *Economic Research-Ekonomska Istraživanja*, 32(1), pp. 1844–1868.

Milburn, T. Schuler, R. Watman, K. (1983). Organizational crisis: Definition and conceptualization. *Human Relations*, 36(12), pp. 1141–1160.

Mitroff, I. (2004). Think like a sociopath, act like a saint. *Journal of Business Strategy*, 25(4), pp. 42–53.

Mitroff, I., Pearson, C., Harrington, C. (1996). *The Essential Guide to Managing Corporate Crises: A Step by Step Handbook for Surviving Major Catastrophes.* Oxford: Oxford University Press.

Mitroff, I., Shrivastava, P., Udwadia, F. (1987). Effective crisis management. *The Academy of Management Executive*, 1(4), pp. 283–292.

Mitroff, I.I., Pearson, C.M. (1993). *Crisis Management.* San Francisco, CA: Jossey-Bass.

Noratikah, M.A., Aizza Maisha, D.A.A., Mus Chairil, S. (2017). Crisis response strategy and crisis types suitability: A preliminary study on MH370. Paper presented at the *International Conference on Communication and Media: An International Communication Association Regional Conference (i-COME'16)*, Kuala Lumpur, Malaysia, 33.

Ono, T., Watanabe, K. (2015). Application of natural disaster information for supply chain resilience. *Journal of Disaster Research*, 10, p. 783.

Papalová, M. (2015). Media impact on crisis communications. Paper presented at *Marketing Identity: Digital Life, Pt II*, Smolenice, Slovakia, pp. 448–459.

Pauchant, T., Mitroff, I. (1992). *Transforming the Crisis-Prone Organization.* San Francisco, CA: Jossey-Bass.

Pearson, C.M., Clair, J.A. (1998). Reframing crisis management. *Academy of Management Review*, 23, pp. 59–76.

Pedersen, C.L. (2019). The 3 myths of employee autonomy. *The European Business Review*, November/December, pp. 60–63.

Pedersen, C.L., Ritter, T. (2020). Preparing your business for a post-pandemic world. *Harvard Business Review*, digital article, 13 April 2020.

Peric, M., Vitezic, V. (2016). Impact of global economic crisis on firm growth. *Small Business Economics*, 46, pp. 1–12.

Perrow, C. (1999). *Normal Accidents. Living with High-Risk Technologies.* Princeton, NJ: Princeton University Press.

Ranghieri, F., Ishiwatari, M. (2014). *Learning from Megadisasters: Lessons from the Great East Japan Earthquake.* Washington, DC: World Bank.

Reason, J. (1990). *Human Error.* Cambridge: Cambridge University Press.

Ritter, T., Pedersen, C.L. (2020). Digitization capability and the digitalization of business models in business-to-business firms: Past, present, and future. *Industrial Marketing Management*, 86(4), pp. 180–190.

Robertson, C., Chetty, S.K. (2000). A contingency-based approach to understanding export performance. *International Business Review*, 9, pp. 211–235.

Rochet, C., Keramidas, O., Bout, L. (2008). Crisis as change strategy in public organizations. *International Review of Administrative Sciences*, 74(1), pp. 63–76.

Rose, A.K., Spiegel, M.M. (2012). Cross-country causes and consequences of the 2008 crisis: Early warning. *Japan and the World Economy*, 24, pp. 1–16.

Rosenthal, U., Kouzmin, A. (1997). Crises and crises management: Toward comprehensive government decision making. *Journal of Public Administration Research and Theory*, 7(2), pp. 277–304.

Sahin, S., Ulubeyli, S., Kazaza, A. (2015). Innovative crisis management in construction: Approaches and the process. *Procedia – Social and Behavioral Sciences*, 195, pp. 2298–2305.

Saito, Y.U. (2015). Geographical spread of interfirm transaction networks and the Great East Japan earthquake [in:] T. Watanabe, I. Uesugi, A. Ono (eds.), *The Economics of Interfirm Networks.* Heidelberg: Springer, pp. 158–161.

Selbst, P. (1978). The containment and control of organisational crises [in:] Sutherland, J. (ed.), *Management Handbook for Public Administrators.* New York: Van Nostrand.

Shiller, R.J. (2012). *The Subprime Solution: How Today*'s *Global Financial Crisis Happened and What to Do About It.* 1st edn., Illustrated, Princeton, NJ: Princeton University Press.

Sienkiewicz-Małyjurek, K. (2015). *Skuteczne zarządzanie kryzysowe.* Warszawa: Difin.

Slatter, S., Lovett, D. (2001). *Restrukturyzacja firmy. Zarządzanie przedsiębiorstwem w sytuacjach kryzysowych.* Warszawa: WIG-Press.

Sobel, P.J., Reding, K.F. (2004). Aligning corporate governance with enterprise risk management. *Management Accounting Quarterly*, 5(2), pp.1–9.

Soininen, J., Puumalainen, K., Sjögrén, H., Syrjä, P. (2012). The impact of global economic crisis on SMEs: Does entrepreneurial orientation matter? *Management Research Review*, 35(10), pp. 927–944.

Starbuck, W.H., Milliken, F.J. (1988). Challenger: Fine tuning the odds until something breaks. *Journal of Management Studies*, 25, pp. 319–340.

Tănase, D.I. (2012). Procedural and systematic crisis approach and crisis management. *Theoretical and Applied Economics*, 5(569), pp. 177–184.

Tutar, H. (2004). *Crisis and Stress Management*. Ankara: Seckin Publishing.

Tutar, H. (2007). *Management in States of Crisis and Stress*. 2nd ed. Istanbul: Hayat Publishing.

Valackiene, A. (2011). Theoretical substation of the model for crisis management in organization. *Engineering Economics*, 22(1), pp. 78–90.

Venette, S.J. (2003). *Risk Communication in a High Reliability Organization: APHIS PPQ's Inclusion of Risk in Decision Making*. Ann Arbor, MI: UMI Proquest Information and Learning.

Waller, M.J., Zhike, L., Pratten, R. (2014). Focusing on teams in crisis management education: An integration and simulation-based approach. *Academy of Management Learning & Education*, 13(2), pp. 208–221.

Wang, W.T., Belardo, S. (2005). Strategic integration: A knowledge management approach to crisis management. Paper presented at the *2014 47th Hawaii International Conference on System Sciences*, 8, Big Island, Hawaii, 252a.

Wawrzyniak, B. (1999). *Odnawianie przedsiębiorstwa. Na spotkanie XXI wieku*. Warszawa: Poltext.

Wenzel, M., Stanske, S., Lieberman, M.B. (2020). Strategic responses to crisis. *Strategic Management Journal*, 41, pp. 7–18.

World Economic Forum. (2019). World Economic Forum on the Middle East and North Africa. www.weforum.org/agenda/2019/04/these-are-the-biggest-risks-facing-middle-east-and-north-africa/ (Access: 12.11.2020).

Xu, S. (2010). The design and implementation of prediction and early warning system based on business management and control. Paper presented at the *2010 International Conference on Computational Intelligence and Software Engineering (CiSE)*, Wuhan, China.

Zając, J. (2018). Unia Europejska wobec konfliktu izraelsko-palestyńskiego w latach 2009–2017. *Rocznik Integracji Europejskiej*, 11, pp. 249–262.

Zapletalová, Š. (2012). *Krizový management podniku pro 21. století*. Praha: Ekopress.

Zelek, A. (2003). *Zarządzanie kryzysem w przedsiębiorstwie. Perspektywa strategiczna*. Warszawa: Instytut Organizacji i Zarządzania w Przemyśle "Orgmasz".

Zhang, L., Wang, L. (2016). Risk application research on risk warning mechanism in organizational crisis management – Taking Vanke Real Estate Co. Ltd., as an example. *Chaos, Solitons and Fractals: The Interdisciplinary Journal of Nonlinear Science, and Nonequilibrium and Complex Phenomena*, 89, pp. 373–380.

Ziarko, J., Walas-Trębacz, J. (2010). *Podstawy zarządzania kryzysowego*. Kraków: Krakowskie Towarzystwo Edukacyjne – Oficyna Wydawnicza AFM.

4 Dominant business risks during the COVID-19 pandemic

4.1. Financial risks

Financial risks are among those that emerged during the global COVID-19 pandemic and had the greatest impact on business enterprises. The key risks in this category include liquidity risk, insurance risk, price risk and credit risk.

4.1.1. Liquidity risk

From the very beginning of the pandemic, enterprises in various sectors had to deal with the instability of financial markets and the uncertainty of current and future revenues as well as cash flows (Marsh, 2020a). Due to financial problems resulting from the crisis triggered by the COVID-19 pandemic, many enterprises around the world, particularly those functioning within supply chains and the industries most affected by operating restrictions (e.g. tourism, catering, etc.), started to face consequences such as a shortage of working capital and a gradual decline in liquidity manifested in the following circumstances:

- the gradually or suddenly weakening ability to settle liabilities in a timely manner (depending on the economic sector and the previous financial situation of the enterprise),
- a decrease in the liquidity of current assets (interrupted production cycles, non-moving inventories, excessive supply).

In many cases, such changes characterized by a violent course resulted in deepening problems with liquidity, sometimes leading to bankruptcy.

Confrontation with a long-term economic slowdown and a drop in liquidity requires active financial risk management, including the implementation of countermeasures in the form of business continuity plans developed previously in the event of a crisis. However, the global COVID-19 pandemic had not been earlier anticipated in specialist analyses and predictive research. According to the 2020 issue of the World Economic Forum's (2020a) annual *The Global Risks Report*, the probability of pandemic occurrence was the lowest in the eight years' period, receiving a score of 2.9 on a 7-point scale. Thus, the impossibility of

DOI: 10.4324/9781003131366-4

predicting a pandemic, combined with the nature of the crisis that it triggered, i.e. enterprises' limited capacity to counteract negative financial consequences, caused grave liquidity problems for many entities, including large ones with a well-established market position.

Responding to liquidity problems during the COVID-19 pandemic, enterprises often resorted to disposing of part of their assets in order to acquire cash necessary to settle overdue liabilities and to cover fixed operating costs. In such a situation, the timing of this type of action is of primary importance. As it turns out, the deepening recession resulting from the pandemic resulted in a rapid fall in the market prices of assets, hence, over time, the possibilities of obtaining additional funds for financing operations from asset disposal were becoming increasingly limited. In its international report entitled *COVID-19: Implications for business* (Craven et al., 2020), the American worldwide management consulting firm McKinsey included guidelines for companies struggling with liquidity problems during the COVID-19 crisis. Enterprises should develop situation development scenarios, taking into account the pandemic context, their individual positions and critical variables that may have the greatest influence on their revenues and cost structure during the subsequent phases of the pandemic. With regard to risk management during the COVID-19 crisis, companies should model their finances (balance sheet, profit and loss account and cash flow) in each scenario developed and identify on an ongoing basis factors that could significantly weaken their liquidity. For each such factor, the enterprise should develop remedial actions, e.g. actions optimizing the relationship between liabilities and receivables that reduce costs, such as asset disposal, mergers or acquisitions.

Also, experts from the consulting firm Deloitte developed a manual for enterprises that provides guidance and suggestions for actions whose implementation may secure their financial liquidity during the COVID-19 pandemic. Such actions include the following (Deloitte, 2020a):

- developing a contingency financing plan,
- reviewing the exposure to currency risk, commodity price risk and interest rate risk (market risk),
- reviewing the creditworthiness of business partners,
- conducting a liquidity analysis, including a stress conditions analysis,
- reviewing possible instruments used to improve liquidity (e.g. factoring and forfaiting),
- identifying cash releasing initiatives,
- releasing cash frozen in working capital,
- implementing appropriate IT tools.

The results of a survey conducted during the pandemic by Marsh (2020a), indicate that maintaining financial liquidity can be one of the key factors determining the survival of enterprises during the COVID-19 crisis. The pursuit of this objective can be supported by effective insurance strategies and risk management strategies, for example strategies for reducing additional costs, borrowing, credit insurance, using credit insurance to protect receivables, using insurance services, cooperation with insurance consultants, or factoring agreements.

In order to accurately estimate the liquidity gap caused by the COVID-19 pandemic, in its policy to combat the coronavirus pandemic addressed to small and medium-sized enterprises (SMEs), the OECD (2020a) provided a list of auxiliary metrics such as a drop in revenues, current costs, access to resources that could bridge the liquidity gap and government support. Furthermore, based on a survey of almost one million companies from 16 European countries, the OECD assessed the risk of a liquidity crisis during the COVID-19 pandemic. The survey showed that government policy tools such as tax deferrals, debt moratoriums, and wage subsidies are important in alleviating enterprises' liquidity problems, including protection against bankruptcy. An overview of the results of selected research on financial liquidity of enterprises during the COVID-19 pandemic is presented in Table 4.1.

However, it turns out that, besides companies that experienced serious liquidity shortages following the crisis caused by the COVID-19 pandemic, there are also enterprises that improved their liquidity in that situation. These include companies from the sectors providing products or services demand for which increased abruptly, for example personal protective equipment, disinfectants, medical oxygen, courier services and online sales services.

4.1.2. Insurance risk

The COVID-19 pandemic had a number of negative effects on claims ratios of individual insurance products, causing significant changes in the perception, assessment and scope of insurance risk. Despite the fact that in most sectors of the economy, the pandemic crisis brought negative consequences, some of them experienced a fall in the number of insurance claims. Table 4.2 presents the main changes in insurance risk affecting various sectors and branches of the economy during the pandemic.

The specificity of the COVID-19 pandemic lies in its exceptionally strong impact on the real economy, as well as the property and accident segments. Many enterprises realized that business interruptions and sometimes critical liquidity and solvency problems had a high cumulative potential and exposed them to the temptation of abuse. It is precisely these factors that cause the pandemic to generate risks that may prove to be uninsurable. These identified limitations on the insurability of risks associated with the pandemic are undoubtedly an impetus for reviewing the structure and methods of financing protection against and resilience to future pandemics (Richter and Wilson, 2020). It turns out that few insurance products providing cover against the pure risk of a pandemic have ever been offered on the market. For this reason, and due to the relative rarity of the emergence of global pandemics of such a magnitude as COVID-19, the majority of enterprises did not have insurance cover for such circumstances. However, there are a few examples of organizations that were able to obtain significant financial compensation thanks to insurance against the consequences of a pandemic. A case

Table 4.1 The results of selected research and surveys on financial liquidity of enterprises during the global COVID-19 pandemic

Author	*Surveyed enterprises*	*Subject of survey*	*Major findings*
Gourinchas et al. (2020)	SMEs from 17 countries	An assessment of the impact of different types of government policy interventions on liquidity and bankruptcy during the COVID-19 epidemic.	• the bankruptcy rate for SMEs during the pandemic was 12.1% (in the absence of government action), while, in non-pandemic conditions, it is estimated that it would have been 4.5%, • the implementation of government aid worth 1.1% of GDP brings the bankruptcy rate back to its pre-COVID-19 level, which means a decrease of 8.75%, • these actions saved approximately 1.5% of GDP in salaries and approximately 5% of employment.
Bircan et al. (2020)	Enterprises from 19 countries	• SMEs' demand for cash and improved liquidity in consequence of COVID-19, • the geographical diversity of challenges to liquidity during COVID-19.	• SMEs' cash decreased below the expected level of 3–7% of total assets (Croatia, Lithuania, Morocco, Serbia, Slovenia and Ukraine) – decrease in liquidity, • SMEs from Bulgaria, the Czech Republic, Latvia, Montenegro, Slovakia reported larger than expected cash buffers – increase in liquidity, • SMEs from Bosnia and Herzegovina, Croatia, Slovenia and Portugal – limited possibility of debt increase, • on average, SMEs from many of the countries surveyed already had limited liquidity buffers at the outbreak of the pandemic.
Revoltella et al. (2020)	SMEs and large-sized enterprises in EU countries	• liquidity problems during COVID-19 are visible as income losses, • the impact of government interventions on pandemic liquidity problems.	• cumulative losses in net income of companies in a three months' lockdown scenario amount to 13–24% of GDP, and more than half of companies face liquidity shortages even after government interventions, • SMEs contend with greater income losses than large-sized companies, calculated as a percentage of total assets (6–11% for SMEs, 2–4% for large enterprises).
McGeever et al. (2020)	SMEs in Ireland	• the sources of liquidity problems during COVID-19, • the size of the liquidity gap during the COVID-19.	• liquidity problems are linked primarily to non-personnel costs, as salary costs have been to a considerable degree compensated for by the government, • for SMEs, the liquidity gap is estimated at EUR 2.4–5.7 billion, • the existing credit facilities provided by the Central Bank of Ireland are unlikely to be sufficient to meet the financing needs of all companies, estimated at EUR 2.4–5.7 billion over three months.

(*Continued*)

Table 4.1 (Continued) The results of selected research and surveys on financial liquidity of enterprises during the global COVID-19 pandemic

Author	*Surveyed enterprises*	*Subject of survey*	*Major findings*
Drechsel and Kalemli-Özcan (2020a; 2020b)	Enterprises in the USA	The liquidity gap in the United States during COVID-19 and political remedies.	• salary costs are regarded as a proxy for the costs to be covered and the liquidity gap with respect to company size, • compensating for salary costs for enterprises employing up to 100 people for 3 months would amount to approximately USD 449 billion; extending this to companies with up to 500 employees would raise the bill to USD 678 billion, • estimates of the American Association of Property Insurance in the USA indicate that the cost of interruptions in the functioning of small enterprises (with fewer than 100 employees) is USD 220–431 billion per month.
Liu and Parilla (2020)	Small enterprises in the USA	Regional diversification of liquidity problems during COVID-19.	• liquidity challenges for small businesses vary greatly from region to region and from city to city, • income losses range from 74% in Buffalo, New York to 58% in Jacksonville, Florida, • similarly, the percentage of small enterprises with cash reserves for up to 4 weeks ranges from 65% (Buffalo, NY) to 38% (Columbus, Ohio).
Schivardi and Romano (2020)	Enterprises of all sizes in Italy	The number of enterprises with liquidity problems and the scale of liquidity problems generated by COVID-19.	• in a mild scenario (i.e. the pandemic crisis ends in September 2020), it is estimated that 50,000 companies would require liquidity support, • in a more pessimistic scenario providing for the pandemic lasting until 2021, this estimate rises to 100,000 enterprises. The liquidity gap would then be between EUR 30 and 80 billion.
Carletti et al. (2020)	Enterprises in Italy	Capital shortages due to COVID-19.	• for a three months' lockdown, it is estimated that the total annual fall in profit will amount to EUR 170 billion, • the percentage of SMEs struggling because of liquidity problems in a lockdown situation (17.2%) is higher than that of large-sized companies (6.4%).
CPB Netherlands Bureau for Economic Policy Analysis (2020a; 2020b)	SMEs in the Netherlands	• liquidity shortages during COVID-19, • the impact of government actions on liquidity problems following COVID-19.	• during the first three months of the pandemic crisis, 30% of SMEs suffered from liquidity shortages of EUR 12 billion. After six months, 48% of SMEs had liquidity problems totalling EUR 30 billion, • even with the support policy measures implemented in a six months' period, 25% of the SMEs sector will experience negative liquidity. In a three-month scenario, this percentage will decrease to 17%.

Table 4.2 Changes in insurance risk caused by COVID-19

Type of insurance	*Changes in claims ratios caused by COVID-19*
motor insurance	Third-party liability insurance – the claims ratio during the lockdown period averaged 50%–70% of the ratio before the pandemic. Such a clear decrease in the claims ratio was primarily a consequence of the lower frequency of traffic accidents (e.g. following travel and movement restrictions), Comprehensive motor insurance – the fall in the claims ratio was smaller than in the case of third-party liability insurance, and amounted to 30%.
travel insurance	In the first acute phase of the pandemic, insurance companies noted an increase in the travel insurance claims ratio, while the introduction of travel restrictions was followed by the freezing of this product group.
property insurance	A clear increase in claims ratios for telemedicine-related products and symptoms of deterioration in insurance for the SME sector.
home insurance	After the introduction of lockdown, there occurred a subtle improvement in claims ratios, while a clear deterioration was witnessed in the case of assistance insurance.
life insurance	Declines in claims ratios for health and group insurance. The causes include, among others: restrictions on the performance of medical procedures and a fall in the number of accidents following lockdown.

Source: the authors' own work based on: Deloitte, 2020b.

in point is the Wimbledon tennis tournament in London, whose organizers had been paying an annual premium of USD 2 million for pandemic insurance for 17 years (since the SARS epidemic). Therefore, the cancellation of the tournament in 2020 resulted in the payout of USD 141 million by event insurers. A similar situation could be observed in the case of the International Olympic Committee (IOC), the organizer of the Tokyo 2020 Olympic Games, which were postponed to 2021. The scope of the insurance cover taken out also included compensation for damage caused by the cancellation of the Games in the event of a pandemic. Consequently, the IOC received compensation to cover part of its losses associated with the postponement (Hartwig et al., 2020).

During the COVID-19 pandemic, a number of changes could also be observed in the broadening range of insurance services offered, for example cyber insurance. The reasons for insurance companies' extending the range of their products include enterprises' willingness to provide insurance cover protecting their businesses and employees against negative consequences of the pandemic crisis, to strengthen their resilience and to search for possible sources of compensation for financial losses in insurance policies already held or to be taken out. *COVID-19: Evolving insurance and risk management implications*, a report prepared by

Marsh (2020b), indicates that the pandemic caused the expansion of the range of insurance services in the areas of property insurance, compensation for cancelled mass events, a great increase in cyber risk caused by the transfer of business activities to the internet as well as increased liability of management teams for the safety of enterprises and employees. According to the analyses published in the OECD (2020b) report entitled *Initial assessment of insurance coverage and gaps for tackling COVID-19 impacts*, this catalogue of insurance services was extended to include insurance against SARS-CoV-2 virus infection, travel insurance in the event of infection during travel or compensation for people losing their jobs as a result of a pandemic. The extension of the range of insurance services offered following the COVID-19 pandemic is presented in Table 4.3.

In conclusion, the COVID-19 pandemic affected the insurance market in two ways: it posed significant threats, but also created development opportunities. The threats include increased claims ratios in the previously mentioned areas of business and people's personal lives, intensifying price pressure, worsening economic conditions (a drop in interest rates, increase in unemployment) and a fall in demand for group insurance. However, what is crucial for insurance companies to prevent a deterioration in financial results is the adjustment of insurance premium levels to the changing profiles of the particular types of risk occurring in consequence of the pandemic. On the other hand, when considering the situation of a pandemic as an opportunity for the insurance market in the medium and long perspective, special attention should be paid to increasing benefits associated with the extension of the range of services offered, increasing customer awareness of the usefulness of typical insurance covers, simplifying general conditions of insurance and using technological transformation and automation to simplify

Table 4.3 The range of insurance against risks related to the COVID-19 pandemic

Type of insurance	*Types of benefits in respect of insured events caused by COVID-19*
Life	Compensation for death caused by COVID-19
Health	Compensation for expenditure on tests for the presence of the SARS-CoV-2 virus and for hospitalization following a COVID-19 infection
Travel	Compensation for the costs of travels and trips cancelled because of Covid-19. Compensation for medical expenses incurred abroad due to a Covid-19 infection
Business activities	Compensation for losses due to the cessation of operations following a lockdown or crisis as a consequence of COVID-19
Employees	Compensation or damages for employees
Management liability	Compensation or damages for shareholders
Public liability	Compensation or damages for affected stakeholders

Source: the authors' own work based on: OECD, 2020b.

compensation, contract conclusion and claim settlement procedures (Deloitte, 2020b).

4.1.3. Price risk

The outbreak of the COVID-19 pandemic, the freezing of economies, lower incomes and lost jobs are factors with considerable influence on the shape of price risk. Purchasing habits around the world changed significantly. According to *Consumers and the new reality*, a global survey conducted by KPMG (2020a) among more than 12,000 consumers in the United States, Brazil, the United Kingdom, Canada, France, Spain, Italy, Germany, Japan, Australia, China and Hong Kong, Spain, a new category of consumer is emerging globally: it is the consumer who significantly reduces their spending in the wake of the pandemic crisis, makes more informed purchasing decisions and expects to be able to do shopping by means of digital technologies. In the new pandemic reality, consumers are paying particular attention to the comfort and safety of shopping and are looking for products and services at competitive prices. These new trends contribute, on the one hand, to the dynamic development of internet commerce and price competition among internet platforms and shops, and, on the other, cause measurable losses for shops operating exclusively as brick-and-mortar establishments. The KPMG's survey also revealed that during the coronavirus pandemic the key factor influencing consumers' purchasing decisions was the ratio of quality to price of products offered (63% of respondents). The other important factors ranked as follows: ease of shopping (42%), trust in the brand (41%) and personal safety (40%). Price is also (after convenience and safety) the third most frequently indicated factor influencing online purchasing decisions concerning food products (just after convenience and safety) and the factor with the greatest influence on online purchasing decisions in the case of non-food products.

The COVID-19 pandemic also triggered steep increases in the prices of products and services in some sectors. One of these is undoubtedly the health services sector, where, according to Eurostat (2020) data, the highest increases were observed in the prices of medical and dental services, while slightly smaller increases were observed in the prices of pharmaceuticals, hospital and sanatorium services, as well as therapeutic equipment and medical devices. The high dynamics of changes in the prices of these services resulted mainly from the need to ensure the sanitary safety of employees and patients, and also from the search for ways of compensating at least partly for losses resulting from the temporary inability of the healthcare system to provide these services during the period of economy freezing.

It was not only in the healthcare sector that the materialization of the price risk during the COVID-19 pandemic was negative for customers. In its analyses, the World Bank (2020) forecast increases in the prices of oil and metals, among other commodities. On the other hand, the transport or food production sectors had to face an unprecedented growth in demand for their products and services, which translated into strong pressure on price increases. Price challenges caused by the COVID-19 pandemic should be considered separately based on three market scenarios for the particular groups of enterprises (Abdelnour et al., 2020):

- companies experiencing a rapid and unprecedented decline in demand (e.g. airlines, hotels, restaurants) and characterized by overcapacity and increased price sensitivity,
- companies facing a rapid growth in demand (e.g. producers of medical supplies, transport companies, the IT sector) and characterized by more opportunities to raise prices, which, however, may have negative legal and reputational consequences,
- companies with suppressed or uneven demand (e.g. the home improvement or landscaping sectors) and with potential for short-term price differentiation to protect and generate added value.

During COVID-19 the price risk in the speculative form materialized positively for the providers of logistics services. Disruptions in the functioning of supply chains and increased demand led to shortages of a number of basic products. This translated into higher prices for transport services, and their providers became key market actors during the global pandemic (OECD, 2020c). From the logistics point of view, factory closures, broken value chains, restrictions on international trade, and restrictions on consumers moving around to purchase goods and services can make transport services providers indispensable for maintaining access to certain product groups in many geographical locations (Motta, 2020).

4.1.4. Credit risk

In the wake of the pandemic crisis, the creditworthiness of both enterprises and individual consumers was undermined. The creditworthiness of businesses was weakened mainly by liquidity problems discussed earlier, while that of consumers by drops in income or redundancies in the sectors that were struck the hardest by the lockdown. Weakened creditworthiness concerns both loans taken out before the COVID-19 pandemic and loans that potential borrowers apply for to compensate for previously unforeseeable drops in revenues following the outbreak of the pandemic. Banks providing credit in this new economic reality bear additional risk (International Monetary Fund, 2020). Thus, they have to review their existing methodology for assessing their customers' capacity to repay loans. According to *Global Banking M&A Outlook H2 2020*, a report presented by KPMG (2020b), one of the direct effects of the pandemic on the world economy is the increased credit risk of both corporate and retail clients of banks. In order to continue to support financially the real economy, banks should be able to skilfully diagnose differences between purely temporary phenomena whose negative consequences will be mitigated in the short-term and longer-term changes that require firm changes in management. The global COVID-19 pandemic brought about changes in the functioning of the entire banking sector. It appeared that the key changes in banks' operations in the new pandemic reality were focused on maintaining profitability, managing the credit risk and the cost of risk, as well as coping with falling interest rates.

The consequence of the COVID-19 crisis in the banking sector was a fall in the valuation of banks and a fall in market prices of their shares. European banks were hit hard: the Euro STOXX index of banks recorded a drop of 40.18%. Slightly smaller decreases were recorded by the STOXX North America 600 banks index (by 31.23%) and the STOXX Asia/Pacific 600 Banks Index (by 26.09%) (KPMG, 2020b). Table 4.4 presents the values of the price to tangible book value ratio (P/TBV) for the world's leading banks in Europe, North America and Asia, before and during the COVID-19 pandemic.

Table 4.4 The P/TBV ratio of the world's leading banks before and during the COVID-19 pandemic

Region	*Bank*	*P/TBV December 2019 (Pre-COVID)*	*P/TBV April 2020*	*P/TBV June 2020*
North America	JP Morgan Chase	2.28	1.53	1.68
	Bank of America	1.78	1.14	1.28
	Citigroup	1.12	0.61	0.75
	Wells Fargo	1.57	0.86	0.85
	Royal Bank of Canada	2.42	1.95	2.10
	Goldman Sachs	1.06	0.80	0.97
Asia	Industrial and Commercial Bank of China	0.70	0.65	0.60
	China Construction Bank	0.72	0.65	0.65
	Agricultural Bank of China	0.55	0.53	0.52
	Bank of China	0.59	0.46	0.43
	Mitsubishi UFJ Financial Group	0.51	0.35	0.39
	HSBC Holdings	0.76	0.74	0.52
Europe	BNP Paribas	0.68	0.35	0.46
	Credit Agricole	0.84	0.43	0.54
	Banco Santander	0.86	0.48	0.53
	Barclays plc	0.52	0.28	0.34
	Lloyds Banking Group	0.62	0.51	0.55
	ING Group	0.80	0.39	0.48
	UBS Group	0.88	0.76	0.77
	Unicredit	0.47	0.26	0.25
	Intesa Sanpaolo	0.90	0.52	0.58
	Banco Bilbao Vizcaya Argentaria	0.78	0.27	0.47
	Skandinaviska Enskilda Banken	1.27	1.00	1.13
	Swedbank	1.25	1.01	1.13

Source: the authors' own work based on: KPMG, 2020b.

Such obvious financial problems faced by banks had a significant influence on changes in credit risk management processes. Thus, credit risk management during the global COVID-19 pandemic underwent significant transformations. The unique features of the recession caused by the pandemic prompted banks to react more quickly and to perform more in-depth analyses simultaneously with the decision-making process. The experience of the early phase of the pandemic allowed banks and other credit institutions to realize that particular sectors were impacted by the crisis differently and caused them to pay greater attention to the finances and business models of individual households and businesses. In order to make the process of assessing creditworthiness and making credit decisions more flexible, leading banks accelerated their digital transformation processing, which gave them the ability to monitor incoming financial data in real time and to automatize the process of making this type of decisions. According to McKinsey's analysis, the COVID-19 crisis resulted in five significant changes to the existing credit risk management processes (Koulouridi et al., 2020):

- changes in creditworthiness assessment at the levels of sectors and subsectors,
- difficulties with distinguishing among potential borrowers within the same sector or subsector,
- strong constraints on information relevant to credit decisions that comes in late and is not automatically taken into account when such decisions are made,
- digital transformation to meet the changing preferences of current and potential customers,
- the emergence of a wave of non-performing loans, which requires a completely new approach to credit management.

4.2. Organizational risks

During the COVID-19 pandemic organizational risks affected almost all enterprises. Depending on the sector represented, the severity of their consequences varied. Within this category, legal and personnel risks played a dominant role.

4.2.1. Legal risk

One of the key actions in response to global crises such as the COVID-19 pandemic is the creation of legislation that would constitute "the heart of the response to COVID-19" (OECD, 2020e). Since such legislation is enacted under extraordinary conditions and applies to many complex social and economic issues, it is essential to ensure its high quality because sloppy legislation could constitute an additional source of legal risk for businesses. Analyzing the law-making process in response to the COVID-19 pandemic, the OECD (2020e) proposed a catalogue of the following recommendations:

- legal regulations created and implemented on an ad hoc basis have to be monitored at an early stage of implementation,

- the processes of creating regulations and, in particular, policies of individual countries should be coordinated, which will make them more effective,
- it is essential to monitor progress in the implementation of newly enacted regulations,
- administrative barriers to law enforcement have to be reduced to a minimum.

On the other hand, the role of enterprises is to actively monitor the quality of adopted regulations and to react to any deficiencies. Similarly, the key importance of legal regulations for the situation of enterprises during the COVID-19 pandemic was emphasized by analysts from Ernst & Young (2020b). In their opinion, the key industries affected by these regulations include the travel, logistics, technology, banking, insurance, hospitality, entertainment and pharmaceutical industries, as well as essential goods manufacturers, distributors and retailers. The main areas subject to regulations are the following (Ernst & Young, 2020b): corporate governance and disclosures, workplace health and safety, employment, data privacy, supply chain and working capital. Regulations that do not meet the criterion of compliance with requirements may be a source of various perturbations for enterprises. Such perturbations include, for example (Ernst & Young, 2020b): trade restrictions resulting in loss of business, additional cost of operations, forceful shutdown of business operations along with fines and penalties levied by the regulators, reputation loss due to negative media reports on failure to adopt preventive or detective measures, damages and compensation to be paid to impacted individuals for not adopting adequate measures, criminal prosecutions against key managerial personnel and/or board members.

Representatives of the consulting company Exigent Group (2020) indicate eight key issues that should be the subject of strategic reflection in enterprises and public organizations, aimed at illustrating the impact of the COVID-19 pandemic on the legal and business risks. These issues form a catalogue of crucial management information that requires an immediate response. They include the following:

- public disclosure: data points for necessary or desirable disclosure for all stakeholders (customers, employees, shareholders, partners etc.),
- corporate governance: senior management and board information on the potential impact of pandemic issues,
- people and HR policies: planning, policies and practices,
- financial management and reporting: treasury issues, additional reporting required by contract partners for financial statements, or by auditors,
- material contracts: supply chain disruptions, fluctuating demand, new contracts to be considered material and/or critical such as PP&E supply contracts,
- insurance and risk management policies: analyse pandemic-related loss coverage and negligence risk,
- continuous due diligence questions: ongoing quality review of PP&E supply and usage; establish process for rapidly raising new diligence questions,

- business operations continuity information: the who, what, where, how and when of business operations, including risks from curbside, contactless or other new business operations options.

An important legal risk factor for enterprises is regulations enacted at the national or regional level and constituting legislators' response to the pandemic. They concerned, among others, the competition and antitrust law (Covington Competition, 2020). For example, in the European Union, emphasis was laid on supporting the economies affected by the pandemic. On 19 March 2020 the European Commission adopted the Temporary State Aid Framework, which was followed by further supporting actions in the subsequent months. The European Union's decision influencing the position of enterprises concerned first of all the allowable forms of support (direct grants, selective tax advantages and advance payments, state guarantees for loans taken by companies from banks, subsidized public loans for companies, safeguards for banks that channel state aid to the real economy, subsidized public loans to companies, member states will be able to grant loans with favourable interest rates to companies. These loans can help businesses cover immediate working capital and investment needs, short-term export credit insurance). In the next step, other forms of support were taken into consideration, for example those strictly related to pandemic prevention and including the following (Covington Competition, 2020): support for COVID-19 related research and development, support for the construction and upscaling of testing facilities, support for the production of products relevant to tackle the COVID-19 outbreak, targeted support in the form of deferral of tax payments and/or suspensions of social security contributions, targeted support in the form of wage subsidies for employees. The application of the indicated legal solutions caused a divergence of the legal risk of enterprises with respect to their size, object of activities and location.

Another new area of legal risk for businesses during the COVID-19 pandemic was the necessity to guarantee consumer products safety compliance, particularly important in consumer product industries. Enterprises in these sectors had to deal with the following issues identified by the US Consumer Product Safety Commission (2020): recalls continue with remedial flexibility, mandatory reporting of substantial product hazards, stay-at home focus and household hazards, product development and compliance enhancements. According to the specific provisions introduced, companies concerned had to supplement and modify their own product safety policies and practices within the time limits indicated.

The analysts from the well-known British law firm Osborne Clarke (2020) carried out an interesting diagnostic survey on the impact of the COVID-19 pandemic on business compliance. It led to interesting and positive conclusions:

- 60% of the respondents agreed with the statement that the impact of COVID-19 would encourage companies to be more compliant overall in the future,
- 64% of the respondents expressed the opinion that the impact of COVID-19 would lead to an increase in health and safety compliance in the workplace,

- 54% of the respondents accepted the conclusion that the impact of COVID-19 would lead to increased emphasis on environmental, social and governance factors.

Moreover, the representatives of the surveyed corporations declared that they had allocated necessary financial resources in their budgets to ensure compliance (Osborne Clarke, 2020).

4.2.2. Personnel risk

The authors of the report published by the global consulting company Gartner (2020) identified managerial challenges related to the impact of the COVID-19 pandemic on the increase in personnel risk exposure. They distinguished the following managerial tasks and issues:

- making the decision to return to the workplace (cooperation of managers and allocation of responsibilities for decision-making, analysis of risks and requirements related to return to the workplace, ensuring safety, change of managerial roles related to return of employees),
- managing employees' health and safety (collecting and analyzing employee data related to test results, temperature measurements and other medical measures, balancing employees' health and safety),
- making cost optimization decision (changes in budget items, reflection on cooperation with external partners, reduction of working hours and external costs),
- managing remote employees (supporting employees in remote work and monitoring results, normalizing self-direction, enabling new relationships, revamping team expectations).

The above list shows that employee management during a pandemic constitutes a multidimensional challenge.

Personnel risk management in a pandemic situation requires close, day-to-day cooperation between employees and managers and integration of their efforts, with the role of employees appearing to be crucial. On the side of employees, the following responsibilities can be indicated (University of Exeter, 2020): familiarizing oneself with the guidelines for dealing with a pandemic situation, completing individual risk assessment sheets, informing the manager about contracting COVID-19 and individual susceptibility to the disease, monitoring the situation on an ongoing basis. Thus, employees are expected to adopt an attitude based on openness, honesty and confidentiality.

One of the key tasks of enterprises is to assess personnel risk exposure. Due to the complexity of the COVID-19 matter, such assessment should take into account a number of recommendations as to the order of actions to be taken, for example (NHS Employers, 2020):

- reflecting on the intelligence available regarding the organization. This would include data on absence due to COVID-19, any worker deaths due to COVID-19, staff survey data, and any pulse survey data,
- consulting with staff networks, trade unions and other key stakeholders for support and advice regarding the approach to be taken to risk assessment and agree how a continued dialogue can be maintained,
- communicating to all workers, whatever their professional background or work area, describing the approach being taken to risk assessment, reassuring them as to the nature of the assessment being undertaken and the support available to them,
- sharing the agreed local risk assessment tool or guidance with all team members to help them identify whether they are in an at-risk group,
- explaining the need for staff to discuss any concerns as a result of the risk assessment guide or any concern or anxiety they might have with their manager (and offer them alternative routes of support prior to these discussions),
- agreeing alternative routes through which individuals might raise concerns or flag the need for a risk assessment discussion,
- providing guidance to those managing services regarding the follow-up conversations about risk with their team members, including the potential responses to protect or support staff,
- reviewing and repeating risk assessments as necessary in line with individual circumstances, emerging evidence and/or national guidance.

The conducted risk assessment should be followed by the preparation of workplaces for COVID-19, including the actions listed in Table 4.5.

The actions listed in Table 4.5. are of a chronological nature and take into account the different levels of personnel risk as well as the place of work.

Representatives of the international certification unit BSI (2020) emphasize that in order to safeguard jobs during the COVID-19 pandemic, enterprises can use the proven ISO 45001 standard. They argue that the ISO 45001 occupational health and safety management system provides a framework to support the successful protection of the mental and physical health of workers. Health and safety awareness as part of the culture of an organization is emphasized with participation of, and consultation with, workers from all levels and functions. This can ensure that, when employed, the management system covers what is needed and is communicated effectively to all involved.

Numerous recommendations addressed to companies in particular sectors have been prepared by the International Labour Organization (ILO). The sectors identified by this institution as requiring the highest degree of additional recommendations and personnel risk management tools under COVID-19 conditions include tourism, health, education, agriculture, mining, shipping and textiles, clothing, leather and footwear. The ILO has developed a general action checklist for the prevention and mitigation of COVID-19 at work, a policy brief on a safe and healthy return to work during the COVID-19 pandemic and ten action

Table 4.5 Actions aimed at preparing workplaces for COVID-19

Group of actions	*Individual actions*
Decreasing worker exposure to COVID-19	• develop an infectious disease preparedness and response plan, • prepare to implement basic infection prevention measures, • develop policies and procedures for prompt identification and isolation of sick people, if appropriate, • develop, implement and communicate about workplace flexibilities and protections, • implement workplace controls.
Classifying worker exposure to COVID-19	• prepare occupational risk pyramid for COVID-19, • classify employees to the following categories: very high exposure risk, high exposure risk, medium exposure risk, lower exposure risk.
Protecting employees classified at lower exposure risk	• additional engineering controls, • administrative controls, • personal protective equipment.
Protecting employees classified at medium exposure risk	• additional engineering controls, • administrative controls, • personal protective equipment.
Protecting employees classified at high or very high exposure risk	• additional engineering controls, • administrative controls, • safe work practices, • personal protective equipment.
Protecting employees living abroad or travelling internationally	• the above standard actions, • follow the travel guidelines for the COVID-19 situation, • follow the guidelines and regulations of host countries for the COVID-19 situation.

Source: the authors' own work based on: U.S. Department of Labor Occupational Safety and Health Administration, 2020.

points for a safe return to work, along with general guidance for employers on COVID-19 prevention (International Labour Organization, 2020a).

Besides safety issues, the personnel risk during the COVID-19 pandemic is also correlated with the changes taking place in the labour markets. The aforementioned ILO monitors the situation and provides forecasts in this respect. Surveys carried out by this organization are used to formulate theses about the impact of the COVID-19 pandemic on the situation of employees, for example, in the context of trade and global supply chains. Such theses include the following (International Labour Organization, 2020b):

- the economic impact of COVID-19 has taken the form of demand and supply shocks, disrupting all tiers of global supply chains and leading to sharp declines in global trade across a broad range of industries and products,

- the contagion effects of the direct shock to trade and global supply chains have exacerbated the crisis for firms and workers around the world, with the most vulnerable consisting of migrants, those who lack social protection and small and medium enterprises,
- the crisis might lead to longlasting structural effects with the potential of the reconfiguration of global supply chains in certain industries, accelerating reshoring and/or near-shoring, diversification of suppliers as well as increased automation.

4.3. Strategic risks

The materialization of business risks during the COVID-19 pandemic undoubtedly forced enterprises to introduce a number of adaptive changes into their management practices. The area of strategic risks comprises different types of risk of primary significance for creating conditions facilitating long-term growth and development. The risks belonging to this category that proved to be the most widespread during the COVID-19 pandemic are the following: business continuity risk, reputation risk and investment risk.

4.3.1. Business continuity risk

Business continuity risk is a category of risk whose realization may jeopardize the enterprise's ability to fulfil its core functions and continue its operations. This type of threat affected many companies during the global COVID-19 crisis. In this respect, the main problems turned out to be a decline in the attractiveness of products or services offered by companies, difficulties with the achievement of main strategic objectives and disruptions in operations forced by the restrictions of lockdowns and sanitary regimes. The consequences of such disruptions included a deterioration in the financial position of companies, redundancies or even bankruptcies. SMEs are particularly vulnerable to the most dramatic effect of the pandemic crisis because of their lower resource potential that could be used to effectively counteract interruptions to business continuity. Research conducted in 17, mainly European countries (Gourinchas et al., 2020) shows that, among SMEs during COVID-19 (in 2020), the average SME Bankruptcy Rate was 12.36%, with an estimated 3.61% in non-pandemic conditions. The highest values of this rate were observed in Italy and France, while the lowest were in Korea and Romania. As far as particular sectors are concerned, it turns out that the highest values of the SME Bankruptcy Rate were recorded in the sectors of administration and entertainment/recreation, while the lowest were in water and waste management and construction.

According to analyses carried out by Deloitte (2020e), in order to ensure the highest possible level of business continuity during the COVID-19 crisis, it is necessary to examine possible scenarios and draw up contingency plans adequate for each identified scenario for the further development of the pandemic. Managing business continuity during a global pandemic requires the integration of approaches to different types of risks, such as infrastructural, cyber, personnel, business, operational, communications and financial risks, in order to ensure continuity of service provision and production operations. This is so because business continuity management provides a strategic framework for continuously increasing the enterprise's resilience to a crisis situation. Among the recommendations for maintaining business continuity, the following can be distinguished (Deloitte, 2020e):

- mapping single points of failure in the enterprise (processes, employees, technologies),
- developing emergency measures and organizational instructions appropriate to the estimated level of risk,
- drawing up emergency response plans (procedures, staff allocation, tools and resources),
- securing areas particularly exposed to risks (e.g. supply chains or functional areas where remote work is not possible),
- preparing for a possible shutdown of the enterprise in consequence of a lockdown,
- preparing plans, procedures and measures to restore business continuity once the crisis is over – disaster recovery plans.

In view of the fact that the crisis caused by the global COVID-19 pandemic acquired a systemic character, enterprises in many sectors faced the challenge of revising and redefining their existing business strategy. Combining this difficult task with the strong time pressure resulting from the dynamic development of the worldwide pandemic in 2020 required that risk be counteracted by strategic actions aimed at developing a greater capacity for maintaining business continuity under conditions of recession. Besides the traditional approach based on measuring the probability of occurrence and impact of individual identified risks, such strategic actions include the following (KPMG, 2020d):

- introducing measures for interconnections among different types of threats and the strength of systemic risk impact,
- assessing and reconstructing the existing risk profile in response to changes caused by COVID-19,
- adapting the business strategy to the reconstructed risk profile,
- identifying risks determining the ability to maintain business continuity and making them the targets of preventive and neutralizing techniques, as well as techniques supporting the resumption of operations after the crisis,
- developing methods of assessing the impact of structural breaks on the formulation, planning and implementation of business strategies,
- creating risk clusters and assessing the impact of the pandemic on changes in the likelihood of the occurrence of related risks.

An example of the application of the above-described approach to strategic risk management based on the creation and analysis of risk clusters during and after the COVID-19 crisis is Business for South Africa (2020), where critical, strategic threats to the recovery of the economy after the COVID-19 crisis were analyzed. Among other things, these actions made it possible to identify investments into law and order and essential services as key factors for de-risking recovery.

4.3.2. Reputational risk

During the COVID-19 pandemic, there was an increased risk of reputational damage and potential damage to long-term relationships with business partners. Communication with customers and other stakeholders during the pandemic should take into account the difficult circumstances in which they have found themselves, those resulting both directly from COVID-19 and its economic consequences. Account should also be taken of the increased impact of social media on customer loyalty, and hence the possibility of weakening or losing reputation. In this exceptional crisis situation, it is recommended that companies have a strategy or policy in respect of forbearance requests in order to ensure that their practices and decisions are defended when they are critically assessed. Enterprises should also be prepared to receive claims relating to, for example, amendments to contracts entered into before COVID-19. Different stakeholder groups may require greater flexibility from their contractors and business partners, even if there is no legal basis for this. Negative reactions to proposals of this type may exacerbate the phenomenon of reputation loss (Baker McKenzie, 2020). Companies' behaviours that negatively affect their reputation during COVID-19 include, for example, abrupt price increases in the first phase of the pandemic for products the demand for which rose suddenly, such as personal protective equipment or disinfectants. Another example of negatively perceived behaviours was rejecting orders for products or services placed by existing customer groups due to protectionist policies such as export restrictions imposed on certain types of medical goods (Deutsche Bank Research, 2020) or food products with a view to meeting the growing domestic demand. Increased domestic demand for food products is a consequence of decreasing production volumes caused by the growing incidence of the disease among workers, disruptions of supply chains, downtime in production operations and the implementation of various restrictive measures (Espita et al., 2020).

The COVID-19 pandemic also exerted influence on Corporate Social Responsibility (CSR). In the period before the pandemic, the number of social and environmental initiatives undertaken by enterprises was growing dynamically. However, the emergence of a global pandemic clearly challenged the validity of some of the previous CSR assumptions, concepts and practices, particularly those related to stakeholders, societal risk, supply chain responsibility and political economy of CSR (Crane and Matten, 2020). Table 4.6 presents major CSR issues during COVID-19, divided into four identified areas.

Nevertheless, the COVID-19 pandemic also provides enterprises with the opportunity to move to more genuine and authentic CSR and undertake initiatives in response to global social and environmental challenges (He and Harris,

Table 4.6 CSR during the COVID-19 global pandemic

CSR area	*Major CSR issues during COVID-19*
Stakeholders	• essential stakeholders of business: frontline workers in healthcare, food service, delivery and public transportation – exposed to infection without necessary protections and remain poorly paid and economically vulnerable, • exacerbating social inequalities leading to growth in precarious work even among ostensibly essential workers, • performing remote work on a large scale, which reveals how much economic value creation depends on the often overlooked and unpaid work at home such as caring for children or the elderly.
Societal risk	• business as one of the sources of societal risk, • the role of business responsibility in preventing the development of the pandemic, • enterprises' problems related to decisions on employee retention/dismissal and the provision of basic services to customers, • highlighting the core function of enterprises consisting in the production of goods and the provision of services that meet society's needs and requirements (e.g. personal protective equipment, vaccines).
Supply chain responsibility	• increased responsibility of supply chains due to growing demand for medical products and shortages due to stockpiling, • production disruptions and stoppages due to sanitary restrictions and lockdowns, • decreases in salaries, loss of employment or lack of social protection for supply chain workers, • problems of supplier factories: cancellation of orders, late payment, demands for discounts.
Political economy of CSR	• challenges related to the organization of cooperation between companies and governments in order to overcome the pandemic, including: protection of employment and safety of workers, production of socially useful products, protection of stakeholders, charitable activities, • assessment of how the systems of particular countries are prepared for coping with pandemic challenges and assessment of the role of CSR in such systems in order to meet the requirements of society as a whole, • challenges related to the perception of business as a dimension of social management as well as to the social and political responsibilities of business.

Source: the authors' own work based on: Crane and Matten, 2020; Lancet, 2020; Lowrey, 2020; Kniffin et al., 2020; Leitheiser et al., 2020; Rhodes and Fleming, 2020.

2020). Such initiatives can have positive effects on the reputation of enterprises, strengthening their credibility and relations with the environment. A case in point is the InterContinental Hotels Group (IHG), one of the leading hotel chains in the world (over 5,900 establishments worldwide). The IHG undertook many CSR initiatives during COVID-19. They extended their IHG True Hospitality for Good programme, whose mission is to provide support to local communities in the event of disasters. The programme is based on a global partnership aimed at supporting food banks and other charitable organizations assisting the most vulnerable victims of the COVID-19 crisis in 70 countries. Furthermore, the IHG Rewards Club was launched. Its members can transfer loyalty points converted into cash to social partners of the True Hospitality for Good programme, such as the International Red Cross and Red Crescent Movement. The IHG also announced its collaboration with #FirstRespondersFirst to provide free accommodation for frontline medical personnel combating the coronavirus and delivery drivers in the United States, China, Australia and the United Kingdom (IHG Our response ..., 2020).

4.3.3. Investment risk

Slowdowns, disruptions and turbulence in global economic activity as a result of the COVID-19 crisis have broad implications for investment management, significantly influencing the shape of investment risk. Strong fiscal policy responses together with an extensive lockdown had a serious negative impact on the investment climate, mainly in terms of foreign investment (Deloitte, 2020f). This is evidenced by data presented in the World Investment Report (Unctad, 2020), which indicated that global flows of foreign direct investment (FDI) were under strong pressure from COVID-19, which resulted in an up to 40% decrease in foreign investment in 2020. These significant resources are forecast to fall sharply from USD 1.5 trillion reached at the end of 2019 to well below the level hit during the global financial crisis of 2008, and to eliminate the weak growth in international investment observed over the last decade. The available data and conducted research also indicate that investment flows to developing countries, which are more reliant on investment in the mining and raw materials processing industries, will suffer the most as investments oriented towards export as well as raw materials mining and processing operations are among those most affected by the global COVID-19 crisis. Furthermore, developing economies are not able to introduce the same intensive economic support measures as those deployed in developed countries. It also turns out that the most affected sectors are those with the highest degree of internationalization (measured as a ratio of gross exports to total output), i.e. electronics (82%), machinery and equipment (80%), textiles and apparel (78%) and automotive (73%). It is estimated that the consequences of the worsened investment climate may last much longer than their direct impact on investment flows. On the other hand, the pandemic could become a catalyst for the structural transformation of international production in this decade and an opportunity for increased sustainability, but this will depend on enterprises' ability to exploit the new industrial revolution and to overcome growing economic nationalism. The main determinant of an assessment of this ability will be international cooperation and the global political climate, which continues to favour cross-border investment. Table 4.7 presents the impact of the COVID-19 pandemic on FDI in both the short-term and long-term perspectives.

In view of the identified impact of the COVID-19 pandemic, investment management leaders should take active actions in the three dimensions of crisis management: responding, recovering and thriving. The concrete steps to be taken to ensure effective investment management during COVID-19 are the following (Deloitte, 2020f):

- to reassure investors during short-term periods of volatility,
- to drive innovation to support the "future of" scenarios,
- to enhance ongoing management of investment and non-financial risks,
- to ensure motivation and productivity of remote workforce.

The COVID-19 crisis also generated significant changes in investments in merger and acquisition (M&A) processes. Globally, the volume of M&A dropped significantly as a result of the crisis caused by the pandemic. For example, M&A levels in the United States fell by more than 50% in the first quarter of 2020 compared to 2019. Parties to pending mergers and acquisitions started to withdraw from planned transactions. For example, Xerox withdrew its USD 34 billion offer for HP to focus on coping with the effects of the COVID-19 pandemic. Similarly, SoftBank terminated its USD 3 billion tender offer for WeWork, pointing to the consequences of COVID-19 as the main reason for their decision. Another

Table 4.7 The impact of the COVID-19 pandemic on FDI

Perspective	*Challenges to FDI*	*Impact of COVID-19 on FDI*
2020 (immediate)	FDI stuck in the lockdown	Slowdown of implementation of ongoing projects due to closures of sites (but also slowdowns in cross-border M&As and new project starts)
2021 (short-term)	FDI with tightening margins for reinvestment	Automatic effect on reinvested earnings, a key component of FDI (50% average worldwide)
	FDI hindered by new investment restrictions	Reduction in cross-border M&A
2022 (medium-term)	FDI navigating severe global economic recession	Shelving of projects, drop in new investment decisions
2030 (long-term)	FDI heading towards increased supply chain resilience and higher degrees of autonomy for critical supplies	Divestment, reshoring, diversion

Source: the authors' own work based on: Unctad, 2020.

example is Hexcel and Woodward, Boeing's suppliers, which cancelled the ongoing USD 6.4 billion merger transaction due to unprecedented challenges caused by the pandemic (Harroch, 2020).

A special role during the COVID-19 pandemic is attributed to the use of M&A strategies to prepare and speed up the recovery of businesses during the post-pandemic period. Experts expect the number of M&A transactions to start growing again after a visible slowdown in the first stages of COVID-19. According to analyses performed by Deloitte (2020g), M&A strategies to be used in the process of post-pandemic recovery can be divided into offensive strategies that can accelerate the transformation of existing business models and defensive strategies that help secure enterprises for the future. Within the range of defensive strategies, the following actions can be distinguished:

- divestments (including managed exit) and separations,
- integration and value creation services,
- investor activism and defence,
- end-to-end distressed M&A.

Offensive strategies comprise the following actions:

- supply chain optimization (particularly recommended for sectors experiencing structural disturbances during the pandemic, such as manufacturing, automotive, energy and resources sectors),
- M&A strategy (especially recommended for sectors experiencing irreversible changes forced by the pandemic, such as specialty retail, hospitality, healthcare, sports and live entertainment sectors),
- disruptive M&A (especially recommended for sectors that are more resistant to the effects of COVID-19, such as consumer products, financial services, tech and telecom sectors),
- alliances and joint venture advisory (sector convergence underpinned by alliances like media, banking and general retail).

Pandemic problems also affect investment funds, which, due to the emerging crisis, lockdown and bankruptcies of many companies, may have difficulties in maintaining the continuity of their operations, investment portfolios as well as existing range and standards of customer service. According to the Ernst & Young (2020a) report *Impact of COVID-19 on investment fund asset valuations*, the main problems facing investment funds during the COVID-19 pandemic are unstable equity markets, growing credit spreads, reduced liquidity of many asset classes, deferred M&A transactions and temporary closure of small financial markets.

4.4. Global risks

Due to the high degree of globalization of the economy, the dynamics of international trade and extensive supranational business cooperation, during the global

COVID-19 pandemic it is also possible to observe the materialization of global risks whose specific nature makes it significantly difficult, and often impossible, to implement mitigation actions. Among these risks, those related to global supply chains as well as technological issues are particularly evident.

4.4.1. Global supply chain risk

Global supply chains are one of the key elements of the economy. In recent years, they have become key elements of competitiveness for many companies. The models of cooperation developed within supply chains, on the one hand, allow enterprises to optimize flows, minimize costs, strengthen resource utilization efficiency and support the inventory management process but, on the other hand, reduce flexibility in dealing with delays and disturbances. Due to the global nature of supply chains, any disruptions in their functioning (e.g. the inability to maintain the continuity of basic processes, problems with delivering goods to the market or providing key services to customers) can have negative implications for the global economy and finances. Such problems were observed, for example, after the earthquake and tsunami in Japan in 2011 and the catastrophic floods in Thailand in 2011 and 2012. The COVID-19 pandemic affected global business cooperation within supply chains even more severely than other crises, often interrupting their continuity or significantly disrupting the efficiency and timeliness of their operations. The overall impact of COVID-19 on global logistics networks is not yet known, but it is already clear that the problems that supply chains are currently experiencing, from the supply of raw materials to the delivery of finished products, will be felt for a long time to come. The COVID-19 pandemic situation is therefore undoubtedly a valid reason for companies to transform their existing supply chain models (Deloitte, 2020c).

The information presented by the World Trade Organization (2020) in the report *Helping SMEs navigate the COVID-19 crisis* shows that SMEs are particularly vulnerable to supply chain disruptions caused by COVID-19. It turns out that the impact of the pandemic crisis on supply chains depends on the country and economic sector. Among SMEs, the sectors such as office equipment, electronics, chemicals, oil, plastics, where imports account for almost 60% of total expenditures, were hit the hardest. In the case of exports, the supply chains of SMEs in the automotive and furniture industries, which export over 40% of their production output through direct or indirect trade channels, turned out to be the most vulnerable. As the data shows, in the sectors most affected by the pandemic, SMEs are more inclined to export than larger companies and are, consequently, more exposed to growing protectionism in these sectors (e.g. in agriculture) (OECD, 2020a).

The first problems with the COVID-19 pandemic, disrupting the functioning of supply chains, were a direct consequence of travel restrictions, quarantine regulations and the gradual introduction of lockdowns in various countries. Initially, enterprises in China faced shortages of labour, spare parts and intermediate products, which disrupted the previously perfect functioning of just-in-time supply chain systems. Due to the scale of Chinese exports such logistical problems were soon followed by negative changes affecting enterprises all over the world, for example in the technology, IT, automotive, consumer goods, pharmaceuticals and other industries (World Economic Forum, 2020 b). The COVID-19 pandemic forced, as it were, many enterprises to introduce a number of deglobalization actions. What could be observed in many parts of the world during its course was the localization or regionalization of supply chains. This was so because the pandemic crisis revealed a very high and risky dependency of the world economy on sensitive nodes in global supply chains. A perfect case in point is China, which accounts for 50–70% of the world's demand for copper, iron ores, metallurgical coke and nickel. Furthermore, it accounts for 60% of global exports of consumer goods and 40% of global exports of TMT (technology, media, and telecoms) products. The problems of global supply chains following COVID-19 have their origins in China. In the first quarter of 2020, numerous cases of downtime were observed in many Chinese factories. On 1 March 2020, many large Chinese companies declared productivity of approximately 90%. The main reason for the drop in productivity was the lower than usual availability of migrant workers. The capacity to transport goods from factories to sea ports was 60–80% of normal levels. Goods arrived at ports with a delay of 8–10 days. It turned out that the Baltic Dry Index (measuring freight rates for cereals and other dry goods around the world) fell by around 15% at the beginning of the pandemic, only to grow by 30% in its subsequent phase. The TAC index, which measures air freight prices, also increased by approximately 15% after February 2020 (Craven et al., 2020; Hedwall, 2020). Moreover, many companies all over the world are dependent on production and supply not only from China, but also from Southeast Asia and other low-cost countries.

Surveys carried out to assess the impact of COVID-19 on GDP declines in 64 countries, on six continents and in 33 industries (Bonadio et al., 2020) revealed also the severity of problems occurring in supply chains. They also aimed to identify what part of a decline in GDP was due to disturbances in international trade. The results indicated that shocks transmitted through global supply chains were responsible for a small part of the fall in GDP. The average share of foreign trade problems in the total estimated fall in GDP was approximately 33%. This means that, on average, each country participating in the survey experienced an 11% fall in GDP due to foreign trade lockdowns alone. It appears that the economies in which the share of problems in international trade in GDP falls is the largest are the most integrated with global supply chains (e.g. Brunei, Kazakhstan, Saudi Arabia, Chile, Colombia – among these five countries, foreign shocks represent on average 57% of the overall GDP decline identified during COVID-19). It also turns out that some countries, such as Japan, Taiwan, Sweden and Greece, which had introduced less stringent lockdowns in response to the pandemic shock, experienced fewer internal economic problems than their foreign trading partners. Another conclusion from the conducted survey is that separating these countries from global supply chains would significantly strengthen their resilience to lockdowns by eliminating the transmission of relatively stronger pandemic shocks from other countries. On the other hand, however, the countries with the most stringent lockdown reduced their labour supply to a greater degree than their foreign trading partners. In such a situation, the supply of domestic expenditures falls more than that of foreign expenditures, so what can be observed is a greater fall in GDP when supply chains are renationalized.

Prepared by Deloitte (2020c), the report entitled *COVID-19: Managing supply chain risk and disruption* divided companies operating in supply chains during COVID-19 into three groups according to the extent to which they had been prepared for disruptions resulting from the pandemic crisis (Table 4.8).

The implementation of new supply chain management techniques is indicated as an important factor in mitigating the problems of supply chains during COVID-19. Traditional linear supply chain models started to evolve into digital supply networks (DSNs), where functional silos are broken down and enterprises can connect to the entire logistics supply network to ensure full visibility, effective

Table 4.8 The degree of preparedness of enterprises functioning in supply chains for combating the effects of COVID-19

Enterprises in supply chains	*Actions implemented by enterprises to reduce the negative impact of the COVID-19 pandemic on supply chains*
Enterprises are better prepared than others to mitigate the impact	• development and implementation of a supply chain management strategy and business continuity strategy, • geographical diversification of supply chains in order to reduce the risk of non-supply from any country or region, • access to key raw materials and goods from multiple sources in order to reduce dependence on one supplier, • development of an inventory management strategy to prevent disruptions in the supply chain.
Enterprises are better prepared than others to respond to this event	• development of strong relationships with key suppliers and implementation of systems to ensure full visibility in logistical supply networks, in order to better understand risk and take action based on their adequate prioritization, • development of flexibility of production and distribution networks so that they can be quickly reconfigured and supply is maintained in line with global demand, • investment in supply chain planning solutions and control towers to better detect and respond to and even anticipate supply chain problems.
Other enterprises are scrambling	• lack of prepared actions aimed at negative consequences of COVID-19 – enterprises dependent on one geographical region or one supplier of key products, materials or goods, • lack of effective inventory management systems, production optimization, customer allocation optimization, • lack of developed flexible logistics networks.

Source: the authors' own work based on: Deloitte, 2020c.

collaboration, flexibility and optimization. This is possible when implementing technological solutions such as the internet of things, artificial intelligence and robotics (Deloitte, 2020c).

Based on the experience gained from the COVID-19 pandemic, enterprises functioning within supply chains should improve forms of cooperation and apply a new approach to global logistical cooperation. To do this, they should, among other things (Hedwall, 2020):

- review their obligations arising from concluded agreements on an ongoing basis,
- include contractual clauses relating to force majeure, tax implications, changes to agreements in the event of extraordinary circumstances and their reversal if the situation stabilizes, as well as relocation costs,
- optimize supply chains and invest in building their resilience,
- develop the capacity to adapt to crisis situations,
- apply a holistic approach to supply chain management, based on both supply and demand patterns.

4.4.2. Technological risk

The changes brought about by the global COVID-19 pandemic caused significant transformations in approaches to technological risk management. In some sectors such as mobile applications development, remote communication and work tools and software development, IT and internet services provision, semiconductor and network equipment manufacture (Deloitte, 2020d), it is possible to observe a positive aspect of technological risk, due to the rapid increase in demand resulting from the relocation of sales channels as well as both business and private communication channels to the online space and due to the extending range of remote work in many enterprises around the world. A case in point is Zoom, one of the world's largest video conferencing platforms, which at the end of Q1 2020 recorded a 354% y/y increase in its base of customers with more than ten employees; at the end of Q2 2020 the growth rate reached 458%. This directly translated into a 169% and 355% y/y revenue growth at the end of Q1 2020 and the end of Q2 2020 respectively (Zoom Reports First ..., 2020; Zoom Reports Second ..., 2020). Respondents participating in the survey conducted by McKinsey (2020), i.e. management teams of many companies from all over the world, declare that during COVID-19 their activities started to be dynamically digitized in various dimensions. The results of this survey indicate that the occurrence of COVID-19 accelerated the digitization of customer interaction, supply chains and internal operations accelerated by approximately four years. Moreover, the introduction of digital products and services was accelerated by about seven years. Table 4.9 shows the average percentage of digitized customer interactions and the percentage of partially or fully digitized products and/or services in enterprises from different parts of

Table 4.9 The average share of digitized customer interactions and partially or fully digitized products and/or services during COVID-19 – a geographical analysis

Average share of:	*June 2017*	*May 2018*	*Dec 2019*	*July 2020*
Global				
digitized customer interactions	20%	20%	36%	**58%**
partially or fully digitized products and/or services	29%	28%	35%	**55%**
Europe				
digitized customer interactions	18%	19%	32%	**55%**
partially or fully digitized products and/or services	26%	25%	34%	**50%**
Asia-Pacific				
digitized customer interactions	22%	19%	32%	**53%**
partially or fully digitized products and/or services	31%	26%	33%	**54%**
North America				
digitized customer interactions	25%	25%	41%	**65%**
partially or fully digitized products and/or services	33%	34%	41%	**60%**

Source: the authors' own work based on: McKinsey, 2020.

the world (and from a global perspective) during COVID-19 in comparison to pre-pandemic periods.

In many sectors of the economy, however, technological risks materialized negatively. During COVID-19 it was possible to observe numerous barriers to the provision of services (due to lockdowns and sanitary restrictions on direct contacts) and the sale of products (due to the limited potential of many sales companies and shops earlier operating exclusively on a brick-and-mortar basis to launch remote sales channels). The character of the aforementioned barriers was financial, infrastructural, legal and organizational. In order to facilitate overcoming such barriers, various countries introduced initiatives aimed at increasing the availability and use of digital tools to strengthen business continuity and resilience in the context of COVID-19. According to the OECD (2020d) report entitled *Policy Options to Support Digitalization of Business Models During COVID-19*, during COVID-19 such actions were introduced in the G20 countries and the most important of them include the following:

- initiatives to improve broadband connectivity for businesses and employees (e.g. in the USA, the Federal Communications Commission granted operators temporary access to the spectrum in the 5.9 GHz band to meet the increased demand for broadband in rural areas during the COVID-19 crisis),
- initiatives to encourage video conferencing, remote work and cloud data processing (e.g. in France, the company France Digital created a set of tools

for remote work and started to provide advice on how to cope with the COVID-19 crisis),

- initiatives to develop e-learning platforms (e.g. China provided funding for training targeted at SMEs and offered free access to online training platforms),
- initiatives to improve access to key digital services and tools important for business resilience (e.g. Italy launched a portal called "Digital Solidarity" providing companies with free access to digital services offered by large private sector enterprises),
- initiatives to accelerate the propagation of electronic payment methods (e.g. enterprises in Saudi Arabia started to develop applications aimed particularly at delivery companies and encouraging them to introduce electronic payments protecting safety and health),
- initiatives to help enterprises to develop e-commerce and online business models to access new markets by means of digital tools (e.g. South Korea launched a special support programme to encourage physical shops to open their online equivalents. In response to the COVID-19 pandemic, the number of beneficiaries and the budget of this programme increased considerably),
- initiatives to use digital tools to help enterprises to gain access to government financing schemes aimed at supporting digital activities to maintain business continuity (e.g. Mexico launched the Fintech Initiative to alleviate enterprises' liquidity problems caused by the pandemic).

In the report entitled *Technology risks in light of COVID-19*, KPMG (2020c) presented a technological risk management process for the COVID-19 pandemic, dividing it into the following: actions strengthening resilience to negative consequences of technological risks, actions aimed at the recovery of functionalities after disruptions caused by the materialization of technological risks and actions developing technological risk management methods in the new pandemic and post-pandemic reality (Table 4.10).

On the basis of research (KPMG, 2020c) conducted during the course of COVID-19, the company identified and classified technological risks faced by enterprises in consequence of the pandemic, and also assessed the probability of their occurrence and their possible impact. The next stage of the research was to identify those areas of technological risk occurrence that require the implementation of active risk management plans (planning of protective, preventive and corrective actions) (Table 4.11). The results of the research may prove to be valuable both during and after the pandemic, especially for business leaders and stakeholders in enterprises exposed to technological risks.

Technological risks that materialize during the COVID-19 pandemic cause the development of new areas of cyber risk management. Analyses conducted by Marsh (Splett, 2020) indicate that work in a home office mode on such a global scale as during COVID-19 may cause numerous problems with access to networks or systems. Furthermore, enterprises using the cloud during such heavy workload periods may have problems with accessing their critical data.

Table 4.10 The three phases of technological risk management during the COVID-19 pandemic

Resilience	• objective: to act dynamically in the environment of rapid technological changes, • tools: stabilization and protection strategies, business continuity, policy of resistance to economic pressure, • the main determinant of undertaken actions: marketplace technology trends, • recommended actions: providing a safe but connected workforce, deploying technology innovations and work-arounds, identifying resiliency challenges and opportunities, experiencing onset of uncertainty.
Recovery	• objective: restoring functional stability, operational transformations, incorporating learning processes and technological transformations, • tools: strategies of adaptation to changing patterns of demand and consumption, • the main determinant of undertaken actions: how technological risk management teams respond to threats, • recommended actions: optimizing and securing technology, supporting new phases of resilience, driving cost and operating efficiencies, demonstrating the technological risk value proposition.
Management in the new reality	• objective: adapting to the changing business environment based on virtual communication, • tools: business resilience improvement strategies, risk management system improvements, strategies to respond to new consumer habits, • the main determinant of undertaken actions: potential future results, • recommended actions: evaluating and continuing innovations, redefining the technological risk operating model, revisiting and re-establishing "new basics".

Source: the authors' own work based on: KPMG, 2020c.

Such situations, among other things, may cause additional costs and productivity losses. Working remotely, organizing video conferences and participating in online training events organized by external entities may expose serious security gaps that could potentially be a source of cyber-attacks. Cyber risk insurers estimated that about 80% of ransomware attacks during COVID-19 were related to remote working. Distance work may also be a reason for poorer compliance with security procedures, which may result in the interception of confidential and sensitive data by unauthorized persons. The COVID-19 pandemic also witnessed an increase in the number of social engineering attacks and computer frauds.

Table 4.11 Technological risks during COVID-19 – likelihood, impact, active action plans

Technology risk domain	*Likelihood*	*Impact*	*Needs action plan*
Strategy & governance	low	high	Yes: assessing and understanding the need for changes in the IT strategy in the light of the response to COVID-19, adapting new work methods and operational models, adapting IT projects to newly approved strategies
Security & data privacy	high	high	Yes: assessment and ongoing monitoring of the management strategies of the teams responsible for data and IT systems security in light of increased cyber threats in consequence of COVID-19
Availability & business disruption	medium	low	No
Emerging technology	medium	low	No
Infrastructure & asset management	low	low	No
Programmes & implementation	medium	high	Yes: in the case of activities halted due to COVID-19, assessment of risk management in terms of business rationale, available technology, personnel, necessary changes, compliance and control rules, finance and cooperation with third parties
Identity & access management	low	medium	No
Operations	low	low	No
Compliance	medium	high	Yes: assessment of actions taken in response to technological changes induced by COVID-19 in terms of their compliance with internal procedures and external legal requirements
Third-party management	high	high	Yes: working with contractors/stakeholders to meet changes in demand for IT services and equipment during COVID-19, including evaluating changes in services, assessing performance, making necessary changes to contracts and operating models, as well as evaluating new risk management strategies and effectively implementing necessary changes

Source: the authors' own work based on: KPMG, 2020c.

References

Abdelnour, A., Babbitz, T., Moss, S. (2020). Pricing in a pandemic: Navigating the COVID-19 crisis. www.mckinsey.com/business-functions/marketing-and-sales/our-insights/pricing-in-a-pandemic-navigating-the-covid-19-crisis (Access: 3.12.2020).

Baker McKenzie (2020). COVID-19 checklist for financial institutions. www.bakermckenzie.com/-/media/files/insight/publications/2020/05/bakermckenzie_covid19-checklist-for-financial-institutions.pdf?la=en (Access: 15.12.2020).

Bircan, C., De Haas, R., Schweiger, H., Stepanov, A. (2020). Coronavirus credit support: Don't let liquidity lifelines become a golden noose. VOX CEPR Policy Portal, https://voxeu.org/article/coronavirus-credit-support-don-t-let-liquidity-lifelines-become-golden-noose (Access: 29.11.2020).

Bonadio, B., Huo, Z., Levchenko, A., Pandalai-Nayar, N. (2020). The role of global supply chains in the COVID-19 pandemic and beyond. https://voxeu.org/article/role-global-supply-chains-covid-19-pandemic-and-beyond (Access: 11.12.2020).

BSI (2020). Health and safety standards. Covid-19 response. www.bsigroup.com/en-GB/topics/novel-coronavirus-covid-19/health-and-safety-standards/ (Access: 9.01.2021).

Business for South Africa (2020). COVID-19 Response Dynamic Risk Assessment Findings. https://home.kpmg/content/dam/kpmg/nz/pdf/2020/05/B4SA-COVID-19-Risk-Findings-Report.pdf (Access: 15.12.2020).

Carletti, E., Oliviero, T., Pagano, M., Pelizzon, L., Subrahmanyam, M. (2020). The equity shortfall of Italian firms in the COVID crisis. VOX, CEPR Policy Portal, VOX CEPR Policy Portal, https://voxeu.org/article/equity-shortfall-italian-firms-covid-crisis (Access: 29.11.2020).

Consumer Product Safety Commission (2020). Consumer product safety compliance during the COVID-19 pandemic (2020). www.cov.com/en/news-and-insights/insights/2020/04/consumer-product-safety-compliance-during-the-covid-19-pandemic (Access: 04.01.2021).

Covington Competition (2020). COVID 19 – US and EU competition law implications. www.covcompetition.com/2020/05/covid-19-us-and-eu-competition-law-implications-12-may-2020/?_ga=2.7833586.1708837955.1609841994-794231767.1609841991 (Access: 4.01.2021).

CPB Netherlands Bureau for Economic Policy Analysis (2020a). Een stresstest van het Nederlandse mkb. www.cpb.nl/sites/default/files/omnidownload/CPB-Achtergronddocument-2juni2020-Een-stresstest-van-het-Nederlandse-mkb.pdf (Access: 29.11.2020).

CPB Netherlands Bureau for Economic Policy Analysis (2020b). Risicorapportage Financiële Markten 2020. Centraal Planbureau, The Hague, www.cpb.nl/sites/default/files/omnidownload/CPB-Notitie-Risicorapportage-financiele-markten-2020.pdf (Access: 29.11.2020).

Crane, A., Matten, D. (2020). COVID-19 and the future of CSR research. *Journal of Management Studies*,, 58(1), pp. 280–284.

Craven, M., Liu, L., Wilson, M., Mysore, M. (2020). COVID-19: Implications for business. www.mckinsey.com/business-functions/risk/our-insights/covid-19-implications-for-business (Access: 29.11.2020).

Deloitte (2020a). 8 kroków do zdrowej firmy. Jak uchronić płynność finansową przed skutkami COVID-19: Sprawne zarządzanie ryzykiem finansowym, gotówką, płynnością oraz kapitałem pracującym sposobem na finansową stabilność przedsiębiorstwa. www2.deloitte.com/pl/pl/pages/press-releases/articles/8-krokow-do-zdrowej-firmy-covid-19.html (Access: 29.11.2020).

Deloitte (2020b). Wpływ pandemii COVID-19 na działalność ubezpieczeniową: szanse i zagrożenia. www2.deloitte.com/pl/pl/pages/financial-services/articles/wplyw-pandemii-COVID-19-na-dzialalnosc-ubezpieczeniowa-szanse-i-zagrozenia.html (Access: 1.12.2020).

Deloitte (2020c). COVID-19: Managing supply chain risk and disruption. www2.deloitte.com/global/en/pages/risk/articles/covid-19-managing-supply-chain-risk-and-disruption.html (Access: 11.12.2020).

Deloitte (2020d). Understanding COVID-19's impact on the technology sector. www2.deloitte.com/za/en/pages/about-deloitte/articles/understanding-covid-19-s-impact-on-the-technology-sector-.html (Access: 14.12.2020).

Deloitte (2020e). COVID-19: Managing risks and ensuring business continuity. www2.deloitte.com/rs/en/pages/risk/articles/covid-19-managing-risk-and-ensuring-business-continuity.html (Access: 15.12.2020).

Deloitte (2020f). Understanding the sector impact of COVID-19. Investment Management. www2.deloitte.com/global/en/pages/about-deloitte/articles/covid-19/covid-19-impact-on-the-investment-management-sector.html (Access: 15.12.2020).

Deloitte (2020g). COVID-19: The M&A role in companies recovery. www2.deloitte.com/br/en/pages/strategy-operations/articles/covid-19-papel-fusoes-aquisicoes-recuperacao-empresas.html (Access: 15.12.2020).

Deutsche Bank Research (2020). Życie po COVID-19. www.db.com/poland/docs/DB_konzept_Zycie_po_covid-19.pdf (Access: 15.12.2020).

Drechsel, T., Kalemli-Ozcan, S. (2020a). A proposal for a negative SME tax. VOX, CEPR Policy Portal, VOX CEPR Poliy Portal, https://voxeu.org/article/proposal-negative-sme-tax (Access: 29.11.2020).

Drechsel, T., Kalemli-Özcan, S. (2020b). Are standard macro policies enough to deal with the economic fallout from a global pandemic? Economics for Inclusive Prosperity, Policy Brief, No. 25, ECNFIP, https://econfip.org/policy-brief/are-standard-macro-policies-enough-to-deal-with-the-economic-fallout-from-a-global-pandemic/ (Access: 29.11.2020).

Ernst & Young (2020a). Impact of COVID-19 on investment fund asset valuations. https://assets.ey.com/content/dam/ey-sites/ey-com/en_gl/topics/emeia-financial-services/ey-impact-of-covid-19-on-investment-fund-asset-valuations.pdf (Access: 30.12.2020).

Ernst & Young (2020b). Regulatory risk management for responding to COVID-19 pandemic (2020). https://assets.ey.com/content/dam/ey-sites/ey-com/en_in/topics/covid-19/regulatory-compliance-india-covid-19.pdf (Access: 6.01.2021).

Espita, A., Rocha, N., Ruta, M. (2020). COVID-19 and food protectionism. https://voxeu.org/article/covid-19-and-food-protectionism (Access: 15.12.2020).

Eurostat (2020). Harmonised indices of consumer prices (HICP). https://ec.europa.eu/eurostat/web/hicp/data/database (Access: 3.12.2020).

Exigent Group (2020). 8 key issues for your company's pandemic risk matrix: What the COVID-19 data explosion means for business & legal risks. www.exigent-group.com/blog/covid-19-legal-risks-8-key-issues-for-your-companys-pandemic-risk-matrix/ (Access: 06.01.2021).

Gartner (2020). GC actions in response to COVID-19. www.gartner.com/en/legal-compliance/insights/coronavirus-resources (Access: 6.01.2021).

Gourinchas, P., Kalemli-Özcan, S., Penciakova, V., Sander, N. (2020). COVID-19 and business failures. www.oecd.org/global-forum-productivity/webinars/Gourinchas-Kalemli-Ozcan-covid-19-and-business-failures.pdf (Access: 15.12.2020).

Harroch, R. (2020). The impact of the coronavirus crisis on mergers and acquisitions. www.forbes.com/sites/allbusiness/2020/04/17/impact-of-coronavirus-crisis-on-mergers-and-acquisitions/?sh=73f57e9f200a (Access: 16.12.2020).

Hartwig, R., Niehaus, G., Qiu, J. (2020). Insurance for economic losses caused by pandemics. *The Geneva Risk and Insurance Review*, 14, pp. 1–37.

He, H., Harris, L. (2020). The impact of COVID-19 pandemic on corporate social responsibility and marketing philosophy. *Journal of Business Research*, 116, pp. 176–182.

Hedwall (2020). The ongoing impact of COVID-19 on global supply chains. www.weforum.org/agenda/2020/06/ongoing-impact-covid-19-global-supply-chains/ (Access: 11.12.2020).

IHG (2020). Our response to COVID-19. www.ihgplc.com/en/about-us/our-response-to-covid-19 (Access: 15.12.2020).

International Labour Organization (2020a). Stop COVID-19 at work! Sector-specific guidance and tools for COVID-19 prevention and control. www.ilo.org/sector/Resources/WCMS_746337/lang--en/index.htm (Access: 10.01.2020).

International Labour Organization (2020b). The effects of COVID 19 on trade and global supply chains. https://labordoc.ilo.org/discovery/fulldisplay?docid=alma995084692902676&context=L&vid=41ILO_INST:41ILO_V2&lang=en&search_scope=ALL_ILO&adaptor=Local%20Search%20Engine&tab=ALL_ILO&query=sub,exact,COVID-19&sortby=date_d&offset=0 (9.01.2021).

International Monetary Fund (2020). Public communication during a financial crisis. Monetary and capital markets. Special series on COVID-19, www.imf.org/en/Publications/SPROLLs/covid19-special-notes (Access: 5.12.2020).

Kniffin, K.M.., Narayanan, J., Anseel, F., Antonakis, J., Ashford, S.P., Bakker, A.B., Bamberger, P., Bapuji, H., Bhave, D.P., Choi, V.K., Creary, S.J., Demerouti, E., Flynn, F.J., Gelfand, M.J., Greer, L.L., Johns, G., Kesebir, S., Klein, P.G., Lee, S.Y., Ozcelik, H., Petriglieri, J.L., Rothbard, N.P., Rudolph, C.W., Shaw, J.D., Sirola, N., Wanberg, C.R., Whillans, A., Wilmot, M.P. and van Vugt, M. (2020). COVID-19 and the workplace: Implications, issues, and insights for future research and action. *American Psychologist*, 76(1), pp. 63–77.

Koulouridi, S., Kumar, S., Nario, L., Pepanides, P., Vettori, M. (2020). Managing and monitoring credit risk after the COVID-19 pandemic. www.mckinsey.com/business-functions/risk/our-insights/managing-and-monitoring-credit-risk-after-the-covid-19-pandemic (Access: 5.12.2020).

KPMG (2020a). KPMG international "consumers and the new reality" report. https://home.kpmg/pl/pl/home/media/press-releases/2020/07/media-press-sklepy-musza-zaoferowac-konsumentom-nowe-powody-do-zakupu-w-trybie-offline-koncentrujac-sie-na-cenie-i-wygodzie.html (Access: 3.12.2020).

KPMG (2020b). Global banking M&A outlook. H2 2020 Report, https://home.kpmg/xx/en/home/insights/2020/07/covid-19-impact-on-banking-m-and-a-2020.html (Access: 10.12.2020).

KPMG (2020c). Technology risks in light of COVID-19. Performing a rapid technology impact assessment. https://advisory.kpmg.us/articles/2020/rapid-tech-impact-assessment-covid-19.html (14.12.2020).

KPMG (2020d). COVID-19 and your strategy. The impact of structural breaks, risk interconnectivity and risk velocity. https://home.kpmg/nz/en/home/insights/2020/04/connecting-strategy-and-risk/covid-19-and-your-strategy.html (Access: 15.12.2020).

Lancet, T. (2020). The plight of essential workers during the COVID-19 pandemic. *The Lancet*, 395, 1587.

Leitheiser, E., Hossain, S.N., Sen, S., Tasnim, G., Moon, J., Knudsen, J.S. and Rahman, S. (2020). Early impacts of coronavirus on Bangladesh apparel supply chains. *RISC Briefing* – April 2020.

Liu, S., Parilla, J. (2020). Small businesses have received uneven relief from COVID-19 federal aid. Brookings Institution, www.brookings.edu/blog/the-avenue/2020/05/29/how-the-paycheck-protection-program-is-coming-to-ground-in-the-nations-large-metro-areas/ (Access: 29.11.2020).

Lowrey, A. (2020). Don't blame Econ 101 for the plight of essential workers. *The Atlantic*, www.theatlantic.com/ideas/archive/2020/2005/why-are-americas-most-essential-workers-so-poorly-treated/611575/ (Access: 15.12.2020).

Marsh (2020a). Improving liquidity during and after the pandemic. https://coronavirus.marsh.com/us/en/insights/research-and-briefings/improving-liquidity-during-and-after-pandemic.html (Access: 1.12.2020).

Marsh (2020b). COVID-19: Evolving insurance and risk management implications. https://coronavirus.marsh.com/us/en/insights/research-and-briefings/covid-19-evolving-insurance-risk-management-implications.html (Access: 1.12.2020).

McGeever, N., McQuinn, J., Myers, S. (2020). SME liquidity needs during the COVID-19 shock. Financial Stability Notes, No. 2, Central Bank of Ireland, https://ec.europa.eu/growth/smes/business-friendly-environment/sme-definition_en (Access: 29.11.2020).

McKinsey (2020). How COVID-19 has pushed companies over the technology tipping point and transformed business forever. www.mckinsey.com/business-functions/strategy-and-corporate-finance/our-insights/how-covid-19-has-pushed-companies-over-the-technology-tipping-point-and-transformed-business-forever (Access: 14.12.2020).

Motta, M. (2020). Price regulation in times of crisis can be tricky. *Daily Maverick*, https://www.dailymaverick.co.za/opinionista/2020-04-22-price-regulation-in-times-of-crisis-can-betricky/ (Access: 3.12.2020).

NHS Employers (2020) Risk assessments for staff. www.nhsemployers.org/covid19/health-safety-and-wellbeing/supporting-staff-health-and-safety/risk-assessments-for-staff (Access: 9.01.2021).

OECD (2020a). OECD coronavirus (COVID-19) SME policy responses. www.oecd.org/coronavirus/policy-responses/coronavirus-covid-19-sme-policy-responses-04440101/ (Access: 29.11.2020).

OECD (2020b). Initial assessment of insurance coverage and gaps for tackling COVID-19 impacts. www.oecd.org/pensions/Initial-assessment-of-insurance-coverage-and-gaps-for-tackling-COVID-19-impacts.pdf (Access: 1.12.2020).

OECD (2020c). Exploitative pricing in the time of COVID-19. www.oecd.org/competition/Exploitative-pricing-in-the-time-of-COVID-19.pdf (Access: 3.12.2020).

OECD (2020d). Policy options to support digitalization of business models during Covid-19: Aneks. *Report for the G20 Digital Economy Task Force*. www.oecd.org/sti/policy-options-to-support-digitalization-of-business-models-during-covid-19-annex.pdf (Access: 14.12.2020).

OECD (2020e). Regulatory quality and COVID-19: Managing the risks and supporting the recovery. www.oecd.org/regreform/regulatory-policy/Regulatory-Quality-and-Coronavirus%20-(COVID-19)-web.pdf (Access: 7.01.2021).

Osborne Clarke (2020). Covid-19: Compliance risk survey 2020. www.osborneclarke.com/insights/covid-19-compliance-risk-survey-2020/ (Access: 4.01.2021).

Revoltella, D., Maurin, L., Pal, R. (2020), EU firms in the post-COVID-19 environment. VOX, CEPR Policy Portal, https://voxeu.org/article/eu-firms-post-covid-19-environment (Access: 29.11.2020).

Rhodes, C., Fleming, P. (2020). Forget political corporate social responsibility. *Organization*, 27(6), pp. 943–951.

Richter, A., Wilson, T.C. (2020). COVID-19: Implications for insurer risk management and the insurability of pandemic risk. *The Geneva Risk and Insurance Review*, 45, pp. 171–199.

Schivardi, F., Romano, G. (2020). *A Simple Method to Compute Liquidity Shortfalls during the COVID-19 Crisis with an Application to Italy*. CEPR COVID Economics: Vetted and Real-Time Papers.

Splett, M. (2020). Ubezpieczenia ryzyk cybernetycznych oraz polisy crime w świetle COVID-19. www.marsh.com/pl/pl/insights/risk-in-context/cyber-crime-COVID-19.html (Access: 14.12.2020).

Unctad (2020). World investment report 2020: International production beyond the pandemic. United Nations Publications, Geneva, https://unctad.org/system/files/official-document/wir2020_en.pdf (Access: 15.12.2020).

University of Exeter (2020). COVID-19 age and personal risk assessment. www.exeter.ac.uk/staff/employment/coronavirus/personalriskassessment/#a0 (Access: 8.01.2021).

U.S. Department of Labor Occupational Safety and Health Administration (2020). Guidance on preparing workplaces for COVID-19. www.osha.gov/Publications/OSHA3990.pdf (Access: 8.01.2021).

World Bank (2020). Impact of COVID-19 on commodity markets heaviest on energy prices; lower oil demand likely to persist beyond 2021. www.worldbank.org/en/news/press-release/2020/10/22/impact-of-covid-19-on-commodity-markets-heaviest-on-energy-prices-lower-oil-demand-likely-to-persist-beyond-2021 (Access: 3.12.2020).

World Economic Forum (2020a). The global risks report 2020. www3.weforum.org/docs/WEF_Global_Risk_Report_2020.pdf (Access: 1.08.2020).

World Economic Forum (2020b). This is the impact of the coronavirus on business. www.weforum.org/agenda/2020/02/why-is-coronavirus-a-global-business-risk/?fbclid=IwAR0vYn4nXe3lCAj3pJu7s6sdvCQ8nYxUiT5i05kW-NfPy6UVpV1l-veUDW0 (Access: 11.12.2020).

World Trade Organization (2020). Helping SMEs navigate the COVID-19 crisis. www.wto.org/english/tratop_e/covid19_e/msmes_report_e.pdf (Access: 11.12.2020).

Zoom Reports First Quarter Results (2020). https://investors.zoom.us/news-releases/news-release-details/zoom-reports-first-quarter-results-fiscal-year-2021/ (Access: 14.12.2020).

Zoom Reports Second Quarter Results (2020). https://investors.zoom.us/news-releases/news-release-details/zoom-reports-second-quarter-results-fiscal-year-2021/ (Access: 14.12.2020).

5 "Risk losers" during the COVID-19 pandemic

Case studies

5.1. Blocked by restrictions

5.1.1. Introduction

In some sectors, possibilities of conducting business activities were blocked by restrictions aimed at preventing the COVID-19 pandemic to a greater extent than in others. Certainly, tourism and hospitality are among these unlucky sectors. Davahli et al. (2020) point out numerous problems that appeared in these sectors: loss of jobs, revenue impact, the COVID-19 spreading patterns in the industry, market demand, prospects for recovery, safety and health, travel behaviour and preference of customers. Kaushal and Srivastava (2021) indicate that the pandemic situation became a real crisis management challenge for managers in these sectors. As Gursoy and Chi (2020) note, the pandemic confronted the hospitality industry with an unprecedented challenge. Unfortunately, strategies aimed at flattening the COVID-19 curve such as community lockdowns, social distancing, stay-at-home orders, travel and mobility restrictions resulted in temporary closures of many hospitality businesses and significantly decreased the demand for businesses that were allowed to continue to operate.

Anti-pandemic regulations also affected the catering sector with great intensity. In virtually every country, far-reaching restrictions were introduced in this sector (COVID-19: a new ..., 2020). Experts estimate that in many establishments profits fell by up to 90%, and nearly 30% of catering businesses may not survive the crisis and will permanently disappear from the country's culinary map (Duże straty ..., 2020). The imposition of restrictions on activities of catering establishments did not go unnoticed by businesses indirectly associated with the industry as they focused on developing solutions to realistically support their partners in the difficult conditions of the pandemic. According to industry organizations, partial rescue for the catering industry could be solidarity behaviours consisting in the following (Gastronomia w czasach ..., 2020): ordering meals for employees, providing employees with vouchers to be redeemed in restaurants, organizing remote company Christmas or New Year events, allowing employees to order meals to be delivered to their homes, ordering meals in restaurants for charitable organizations, purchasing vouchers for employees redeemable after the catering lockdown, providing support

DOI: 10.4324/9781003131366-5

through cooperation, e.g. writing off arrears, dividing payables into instalments, amending rental or lease agreements, introducing favourable solutions concerning food supplies such as collection of expired products, making friendly arrangements concerning changes in contracts, introducing promotions, providing goods or services free of charge, offering special conditions of access to online catering services or purchase of new equipment necessary to open a new sales channel.

The list of businesses blocked by restrictions also undoubtedly includes department stores and shopping centres. It is worth noting that restrictions imposed on the functioning of such retail outlets accelerated the development of e-commerce (Will COVID-19 …, 2020). Thus, the existing situation will force many businesses to change their modes of operation. This may lead to bankruptcies, closures, consolidations and liquidations within this once formidable segment of the retail industry (Can the shopping …, 2020).

5.1.2. AccorHotels and Hotele Gołębiewski case studies

5.1.2.1. AccorHotels

AccorHotels is an international hotel group based in France. It dates back to 1967, when Paul Dubrule and Gérard Pélisson founded Société d'investissement et d'exploitation hôteliers (SIEH) and opened the first Novotel hotel near Lille, France. Today, AccorHotels runs 5,100 hotel establishments located in 110 countries and employs around 300,000 people. Besides Novotel hotels, the group is the owner of many other prestigious brands such as Mercure and Ibis. In the spring of 2020, the management team of AccorHotels took a number of dramatic decisions, including (Coronavirus (COVID-19) …, 2020): suspending the hiring programme, dismissing 75% of the global teams at the headquarters in the second quarter of 2020 (this resulted in a EUR 60 million reduction in expenses). The group's revenues in the first part of 2020 fell by 17% compared to the same period in 2019. To differentiate itself during the difficult period of the pandemic, AccorHotels introduced the "ALL Safe Officer" programme under which a Health and Safety Officer was appointed in each hotel to ensure that the highest standards of cleanliness and hygiene were observed. AccorHotels wanted to demonstrate that it was operating in a "COVID safe" environment, meaning that it was likely to be able to attract more guests than its local competitors. During the 2020 holiday season, the group's managers planned to lay off an additional 1,000 people (and this despite the partial opening of hotels in many countries) as part of a plan aimed at reducing costs by EUR 200 million per year (Hotel group …, 2020). After AccorHotels reported that its operating result for the first half of 2020 had been a loss of EUR 227 million, its CFO Jean-Jacques Morin diagnosed that "it is difficult to implement austerity measures in our industry without affecting staff" (Hotel group …, 2020). The occupancy rate in the group's hotels fell to 14.7% in the second quarter and 31.0% in the first half of 2020. The crisis also prevented Accor from presenting any forecast of its performance in the coming months. This is best reflected in a quote from the group's CEO Sébastien Bazin, who said,

> It's a little strange that at this stage, six months in, we simply have no idea whether the number of 1.5 billion travellers we accommodated in the last years and months of 2019 will fall to 600 million or whether it will fall by 80% to 320 million.
>
> (Accor CEO ..., 2020)

The group's recognizability visibility was further affected by a significant reduction in booking cancellation periods, with 60% of bookings made less than five days in advance (as of August 2020) compared to at least ten days in 2019. This uncertainty also took its toll on shareholders, whom the company was unable to provide with guidance for the full year, something it had traditionally done during a presentation of financial results for the first half of a year. At present a similar problem concerns a forecast for the year 2021.

5.1.2.2. Hotele Gołębiewski

Hotele Gołębiewski is a Polish chain of luxury hotels located in tourist destinations. The hotels are owned by a Polish businessman, Tadeusz Gołębiewski, who started his business adventure in the confectionery industry and entered the hotel market in 1989. The Gołębiewski hotels are located in Mikołajki, Białystok, Wisła and Karpacz. The hotel in Pobierowo remains unfinished and still under construction. The hotels were shut down in mid-March 2020. The lifting of some restrictions by the Polish government did not result in their reopening. This was because, as their owner pointed out, from his perspective there was no point in opening hotels if catering or entertainment establishments were not allowed to conduct their business activities at the same time (Tadeusz Gołębiewski ..., 2020). Before the pandemic the hotels employed an average of 950–1000 people. The owner decided not to dismiss his employees. This decision, however, entailed the necessity of covering payroll costs of approximately EUR 800,000 over three months. As the company did not have sufficient own funds to finance the aforementioned costs, another solution was necessary. The owner declared:

> I have this money, I've taken loans from banks. Fortunately, my creditworthiness is very good, and I have a lot of real property, which was pledged in full, even my home. I think this money will allow me to open the hotels.
>
> (Tadeusz Gołębiewski ..., 2020)

In a statement for the local media made on 7 May 2020, Tadeusz Gołębiewski assumed that it would take him a dozen or so years to repay the loan, and about three years to recover the losses caused by the pandemic (Koronawirus uderzył ..., 2020). The problems caused the suspension of the construction project in

Pobierowo, where, in the middle of a forest, Gołębiewski had been building the largest hotel on the Polish coast, and the funds allocated for this investment were diverted to saving the already existing hotels. The overall crisis caused by the COVID-19 pandemic deprived the hospitality industry of customers. Additionally, the business model adopted by Tadeusz Gołębiewski was very risky, but had turned out to work well before only because there was no dramatic crisis in Poland for 30 years. One of the reasons why Tadeusz Gołębiewski is not on the list of the richest Poles is that he builds all his hotels on credit and then pledges them as security for subsequent credits (Koronawirus wykończy ..., 2020). A big source of additional problems is the fact that the enterprise Hotele Gołębiewski was targeting large, corporate customers that organized various types of events and training courses for their employees in the hotels. Meanwhile, this segment of the industry was struck particularly hard by the coronavirus. In another interview conducted in December 2020, Tadeusz Gołębiewski admitted that he was on the verge of bankruptcy. He reiterated that the cost of maintaining his hotels and restaurants during the pandemic was enormous. He added that he would hold out for a maximum of one more month and then he might have to declare bankruptcy (Koronawirus. Właściciel ..., 2020). In connection with the challenges that Hotele Gołębiewski has to cope with, analysts of the hospitality market in Poland emphasize that they are to a considerable extent a consequence of not only the pandemic but also the owner's grandiosity.

5.1.3. Pizza Hut and Gastromall Group case studies

5.1.3.1. Pizza Hut

Pizza Hut was founded in 1958. The company's global expansion actually began in the early 1980s when restaurant guests began to be served pizza on pan dough – thick yet fluffy on the inside and crispy on the outside. Pizza Hut's largest franchisee, the American company NPC International Inc. filed for bankruptcy in a Texas court. NPC had opened its first Pizza Hut restaurant in 1962, and by the date of the bankruptcy filing it had operated as many as 1,225 of them across the United States. The company was not able to withstand the competitive pressure in the restaurant industry that followed the coronavirus outbreak and the weeks-long lockdown (Pizza Hut zaatakowana ..., 2020). Nevertheless, Pizza Hut will not go completely out of business because the company was given a chance – it needs to execute a plan providing for the repayment of debts and an increase in revenues. NPC's debts amounted to USD 900 million. The company managed to negotiate a restructuring agreement with about 90% of its largest creditors and 17% of so-called secondary lenders. The debt reduction plans involve offering shares in the company to first-lien lenders, and these are likely to give the potential bankrupt a cash injection. In addition, some of the restaurants operated by NPC will be sold. Other markets also experienced significant problems. For example, in the UK, Pizza Hut was forced to close 29 out of its 244 restaurants and to dismiss 700 employees (Lloyds Bank ..., 2020). Similarly to the situation in the American market, the British Pizza Hut restaurant chain was forced to restructure its debt under a bankruptcy contract that provided for the loss of many jobs. The British company hired restructuring specialists Alvarez & Marsal to explore business options including, for example, a company voluntary arrangement (CVA), an agreement with creditors to reduce debt, often providing for reduced lease payments (Pizza Hut considers ..., 2020).

5.1.3.2. Gastromall Group

Gastromall Group is a Polish family-owned company that is developing under the franchise model. The portfolio of Gastromall Group comprises such restaurant chains as Olimp, City Break, Bubble Bistro, Bistro Durum, Isto, Deli Sandwich and a few other brands. On the eve of the COVID-19 pandemic, the company, known particularly for its chain of Olimp restaurants, operated a total of 70 food outlets in shopping malls and 55 employee canteens in office buildings across the country (Jeden ..., 2020). The company provided employment to over 500 people and cooperated with thousands of business partners, contractors and suppliers. According to Gastromall's CFO Kamil Majewski, the initial shutdown of shopping centres in Poland, announced by the government on 14 March 2020, came as quite a surprise to the company (Jeden ..., 2020). Announced only two days in advance, the decision forced the company to close its establishment virtually overnight in compliance with the authorities' restrictions and recommendations. In the first period of mall closures, this one of the most popular and fastest-growing catering groups in Poland lost 99.33% of its revenues. However, it had to continue to finance huge fixed costs such as payroll, rent for premises, costs of electricity and gas, as well as costs of servicing loans taken out for the creation of restaurants, their equipment, etc. (Jeden ..., 2020). A few months later, Piotr Niemiec, CEO of Gastromall Group, described the company's position, saying:

> In the current situation all catering companies are in deep trouble. Our revenues equalled zero for two months, and since the suspension of the lockdown the revenues of shopping centres have amounted to just 10% of those generated last year. Thus, the overall picture does not instil optimism in anybody. The rates of rent are an additional burden. So, unless government assistance is stepped up and extended to large companies, there is a risk that businesses will start to go bankrupt. This will entail gigantic unemployment, because this situation will also affect our suppliers and contractors.
>
> (Gastronomia balansuje ..., 2020)

The company's position was partially improved by the legislation that temporarily exempted such entities from lease agreements with shopping centre operators. At the same time, the new regulations did not apply to similar lease agreements between business and owners of office buildings. Piotr Niemiec described this problem as follows:

> The situation is further exacerbated by the necessity to negotiate with each office building owner separately. These owners are often foreign funds that do not want to sit down at the table at all, show a lack of understanding, or break off negotiations, demanding payment for space that remains empty.
>
> (Koronawirus w Polsce ..., 2020)

His company paid more than EUR 300,000 for the rental of office space that stood empty because its former occupants were required to work from home.

5.1.4. JCPenney and M1 Shopping Centres case studies

5.1.4.1. JCPenney

JCPenney is an interesting example of a department store chain that weathered the COVID-19 pandemic rather badly. In the first quarter of 2020, the company's revenues fell by 53%. This decline was predictable given that all of the company's 846 department stores were closed for half of the quarter due to the COVID-19 pandemic. The stores did not open until mid-May, yet the company's losses continued to grow. JCPenney had already been generating regular losses before the pandemic. Its latest profitable year was 2010, and its net losses since then have grown to USD 4.5 billion (The coronavirus ..., 2020). After the summer of 2011 the company recorded a net profit in only five quarters, always during the Christmas shopping season. In June 2020, the company began a deep restructuring of its assets, notifying the bankruptcy court of the planned closure of 154 department stores in the first phase of the process. The company's management formulated an objective based on retaining the best performing establishments and the flagship eCommerce store jcp.com (JCPenney ..., 2020). Jill Soltau, the CEO of JCPenney expressed her hope for the successful implementation of corrective actions, saying:

> While closing stores is always an extremely difficult decision, our store optimization strategy is vital to ensuring we emerge from both Chapter 11 and the COVID-19 pandemic as a stronger retailer with greater financial flexibility to allow us to continue serving our loyal customers for decades to come.
>
> (JCPenney ..., 2020)

To implement the financial restructuring plan, the company filed voluntary petitions for reorganization under Chapter 11 of the US Bankruptcy Code (Restructuring Information, 2020). In another statement, Jill Soltau implied the significant impact of the COVID-19 pandemic on speeding up difficult decisions:

> Until this pandemic struck, we had made significant progress rebuilding our company under our Plan for Renewal strategy – and our efforts had

> already begun to pay off. While we had been working in parallel on options to strengthen our balance sheet and extend our financial runway, the closure of our stores due to the pandemic necessitated a more fulsome review to include the elimination of outstanding debt.
>
> (Long-struggling ..., 2020)

The situation triggered by the pandemic crisis exposed the shortcomings of the company's previous restructuring efforts, particularly the lack of analyses examining the profitability of individual retail outlets.

5.1.4.2. M1 Shopping Centres

M1 Shopping Centres are establishments that bring together both large and small format stores, as well as service outlets. The first M1 Shopping Centre was opened in 1997, and currently the M1 chain consists of nine shopping malls operating in central and southern Poland (M1 ..., 2020). Studying the impact of COVID-19 on the position of Polish shopping centres, PwC analysts showed that their owners lost about 30–35% of annual revenues (without taking into account the second lockdown that was in force in the period from 7 to 27 November 2020). At the same time, they had to bear fixed costs for property maintenance and management, as well as debt service. Following the second period of restrictions imposed on shopping centres from 7 to 27 November 2020, the landlords' losses started to come closer to the dangerous level, threatening their liquidity and seriously increasing the risk of bankruptcy (Centra handlowe na ..., 2020). Of great importance for the situation of M1 Shopping Centres were the Polish government's decisions that introduced a provision under which, during the period of the prohibition on the conduct of business activities, the mutual obligations of parties to rental agreements are suspended. This meant that no charges could be collected from tenants. At the same time, despite huge losses, shopping centre owners continued to incur a variety of fixed costs. Financial losses were growing because in the spring of 2020 the so-called COVID Law introduced rent abolition for tenants, simultaneously depriving the owners and managers of shopping centres of access to the anti-crisis and financial shields provided by the government (PRCH szacuje ..., 2020). Another problem recognized by the Polish Council of Shopping Centres was the pandemic-induced decline in the number of customers visiting shopping centres during their opening hours. The data collected by this organization showed that between 10 and 16 August 2020 the frequency of customer visits to shopping centres in Poland measured by means of the footfall index equalled on average 70–80% of that in 2019. One week earlier it was 70–84%, and two weeks earlier – 76–94% of the value of the index in 2019 (Centra handlowe mają ..., 2020). The related problem was tough negotiations that the managers of M1 Shopping Centres had to conduct with their tenants. Unfortunately, their inevitable result was the lowering of rents.

5.2. Too inert to protect themselves

5.2.1. *Introduction*

The COVID-19 pandemic also had an indirect negative impact on certain groups of enterprises. They are indirect victims of pandemic-related sanitary restrictions and new legal regulations. Their business activities depend on the changes in the economy and consumer behaviour forced by the pandemic. These are most often enterprises experiencing a sharp drop in demand for their products or services or unable to continue their operations to the same extent as before the pandemic. Due to the clear and narrow character of their business dependent on customers or suppliers directly affected by the pandemic, such enterprises were in many cases unable to effectively counteract the negative effects of the pandemic and protect themselves against losses. Enterprises that proved to be too inert to protect themselves from the negative consequences of the global pandemic crisis in their operations include retail chains, luxury goods enterprises and companies representing the petrochemical sector.

Hit by the pandemic, retail chains did not have any serious opportunities for compensating for their losses suffered mainly due to lockdowns imposed on local economies all over the world. According to Unctad (2020), the coronavirus pandemic caused a 3% decline in global trade in the first quarter of 2020. Fashion chains were hit particularly hard as they were forced to liquidate many of their brick-and-mortar establishments, which deprived them of a considerable proportion of current sales revenues. Losses of this magnitude could not be compensated for by the rapid implementation of new business strategies in online commerce.

Significant losses as a result of the pandemic were also noted in the luxury goods market. Manufacturers of such products suffered considerable losses indirectly, mainly due to the decline in average incomes of previously more affluent customer groups. According to estimates by Bain & Company (2020), sales of luxury goods (including clothing, accessories, jewellery, watches or cosmetics) fell by 23% in 2020 compared to 2019, to the levels recorded in 2014.

Serious problems were also observed in the petrochemical industry. Oil companies and other enterprises involved in the wholesale and retail of petroleum products were strongly affected by the pandemic, mainly as a result of the global decline in oil production, prices and demand, as well as pandemic restrictions on movement and transport. According to McKinsey (2020), demand for refined products fell by at least 20% as a result of the pandemic. These developments, among others, triggered an unprecedented crisis in the oil and gas industry.

5.2.2. *Inditex and LPP case studies*

5.2.2.1. *Inditex*

Inditex is one of the world's largest fashion retailers, with origins dating back to 1963. Its headquarters is in Arteixo, Spain. The flagship brand of the holding is Zara. Other brands owned by Inditex include Pull&Bear, Bershka, Stradivarius,

Oysho, Zara Home, Massimo Dutti and Uterqüe. In total, the holding has over 7,000 brick-and-mortar outlets located in 96 markets. In addition, it sells goods through its online platform in 202 markets. Inditex cooperates with 1,985 suppliers and 8,155 factories worldwide (Inditex around ..., 2020). Due to the outbreak of the COVID-19 pandemic, Inditex recorded a significant loss of EUR 409 million in the first quarter of 2020. These losses were mainly due to sanitary and lockdown restrictions that reduced opportunities for sales in stationary brick-and-mortar shops. In response to the pandemic restrictions, in order to at least reduce the scale of losses suffered, the company stepped up online sales (a 50% increase in online sales was recorded in the first quarter of 2020), but unfortunately, despite these efforts, the holding reported a 44% decrease in total sales in this period. In connection with online sales, the Inditex Group's net profit in the second quarter of 2020 was EUR 214 million, which lowered its losses incurred in the first half of the year, nevertheless the losses remained at an alarming level of EUR 195 million. In May 2020, 87% of the Group's retail outlets were shut down. Formulating its approach to managing the pandemic risk, the Group's management opted for the integration of its brick-and-mortar shops and online sales platform as the strategy underpinning the business model for the new economic situation. Furthermore, the three pillars of the Group's business model adapted to the pandemic were indicated: flexibility, digital integration and sustainability. During the pandemic, Inditex comprehensively developed its own IT platform (Inditex Open Platform). An integrated inventory management system (SINT) was also implemented, which gave customers access to the Group's entire assortment of products. Several retail outlets implemented the "Store Mode", a tool that proves the importance of online shop integration for customer service. The Group also undertook to modernize digitally some of its retail outlets, for example by opening large-format stores, and disposing of smaller outlets that were not suitable for a fully integrated model. Given the scale of the pandemic problems, Inditex, presenting the Group's plans for 2020–2022, indicated the need for incurring further considerable capital expenditures in the amount of EUR 1 billion for the development of online operations and EUR 1.7 billion for the further integration of the store platform (Inditex returns ..., 2020; Inditex 1Q20 ..., 2020).

5.2.2.2. LPP

LPP is one of the largest Polish clothing companies managing five brands: Reserved, Cropp, House, Mohito and Sinsay. It has over 1,700 brick-and-mortar shops in 25 countries (apart from Poland also in other European countries, Asia and the Middle East), and provides access to its online shop in 30 countries (LPP w liczbach, 2021; LPP na świecie, 2021). As a result of the restrictions imposed in the wake of COVID-19, approximately 95% of LPP retail outlets were closed in 21 of the 25 markets in which the company operates. This clearly translated into the company's financial position, mainly the lack of revenues from brick-and-mortar sales. The only remaining source of revenues was online sales, which during the pandemic increased by 150% compared to the previous year. Nevertheless, this impressive increase did not compensate for the losses incurred. In such a problematic situation, the company's main objective became maintaining financial liquidity and continuity of business processes. Due to the developing pandemic and its impact on the further functioning of the sector, the LPP management tried to plan a post-crisis recovery scenario. This scenario is based on three key elements: support for sales in the e-commerce channel, strict cost discipline (mainly reduction of capital expenditures by over PLN 600 million in 2020) as well as optimization of logistics processes and areas supporting the company's operations during both the epidemic and the recovery period. The savings on capital expenditures significantly slowed down the development of the retail outlet network and postponed until later date many new openings, the expansion of the company headquarters and the construction of a new distribution centre. The applied reductions also comprised personnel costs in the sales network and the company headquarters, as well as rental costs. These measures were taken in order to prevent collective redundancies. Furthermore, the company attempted to initiate the process of forecasting customer preferences during the pandemic (taking into account the weakening of customers' purchasing power as a result of reductions or loss of salaries following the pandemic crisis) and preparing orders for subsequent seasons on this basis (LPP podsumowuje ..., 2021).

5.2.3. *Kering and Wittchen case studies*

5.2.3.1. Kering

Kering is a global luxury group managing the development of numerous renowned fashion houses specializing in leather goods, jewellery and watches, including Gucci, Saint Laurent, Bottega Veneto, Balenciaga, Alexander McQueen, Brioni, Boucheron, Pomellato, Dodo, Qelin, Ulysse Nardin, Girard-Perregaux, and Kering Eyewear (Discover Kering, 2021). The COVID-19 pandemic had a very strong impact on the Group's business, mainly in the first quarter of 2020. The main causes were lockdowns imposed in many of the markets where the Group operates and the necessity to shut down a number of retail outlets, first in the Asia-Pacific region starting in February 2020 and subsequently, due to the rapidly deteriorating situation, also in Europe and the United States starting in March 2020. Revenues from the directly operated stores of the Luxury Houses fell by 19.5% on a comparable basis. What contributed to the huge volume of losses was also a halt in tourism and the need to close some manufacturing and logistics facilities. Problems with distribution were also revealed. Due to the lack of access to a large proportion of its brick-and-mortar shops, Kering recorded an increase in e-commerce of more than 20% in the first quarter of 2020, but despite this impressive growth, consolidated revenues fell by 15.4% (as reported) and by 16.4% (on a comparable basis). During the same period, sales in the wholesale network fell by 6.8%. The particular brands owned by Kering also suffered high losses. For example, in the first quarter of 2020 Gucci's revenues decreased 22.4% as reported and 23.2% on a comparable basis, while in the case of Yves Saint Laurent revenues fell by 12.6% and 13.8% respectively. In order to limit the scale of the losses incurred, Kering initiated a series of managerial measures with a view to ensuring the continuity of the Group's operations and the possibility of responding adequately to various pandemic development options. Within the range of such measures, adapting the cost base and preserving the cash position were indicated as priorities. Another challenge that Kering had to face during the pandemic was also a skilful combination of a long-term vision with near-term imperatives. Group-wide business continuity plans were also developed for human resources, inventory management, logistics and merchandising. In order to defend itself in any way from the enormous scale of losses, Kering also implemented cost-cutting measures to optimize the positioning of the Group before the expected gradual restoration of productivity levels (In a quarter ..., 2021).

5.2.3.2. Wittchen

Wittchen is a Polish manufacturer of exclusive high quality leather products. In its category, it is one of the most recognizable brands on the European market. The company sells its products through a chain of traditional retail outlets and an online shop (Wittchen – o firmie, 2021). As a result of the coronavirus pandemic spreading in Poland and all over the world, the company suffered severe losses visible, among other things, in a decline in consolidated sales revenues. Between January and September 2020, Wittchen reported a 24% decrease in revenues compared to the same period in 2019 in the retail segment (sales in showrooms, in online shop and other retail units) and a 45% decrease in the B2B segment (domestic sales and export sales to companies and corporate customers). The losses were largely due to the impossibility to sell goods in retail outlets located in shopping centres. Only in the segment of other revenues (sales not classified elsewhere and revenues from office space rental) did Wittchen record a 32% increase in revenues. In the initial phase of the pandemic, the company had a significant inventory of goods located in its warehouses and the logistics centre, which constituted some form of rescue allowing the company to continue operations in the event of possible interruptions in the provision of transport services. Furthermore, during the pandemic the company tried to intensify its online sales, which account for a significant share in the revenue structure of the Wittchen capital group. To this end, measures were also taken to support and promote sales in Wittchen's online shops in Poland and abroad, as well as sales on various marketplaces in order to compensate, at least to some extent, for unrealized sales in brick-and-mortar shops. However, the development of e-commerce involved the necessity to incur high additional costs (Wittchen Raport bieżący nr 21, 2020; Wittchen Raport bieżący nr 5, 2020; Wittchen Skonsolidowany Raport ..., 2020; Wittchen zapłaci ..., 2020).

5.2.4. BP and LOTOS case studies

5.2.4.1. BP

BP is a British petrochemical company, one of the largest in the world. It produces, distributes and sells gasoline, transport fuels, chemicals and alternative sources of energy such as wind and biofuels in many markets around the world. The company's assets include production platforms, refineries, ships, corporate offices, wind farms, research facilities and retail service stations (The BP brand, 2021). The global COVID-19 pandemic took its toll on BP's performance, as it did on most companies in the sector. The results for the second quarter of 2020 show that the underlying replacement cost loss amounted to USD 6.7 billion, compared to USD 2.8 billion profit for the corresponding period of 2019. At the same time, oil trading generated a loss of USD 16.8 billion, compared to a 2019 profit of USD 1.8 billion. These losses were primarily driven by non-cash upstream exploration write-offs, mainly resulting from the review of BP's long-term strategic plans and changes in long-term pricing assumptions. Other causes included lower oil and gas prices, very weak refining margins, reduced oil and gas production and significantly reduced demand for fuels and lubricants during the pandemic. During the course of COVID-19, the company managed to raise funds from, among other things, the agreed sale of BP's petrochemicals business to INEOS and the sale of BP's extraction assets in Alaska, but this did not compensate for the very large scale of losses incurred. Responding to the effects of the pandemic, BP re-designed its action plans and, for example, introduced measures aimed at reducing annual cash costs by USD 2.5 billion by the end of 2021. In addition, the company issued hybrid bonds with a view to diversifying its capital structure, supporting its credit rating at the investment level and strengthening its finances (Second quarter ..., 2020). The priority of the company's operations during COVID-19 was to try to maintain the supply of energy, fuel and essential petrochemical raw materials. For this purpose, each BE operating site (be it an offshore platform or a petrochemical facility) undertook to develop business continuity plans (COVID-19 BP response, 2020).

5.2.4.2. LOTOS

LOTOS is a Polish capital group and one of the most modern petrochemical companies in Europe, engaged in extraction and processing of crude oil as well as wholesale and retail of petroleum products such as petrol, oils, aviation fuel and asphalts. The company owns and operates over 500 service stations. Like all enterprises in the industry, LOTOS was severely affected by the pandemic. EBITDA LIFO (net of non-recurring events) in the second quarter of 2020 was 93% lower than in the same period in 2019 (declines were recorded in the production, trading and extraction segments). The company indicated the weakening of margins for refinery products and low crude oil and natural gas prices during the pandemic as the main reasons for the losses. The difficult macroeconomic environment, both domestically and globally, meant that it was not possible to fully implement the LOTOS 2020 strategy (a marked decline in volumes allocated to the retail channel, mainly with respect to petrol and diesel sold to service station chains). Furthermore, the balance and liquidity of international economic exchange relations were significantly disturbed. Despite a significant drop in domestic demand, in order to neutralize to some extent the negative effects of the pandemic on its business activities, the company, among other things, optimized the operations of its refinery in order to adjust production outputs to the market situation (thanks to which capacity utilization was maintained). Taking advantage of the technological flexibility of its refinery installations, LOTOS was able to adjust its output of petroleum products to market demand. Also, the seaside location of its refinery allowed the company to counter the negative changes in demand on the domestic market with increased sales volumes in sea exports, which contributed to the maintenance of a higher level of oil processing and the optimization of the refining margin during the peak period of the COVID-19 pandemic, which, however, was not enough to compensate for the huge scale of losses resulting from problems associated with the COVID-19 pandemic (LOTOS Skonsolidowane …, 2020; LOTOS Komentarz …, 2020).

5.3. Too traditional to change

5.3.1. Introduction

Another group that clearly lost out during the global COVID-19 pandemic are those companies whose traditional form of business, unchanged for years, provides limited opportunities to undertake various forms of combat against its negative consequences. These are usually entities that were not directly burdened with pandemic sanitary restrictions, but incurred losses indirectly as if "hit by a pandemic ricochet". Such enterprises include various types of financial institutions, banks and real estate sector enterprises that are unable to neutralize the effects of the pandemic, for example by changing their assortment strategy or moving their core activities to the remote work area.

It is estimated that the banking sector is suffering and will continue to suffer the long-term consequences of the crisis caused by the COVID-19 pandemic. According to an international survey of European banks conducted by Deloitte (2020a), the economic impact of the pandemic on the banking sector is to be experienced for at least 12 months. Moreover, the year 2020 witnessed a significant decline in the volume of credits granted as compared to that of 2019 and a tightening of credit conditions, both for retail customers and non-financial enterprises, mainly as a result of worsened economic forecasts, increased credit risk and a decrease in risk levels acceptable to banks. The survey also indicated an increase in the number of non-performing credits granted to both individuals and corporations. The increase is relatively small, but its consequences may be quite serious. Another important problem for banks is threats to the liquidity and solvency of borrowers coping with pandemic constraints. It is estimated that 5%–20% of borrowers will require debt restructuring in the next 12 months.

The real estate sector was clearly affected by the pandemic, mainly for the following reasons: the strong correlation between the financial performance of developers and national economies, the significant exposure of real estate investment managers to perceived problems in sectors such as hotel and leisure as well as retail and office investment, rising costs and reduced investment opportunities, redundancies in the construction industry, material supply problems and tenants cut from their sources of income. All these reasons made the existing business models in the sector obsolete (KPMG, 2020; Deloitte, 2020b), negatively affecting different segments of the real estate market in particular countries. In the UK, for example, construction output fell by 40% in April 2020, while in the US the number of initiated construction and housing projects fell by 30% in the same period. The activity of the construction sector also fell sharply during this period, for example in France by more than 45%, in Germany by almost 20% and in Italy and Ireland by 45% (OECD, 2020).

5.3.2. Santander and Alior Bank case studies

5.3.2.1. Santander

Santander is a retail bank operating in ten core markets where it has high market shares: Spain, Santander Consumer Finance, Poland, Portugal, the United Kingdom, Brazil, Mexico, Chile, Argentina and the United States. It employs almost 200,000 people and its customer base in Europe and the Americas is estimated at around 145 million (Santander Key ..., 2021; Santander Where ..., 2021). Like most financial institutions, Santander was affected by the global COVID-19 pandemic. This is clearly visible in the bank's financial results. In the first quarter of 2020, Santander recorded attributable profit of EUR 331 million, which was 82% less than in the corresponding period in 2019, after incurring a net charge of EUR 1,646 euros, primarily due to overlay provisions of EUR 1,600 million related to COVID-19 based on the expected deterioration of the macroeconomic conditions arising from the health crisis. In the second quarter of 2020 the situation continued to be difficult. With respect to the geographical location of the bank's branches, in the first half of 2020 Santander recorded the following decreases in its underlying attributable profit (compared to the first half of 2019): 54% in Europe, 29% in North America and 13% in South America. Commenting on the bank's position at the end of the first half of 2020, Ana Botín, Group Executive Chairman of Banco Santander, said, "The past six months have been among the most challenging in our history". During the pandemic, Santander was able to provide financial support to individual customers and enterprises affected by the crisis. The average number of new loans granted each day to SMEs and corporations increased by more than 100%. In order to adjust to functioning in the conditions of the pandemic, Santander sought to intensify the digitalization of its sales channels (digital sales amounted to 43%). As a result, the number of digital customers increased to 38.3 million, compared to 37 million in 2019. Furthermore, attempting to reduce the scale of the negative impact of the pandemic, Santander implemented actions focused mainly on its employees, customers, shareholders and society at large. One of the priorities in such actions was ensuring service provision continuity and adequately responding to changes in the environment to adapt the financial solutions offered to the needs of individual customers and businesses. Another priority in the bank's operations under the pandemic conditions was providing customers with liquidity, which was possible thanks to, among other things, successful implementation of remedial measures introduced by governments (e.g. credit facilities with public guarantees). In most countries of its operations, Santander began to offer moratoria on loan repayments with grace periods of up to several months. Furthermore, following the recommendation of the European Central Bank and in order to provide necessary flexibility to increase lending, the Bank decided to cancel the payment of dividend for 2019 (Santander reports ..., 2020; Santander Coronavirus, 2020; Santander Results, 2020; Santander Quarterly ..., 2020).

5.3.2.2. Alior Bank

Alior Bank is a universal bank operating in the Polish market. The number of customers is over 4.2 million. The bank's offer is tailored to the needs of both individual and business customers (Alior Bank informacje ..., 2021). Especially in the first half of 2020, Alior Bank's operations were conducted under pressure from difficult economic conditions caused by the COVID-19 pandemic. The problems faced by the bank were reflected, among others, in its financial results. Alior Bank closed the first half of 2020 with a loss of PLN 513 million, which meant a decline in the financial result by more than 650% in comparison to the same period in 2019. This sudden negative change was triggered, among other things, by external factors such as an interest rate reduction. Despite the very unfavourable conditions causing a colossal loss, the Bank managed to maintain its cost efficiency (operating costs decreased by 3% compared to 2019). Alior Bank tried to some extent to adapt to the new operating conditions, maintaining its activity in important market segments. After the first half of 2020, better trends in the sales of the Bank's new key products could be observed (e.g. mortgage loans or products for the SMEs sector). This trend was the result of the fact that the percentage of the bank's business customers from industries sensitive to the development of the pandemic and its consequences was only 13%. During the pandemic, Alior Bank took advantage of the government programmes such as the PFR Financial Shield and the temporary deferment of repayments of cash loans, mortgage loans and credits for business entities. Alior Bank also pursued a conservative approach to risk at the time. Due to the emerging high costs associated with the pandemic, the bank's management decided to make relevant provisions and write-downs in its ledgers. In order to cope with losses related to the pandemic, the bank introduced changes in its tariff of fees and commissions to strengthen an increase in commission income, increased the level of cross-selling of transactional products, optimized deposit interest rates, changed credit margins, developed automated processes and remote customer service processes (sales of personal accounts and savings accounts through remote channels increased by 141%) as well as optimized logistics and consulting costs. However, all these measures did not neutralize the large scale of pandemic losses (Alior Bank Wyniki ..., 2020).

5.3.3. *Simon Property Group and Archicom case studies*

5.3.3.1. *Simon Property Group*

Simon Property Group is an American real estate investment company focusing primarily on the commercial segment. It operates a number of shopping centres and owns shops, restaurants, entertainment venues and other mixed-use establishments in North America, Europe and Asia (About Simon, 2021). Problems associated with the pandemic began to affect Simon Property Group in March 2020, when commercial facilities and retail outlets were being temporarily closed. Another challenge was a threat of bankruptcy or insolvency of tenants. Changes caused by the pandemic were immediately reflected in the group's financial results for the first quarter of 2020. They showed significant declines in total revenue, consolidated net income and net income attributable to common stockholders compared to the same period in 2019. Despite a loss of nearly 10,500 shopping days in its US portfolio, thanks to the measures implemented to limit the negative effects of COVID-19, the situation started to improve somewhat in the second quarter and the company was able to return partly to its investment activity, mainly due to the reopening of many outlets, good relationships with the cooperating brands, a portfolio with a strong mix of geographic locations and product types, as well as its previously developed leadership position in the commercial real estate sector. In order to combat many negative consequences of the COVID-10 crisis, the company took measures aimed at cost reduction and liquidity enhancement. The company was forced, among other things, to reduce its corporate expenses, operating costs of commercial establishments and payroll costs and reduce management and employee compensation until market conditions improved. In addition, Simon Property Group implemented a temporary freeze on company hiring efforts. More than 1 billion US dollars for redevelopment and new development projects were suspended or shelved as a result of pandemic issues. The company also borrowed USD 3.75 billion under its revolving credit facilities (Simon Property Group Reports First ..., 2020; Simon Property Group Reports Second ..., 2020).

5.3.3.2. *Archicom*

Archicom is a Polish developer operating on the residential and commercial real estate market. The company has more than 30 years of experience and has successfully completed more than 150 investment projects, including the construction and sale of approximately 6,000 housing units. The company specializes in the construction of residential estates and office buildings in the five largest cities in Poland (Archicom o nas, 2021). The COVID-19 pandemic seriously impacted Archicom's operations and its financial results. The main causes of problems were changes in the following: demand for new housing units and rental of offices, demand for investment in office buildings, the purchasing profiles and attitudes of customers, the pace of construction work, bank financing for purchasers of apartments, the pace of issuing administrative decisions leading to the acquisition of building permits and occupancy permits, the process of separating and transferring ownership of apartments to purchasers and the sale of real property, the access to sources of financing, as well as the availability of the company's own employees and those of its business partners. These numerous problems faced by Archicom during COVID-19 caused a situation in which the company was able to continue its construction operations in the first quarter of 2020, but also recorded negative operating cash flows due to declining sales (mainly in March 2020). At the end of the first quarter net operating cash flows fell to PLN –12.1 million compared to PLN 0.9 million at the same time in 2019. There was also an increase in the volume of long-term debt financing accompanied by a decreasing amount of advances from customers. In order to counteract the negative effects of the pandemic, the management was analyzing the enterprise's position on an ongoing basis, paying particular attention to actions supporting the timely execution of construction projects and closer cooperation with subcontractors. In view of the unfavourable economic situation during the pandemic and the many negative consequences for the company, the management decided to suspend its dividend policy and not to pay dividend for 2019. During COVID-19, Archicom supplemented its strategy with an item providing for the company's focus on ensuring the safety of conducting business activities in new economic conditions. Due to financial constraints, stricter purchasing criteria were also implemented and a new expansion strategy was developed under pressure exerted by new operating conditions. With respect to financing, the company implemented a corporate bond issue plan, monitored costs and cash flows on an ongoing basis and secured for around 70% of its investment projects. The company also attempted to accelerate design work and took advantage of administrative measures provided under the "Tarcza 2.0". Responding to significant declines in sales caused by the pandemic, the company made efforts to manage prices dynamically, prepared promotional programmes and introduced its own Archicom Defence Shield project (Archicom Wpływ pandemii ..., 2020; Archicom prezentacja wyników 1Q'20, 2020; Archicom prezentacja wyników 2Q'20, 2020).

5.4. Opportunity wasters

5.4.1. Introduction

Strange as it may seem, for some sectors, the occurrence of the COVID-19 pandemic meant the emergence of new business opportunities. One of these is the furniture sector. According to some forecasts presented in the early spring of 2020, the COVID-19 pandemic was to cause a decline of up to 35% in the sales of furniture and the disappearance of many jobs. The only way to save the industry was the opening of furniture outlets on Sundays and the intensification of online sales, which at that time did not exceed 10% of the industry's total sales volume (Sprzedaż ..., 2020). According to the forecasts updated at the end of the year, the value of the marketed production of the furniture industry was to rise by a few percentage points in comparison to that of 2019. Three factors were mentioned as working in favour of the industry: the opening up of trade faster than initially forecast, expenditures on home furnishings as a consequence of cancellation of holidays, and favourable exchange rates for the currencies of the countries with the highest furniture production (Branża meblarska ..., 2020). Of great importance was also the release of aid measures allowing furniture companies to maintain liquidity and employment until the gradual opening of the economies of the most important export markets (Branża, która ..., 2020).

The position of the construction sector was partly similar to that of the furniture sector. The construction industry was also forecast to suffer from the consequences of the pandemic. Therefore, it was emphasized that each entity involved in an investment process (regardless of whether an investment project was a public or private enterprise) should adequately secure its interests by implementing a well-thought-out strategy of action, adequately and regularly documenting the factual or potential impact of the circumstances associated with COVID-19 on the performance of the contract, and notifying the contracting party thereof (Czy COVID-19 ..., 2020). Meanwhile, the construction sector in many countries continued its operations despite the epidemic, which gave it a much better position than that of the other sectors that were forced to suspend their operations. The construction sector also maintained high liquidity and turned out to be much better prepared for the current crisis than the previous ones (Szybka ..., 2020). The position of the transport sector was similar to that of the construction sector. It was allowed to continue its business activities despite the ongoing pandemic.

5.4.2. FORTE and Erbud case studies

5.4.2.1. FORTE

FORTE is a Polish enterprise and one of the largest European manufacturers of self-assembly furniture. The company has five modern production plants located in Poland, with a total production area of 143,000 m^2 and a storage area of 103,000 m^2 (FORTE o ..., 2020). During the 27 years of its activity, FORTE has acquired approximately 4,500 corporate customers in 40 countries around the world. Exports account for about 80% of FORTE's production output. After the outbreak of the pandemic, the management decided to introduce a so-called economic stoppage as of 24 March 2020, forecasting simultaneously its negative impact on the company's financial and operation position (Raporty ..., 2020). FORTE felt the first consequences of the pandemic very soon. They were visible in the summary of the financial results for the first quarter of 2020. Sales revenues for the period from January to the end of March 2020 were 13.5% lower than in the corresponding period of 2019. In March alone, COVID-19 caused a drop in turnover by 42% in comparison to March 2019 (Fabryki ..., 2020). Reacting to the spread of the coronavirus, the management engaged in negotiations with its banks to extend the repayment periods for the capital instalments of investment credits payable in March and the second quarter of 2020. In a communication addressed to investors and presenting its forecast for the subsequent quarters of 2020, the management board wrote:

> The effects of the COVID-19 coronavirus pandemic announced by the World Health Organization and the consequent actions taken by both the Polish government administration, including restrictions imposed on the operation of retail outlets and shopping centres with a surface area of more than 2,000 m^2, and the governments of other European countries will have a significant negative impact on the future financial results of the capital group, with particular emphasis on the second quarter of 2020.
>
> (FORTE spodziewa ..., 2020)

The reasons indicated in the communication accounted for only part of the company's problems. The major problem was the structure of customers, which was dominated by enterprises buying office furniture made of particle board. This group of customers (as opposed to individual clients) stopped purchases in the period of the pandemic, responding to growing uncertainty and transition to remote working.

5.4.2.2. Erbud

Erbud is also a Polish company listed on the Warsaw Stock Exchange. The company represents the construction sector. In the first half of 2020, Polish construction companies listed on the Warsaw Stock Exchange showed a combined 8% increase in revenues as compared to the same period of 2019. For example, Budimex, the biggest player in the sector, reported a 15% increase in revenues, to PLN 3.7 billion. A similar 13% increase was reported by Mostostal Warszawa. The revenues of Unibep grew by 1.2%. However, there were construction companies that experienced a decrease in their turnover. One of them was Erbud, whose revenues fell by 9.5% (Budowlanka ..., 2020). It should be noted that the construction sector in Poland continued to operate despite the pandemic. Erbud, like other construction companies, experienced operational disruptions such as transport restrictions and temporary supply chain interruptions. There was also a problem of the deteriorating availability of workers from Ukraine and work was being performed more slowly due to the health regime requirements (Budowlanka ..., 2020). Moreover, the company was exposed to reputational risk when analysts from the Santander and Trigon brokerage houses indicated a number of Polish companies listed on the Warsaw Stock Exchange and with the greatest exposure to the negative impact of the economic crisis caused by the coronavirus. Among these companies, Erbud was the only representative of the construction industry (Sektor budownictwa ..., 2020). During the pandemic, several major sources of the company's problems were revealed. Firstly, Erbud operates as a parent company for a dozen or so enterprises functioning within a framework of a capital group. Some of them operate in markets where the pandemic caused a temporary suspension of construction operations. Secondly, Erbud's portfolio contains a considerable proportion of enclosed structures (including those to be erected abroad), and this segment of the market was hit particularly hard by the pandemic. The total share of such projects in Erbud's turnover is approximately 63%. And thirdly, the drop in Erbud's sales was triggered by decisions made by private customers, who evidently reduced their investment plans in view of the pandemic. Thus, Erbud, unlike the majority of Polish construction companies, did not take advantage of the opportunities arising from the fact that the sector was spared major restrictions and allowed its financial performance to deteriorate. Some analysts estimate the company's survival capacity at only 4 months (Budowlanka ..., 2020).

5.4.3. Uber and Jack Wolfskin case studies

5.4.3.1. Uber

Engaged primarily in offering an application for transporting people over short distances in urban environments by pairing a driver with a passenger, Uber found itself in serious trouble as a result of the COVID-19 pandemic (Koronawirus: Uber i Airbnb ..., 2020). The company offered its services in as many as 785 metropolitan areas in 63 countries around the world, and global demand for its services as a result of the pandemic dropped by as much as 80%. Many countries introduced lockdowns and restrictions enforcing social distancing among people. Travel restrictions became a core element of strategies to combat COVID-19. In some countries, particularly in Europe, people were forbidden to leave their place of residence without a clear and compelling reason. In May 2020, the Times and TechCrunch announced layoffs at Uber. At the same time, the world learned that Uber was abandoning several projects it had been developing recently. The company planned to close or merge 45 offices around the world. Two weeks earlier it had announced its plan to lay off 3,700 customer service department employees. This was more than 25% of Uber's total workforce (Koronawirus. Uber zwolni ..., 2020). Many of the remaining employees either were asked to take unpaid leave or had their salaries halved. Aware of the difficult situation, the management decided to refocus the company's operations on passenger transport and food delivery. While Uber's general problems did not come as a surprise, what analysts did not expect was the difficulties faced by Uber Eats, Uber's subsidiary offering online food ordering and delivery services. Lockdowns in many countries caused a growth in demand for such services as restaurants and bars were able to function on a takeaway basis only. However, it turned out that this emerging trend sharply intensified competition in this market (Uber rides ..., 2020). Uber Eats failed to cope with this competition and consequently disappeared from 8 markets worldwide (the Czech Republic, Romania, Ukraine, Uruguay, Honduras, Egypt, Saudi Arabia and the United Arab Emirates) in June 2020. The management reported that it "does not see the opportunity to become number one in these markets" and "its growth strategy aims to focus energy and resources on the most promising markets" (Coronavirus: Uber customer ..., 2020). As part of its strategy to reposition Uber Eats, the company launched an application that allowed users in certain cities in the United States, Canada, Brazil, Chile, Colombia and Peru to order groceries (Coronavirus: Uber customer ..., 2020). This was the consequence of the prior acquisition of a majority stake in the Chilean start-up Cornershop. Unfortunately, the partially positive effects of changes in the management of Uber Eats did not offset the problems confronting the whole corporation.

5.4.3.2. Jack Wolfskin

Jack Wolfskin products are currently sold in more than 500 shops and more than 4,000 retail outlets worldwide. In Europe, the company has 234 shops (161 in Germany, 13 in Austria, 12 in Russia, 6 in Switzerland, 9 in Great Britain, 6 in Italy, 8 in Belgium, 10 in Poland, 3 in Luxembourg, 3 in Ukraine, 2 in the Netherlands and 1 in France). There are 313 Jack Wolfskin establishments in Asia (308 in China, 4 in Japan and 1 in Mongolia). The decision to close shopping malls automatically resulted in the closure of many shops specializing in outdoor equipment. Not only Jack Wolfskin but also other brands such as The North Face and Mammut had to suspend their sales activities. Retail outlets were involved in administrative work only (Koronawirus i branża ..., 2020). It should be noted that Jack Wolfskin located the overwhelming majority of its outlets in shopping malls, which prevented the company from generating revenues in traditional brick-and-mortar establishments located outside shopping centres. In general, restrictions or blockades imposed on sports activities generating demand for outdoor clothing and equipment, for example skiing, were bad news for the whole sector represented by Jack Wolfskin (Sprzedawcy ..., 2020) as it meant a significant decline in sales of skiing apparel and equipment. On the other hand, however, in response to the existing restrictions, interest in alternative activities, such as skitouring, increased dramatically. Nevertheless, due to the relatively weak image of the Jack Wolfskin brand, in this segment of the market it was companies such as Dynafit and Salewa that took advantage of the indicated tendency. The COVID-19 pandemic caused a shift of a considerable share of sales transactions to the e-commerce domain. In one of the lists showing the 100 fastest-growing and 100 fastest-declining product categories in e-commerce during the pandemic, clothing products were in the latter group, which shows that customers are not particularly inclined to purchase clothes on a remote basis (E-commerce ..., 2020). Thus, it can be said that due to the lack of diversification in terms of shop locations, insufficient product diversification, and brand image deficiencies, Jack Wolfskin was unable to discount the opportunities arising during the COVID-19 pandemic.

5.5. The key failure factors of the analyzed enterprises during the COVID-19 pandemic

Based on the analysis of the risk management practices presented above, we identified and grouped the key failure factors (Figure 5.1). All factors are divided into seven groups. Three of the seven groups comprise factors that originate from the business environment. These are legal and economic factors, sectoral determinants and customers. The other four groups include factors of an internal character. These are factors related to enterprises' finances, resources, management and sales.

5.5.1. *Law and economics*

The first group consists of legal and economic factors. These have their source in legal regulations introduced in response to the COVID-19 pandemic. Such regulations resulted, for example, in the introduction of sanitary restrictions making it difficult to conduct normally business activities, the imposition of a total prohibition or various limits on the conduct of business activities, the exclusion of particular enterprises from assistance and support programmes and the implementation of a strict ban on collecting fees from business partners. The companies under analysis were also partly affected by the problem of falling interest rates. It was the enterprises nicknamed "blocked by restrictions" that were particularly exposed to the negative impact of the aforementioned factors. Additionally, one of the FORTE manufacturing plants turned out to be a pandemic hot spot, which resulted in a complete suspension of operations there.

5.5.2. *Sector*

The problems of some of the studied enterprises were caused by factors closely related to the specific character of their respective sectors. Such factors include declines in prices and margins influencing negatively financial results (this concerns, for example, shopping centres such as M1, the petrochemical industry represented by BP and LOTOS, banks such as Santander and Alior Bank, outdoor clothing and equipment shops such as Jack Wolfskin), a serious destabilization of demand in the case of practically all of the enterprises analyzed, logistics problems typical of petrochemical companies and luxury goods enterprises (e.g. Kering and Wittchen) and a global decline in supply (dangerous particularly for the petrochemical sector).

5.5.3. *Customers*

A significant part of the problems faced by the companies were related to their customers. The following factors can be mentioned here:

- customers' declining purchasing capacity, which affected numerous companies representing "blocked by restrictions", "too inert to protect themselves", "too traditional to change", and "opportunity wasters",

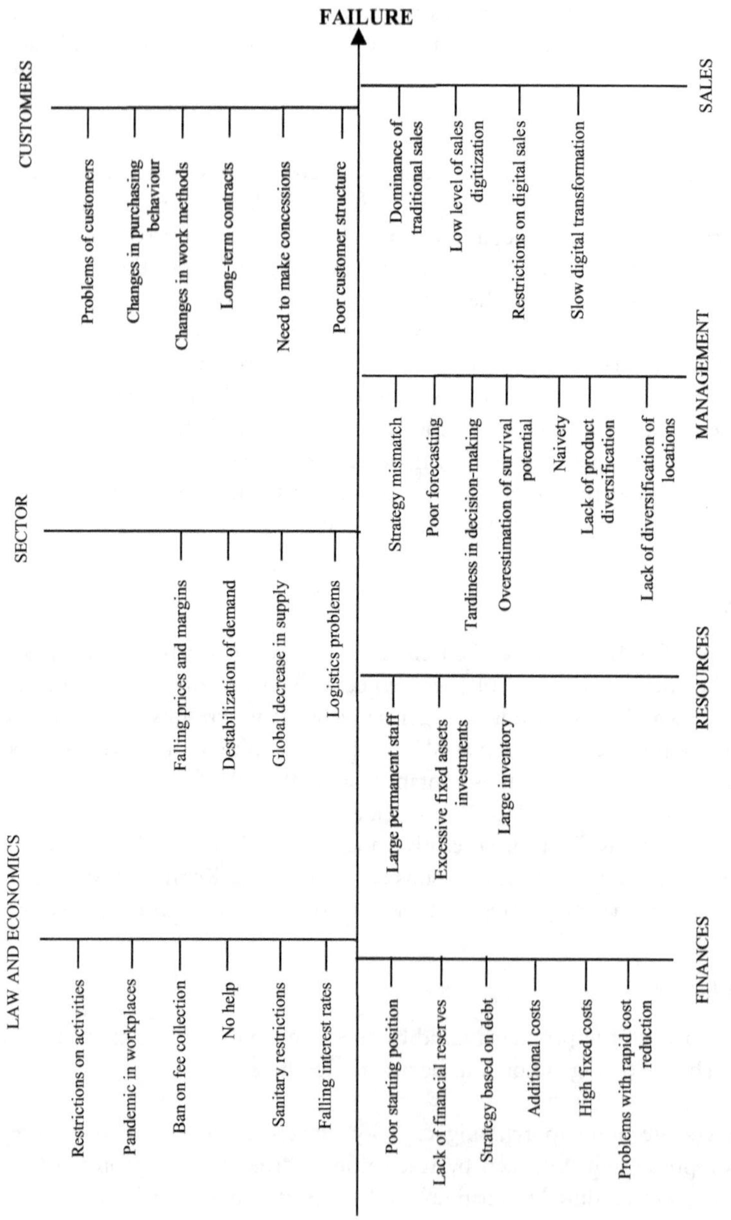

Figure 5.1 Factors determining the failures of the enterprises under analysis during the COVID-19 pandemic

- changes in shopping behaviours consisting, among others, in a shift from traditional "brick-and-mortar" shopping to electronic transactions (especially in the case of shopping centres, retail chains, luxury goods enterprises, banks and outdoor clothing and equipment shops),
- changes in work methods involving the popularization of remote work, which in turn translated into a decline in demand for office space (this factor influenced construction companies such as Erbud and real estate enterprises such as Simon Property Group and Archicom),
- long-term contracts restricting cost-cutting opportunities, particularly in the case of shopping centres,
- the need for concessions, for example in renegotiating contract terms; also typical of shopping centres,
- a poor customer structure due to inadequate diversification (especially in the case of construction enterprises such as Erbud).

5.5.4. *Finances*

The most common symptoms of the problems of the analyzed companies were those of a financial nature. But financial factors were also among the causes of such problems. Some of the enterprises discussed above had already been in a bad financial position before the pandemic (particularly JCPenney). A large proportion of them had negligible financial reserves and used financial strategies based on a high financial leverage ratio (for example Hotele Gołębiewski and Gastromall Group). Due to the outbreak of the COVID-19 pandemic, some companies, such as banks or retail chains, had to incur additional operating costs. Virtually all of the companies had high fixed costs and serious problems with their reduction in a short period of time, with the result that falling revenues were not matched by a corresponding fall in operating costs.

5.5.5. *Resources*

The reasons for the failures of the analyzed companies also included factors related to their resources. As was previously the case with the high level of fixed costs, all surveyed enterprises had large permanent staff. Some of them had invested too much in fixed assets in the period before the outbreak of the COVD-19 pandemic. This problem was particularly evident in the case of Hotele Gołębiewski. Some companies also had large inventories of raw materials and finished products (e.g. retail chains, luxury goods enterprises, outdoor clothing and equipment shops). This foreshadowed problems with selling the available stocks and, consequently, additional pressure on lowering prices and margins.

5.5.6. *Management*

Management dysfunctions contributed significantly to the problems faced by the companies discussed above. They include the following:

- strategy mismatch manifesting itself in principle in all groups of the enterprises characterized, among other things, by low mobility and a lack of preparation for continuing business activities in a crisis situation,
- poor forecasting, which concerned both the inability to anticipate a possible crisis and errors in the assessment of its intensity and duration (the latter was particularly visible in the cases of Hotele Gołębiewski and Gastromall Group),
- naivety and tardiness in decision-making, which together account for insufficient urgency in responding to the crisis and insufficient measures taken to counteract its consequences,
- overestimating survival potential, for example Hotele Gołębiewski,
- the lack of product diversification (e.g. in construction enterprises) and the lack of diversification of locations (especially visible in the case of retail and catering businesses with a significant part of establishments located in shopping centres).

5.5.7. Sales

Sales policies followed by the studied enterprises were the source of various factors limiting the possible range of their activities under the COVID-19 crisis. This concerns in particular the sales model dominant in the period before the pandemic, based on brick-and-mortar shops and characteristic of retail chains, catering businesses, luxury goods enterprises as well as outdoor clothing and equipment shops. Consequently, the twin factor was the low level of digitalization of sales processes. The necessity to switch to remote forms of sales revealed weaknesses such as insufficiently rapid digital transformation or objective obstacles to its implementation, such as in the case of shopping centres.

Thus, the conducted case studies revealed a very diverse collection of factors that contributed to the failure of the companies during the COVID-19 pandemic. They also allowed the identification of different profiles of the companies with respect to their risk exposure. Such profiles were determined by a variety of factors of an individual (typical of a given company company), sectoral (specific to the sector in which a company operates), local (for example, linked to particular governments' decisions concerning the introduction of restrictions or the provision of financial assistance) and eventually general (applicable to all enterprises all over the world) character.

References

About Simon (2021). https://business.simon.com/about (Access: 7.01.2021).

Accor CEO: COVID-19 impact 'global, sudden, violent and unprecedented' (2020). www.spglobal.com/marketintelligence/en/news-insights/latest-news-headlines/accor-ceo-covid-19-impact-global-sudden-violent-and-unprecedented-59766192 (Access: 18.01.2021).

Alior Bank informacje o banku (2021). www.aliorbank.pl/dodatkowe-informacje/o-banku.html (Access: 5.01.2021).

Alior Bank Wyniki finansowe w I półroczu 2020 roku pod presją trudnych warunków ekonomicznych spowodowanych pandemią (2020). www.aliorbank.pl/aktualnosci/2020-08-19-wyniki-finansowe-alior-banku-w-I-polroczu-2020-roku.html (Access: 5.01.2021).

Archicom o nas (2021). www.archicom.pl/poznaj-archicom/o-nas/ (Access: 7.01.2021).

Archicom Prezentacja wyników 1Q'20 (2020). www.archicom.pl/dla-inwestora/wp-content/uploads/sites/3/2020/06/Archicom-prezentacja-1Q20_02.06.2020_final.pdf (Access: 7.01.2021).

Archicom Prezentacja wyników 2Q'20 (2020). www.archicom.pl/dla-inwestora/wp-content/uploads/sites/3/2020/10/Archicom-prezentacja-2Q20_21.09.2020-FINAL.pdf (Access: 7.01.2021).

Archicom Wpływ pandemii wirusa SARS-CoV-2 na działalność i wyniki finansowe Spółki (2020). www.archicom.pl/dla-inwestora/wp-content/uploads/sites/3/2020/03/RB-13_Wp%C5%82yw-pandemii-wirusa-SARS-CoV-2-na-dzia%C5%82alno%C5%9B%C4%87-i-wyniki-finansowe-Sp%C3%B3%C5%82ki.pdf (Access: 7.01.2021).

Bain & Company (2020). Covid-19 crisis pushes luxury to sharpest fall ever but catalyses industry's ability to transform. www.bain.com/about/media-center/press-releases/2020/covid_19_crisis_pushes_luxury_to_sharpest_fall_ever_but_catalyses_industrys_ability_to_transform/ (Access: 30.12.2020).

Branża, która oszukała pandemię: polscy producenci mebli biją rekordy mimo koronawirusa (2020). https://300gospodarka.pl/news/branza-ktora-oszukala-pandemie-polscy-producenci-mebli-bija-rekordy-mimo-koronawirusa (Access: 24.01.2021).

Branża meblarska wygrywa z koronawirusem (2020). www.oigpm.org.pl/797/branza-meblarska-wygrywa-z-koronawirusem (Access: 24.01.2021).

Budowlanka odczuje skutki pandemii (2020). https://biznes.interia.pl/nieruchomosci/news-budowlanka-odczuje-skutki-pandemii,nId,4839292 (Access: 25.01.2021).

Can the shopping mall survive? (2020). *The Edge Magazine*, 5, pp. 20–23.

Centra handlowe mają problemy. Wielu klientów nie wróciło, a kredyty trzeba spłacać (2020). https://businessinsider.com.pl/finanse/handel/problemy-centrow-handlowych-przez-epidemie-wielu-klientow-nie-wrocilo/6tghlsn (Access: 21.01.2021).

Centra handlowe na zakręcie. Wpływ COVID-19 (2020). www.pwc.pl/pl/pdf-nf/2020/raport-o-centrach-handlowych-2020.pdf, (Access: 22.01.2021).

Coronavirus (COVID-19) case study: Impact of COVID-19 on Accor and its response (2020). https://store.globaldata.com/report/gdtt0363mi--coronavirus-covid-19-case-study-impact-of-covid-19-on-accor-and-its-response/ (Access: 18.01.2021).

Coronavirus: Uber customer activity falls sharply (2020). www.bbc.com/news/business-53687422 (Access:18.01.2021).

COVID-19: A new lockdown for Polish gastronomy (2020). https://retailmarketexperts.com/en/news/covid-19-a-new-lockdown-for-polish-gastronomy/ (Access: 18.01.2021).

Covid-19 BP response (2020). www.bp.com/en/global/corporate/news-and-insights/covid-19-bp-response.html (Access: 2.01.2021).

Czy COVID-19 to czarny łabędź branży budowlanej? Perspektywa inżyniera i prawnika (2020). www.rynekinfrastruktury.pl/mobile/czy-covid19-to-czarny-labedz-branzy-budowlanej-perspektywa-inzyniera-i-prawnika-71316.html (Access: 25.01.2021).

Davahli, M.R., Karwowski, W., Sonmez, S., Apostolopoulos, Y. (2020). The hospitality industry in the face of the COVID-19 pandemic: Current topics and research methods. *International Journal of Environmental Research and Public Health*, 17, 7366, pp. 1–20.

Deloitte (2020a). COVID-19 CEE banking sector impact survey. First symptoms of the coronavirus outbreak. www2.deloitte.com/pl/pl/pages/financial-services/articles/Wplyw-COVID-19-na-sektor-bankowy-w-Europie-Srodkowo-Wschodniej.html (Access: 30.12.2020).

Deloitte (2020b). Moving towards the future, how can property developers respond to liquidity challenges? www2.deloitte.com/cn/en/pages/financial-services/articles/how-real-estate-companies-tackle-cash-flow-challenges-during-2019-covid.html (Access: 7.01.2021).

Discover Kering (2021). www.kering.com/en/group/discover-kering/ (Access: 1.01.2020).

Duże straty branży gastronomicznej z powodu COVID-19 (2020). https://mojafirma.infor.pl/wiadomosci/5147680,Duze-straty-branzy-gastronomicznej-z-powodu-COVID19.html (Access: 18.01.2021).

E-commerce w trakcie COVID-19 – które branże rosną, a które maleją? Poznaj dane z Polski i ze świata. (2020). www.ekomercyjnie.pl/ecommerce-koronariwus-branze-rosna-spadaja-polska-swiat/ (Access: 26.01.2021).

Fabryki Mebli Forte ze stratą. Koronawirus wymusił czasowe wstrzymanie produkcji (2020). www.money.pl/gielda/fabryki-mebli-forte-ze-strata-koronawirus-wymusil-czasowe-wstrzymanie-produkcji-6512824703158401a.html (Access: 20.01.2021).

FORTE, o firmie (2020). http://ww2.forte.com.pl/pl/index/o-firmie (Access: 23.01.2021).

Forte spodziewa się znaczącego pogorszenia wyników, szczególnie w II kw. 2020 (2020). https://forsal.pl/artykuly/1460749,forte-spodziewa-sie-znaczacego-pogorszenia-wynikow-szczegolnie-w-ii-kw-2020.html (Access: 22.01.2021).

Gastronomia w czasach pandemii COVID-19. 7 praktycznych wskazówek dla biznesu (2020). www.pulshr.pl/restrukturyzacja/gastronomia-w-czasach-pandemii-covid-19-7-praktycznych-wskazowek-dla-biznesu,78274.html (Access: 18.01.2021).

Gastronomia balansuje na skraju bankructwa (2020). www.propertynews.pl/biura/gastronomia-balansuje-na-skraju-bankructwa,82842.html (Access: 21.01.2021).

Gursoy, D., Chi, C.G. (2020). Effects of COVID-19 pandemic on hospitality, industry: Review of the current situations and a research agenda. *Journal of Hospitality Marketing & Management*, 29(5), pp. 527–529.

Hotel group Accor to cut 1,000 jobs after coronavirus loss (2020). www.reuters.com/article/uk-accor-results/hotel-group-accor-to-cut-1000-jobs-after-coronavirus-loss-idUKKCN25025M (Access: 18.01.2021).

Inditex 1Q20 sales drop limited to 44% despite up to 88% of stores closed (2020). www.inditex.com/article?articleId=648065&title=Inditex+1Q20+sales+drop+limited+to+44%25+despite+up+to+88%25+of+stores+closed (Access: 31.12.2020).

In a quarter heavily impacted by COVID-19, Kering demonstrates its solidity (2021). www.kering.com/en/news/in-a-quarter-heavily-impacted-by-covid-19-kering-demonstrates-its-solidity (Access: 1.01.2021).

Inditex around the world (2020). www.inditex.com/en/about-us/inditex-around-the-world#continent/000 (31.12.2020).

Inditex returns to profitability and generates €734 million net cash in the second quarter (2020). www.inditex.com/en/article?articleId=653527&title=Inditex+returns+to+profitability+and+generates+%E2%82%AC734+million+net+cash+in+the+second+quarter (Access: 30.12.2020).

JCPenney provides update on store optimization strategy (2020). https://ir.jcpenney.com/news-events/press-releases/detail/618/jcpenney-provides-update-on-store-optimization-strategy (Access: 21.01.2021).

Jeden z największych pracodawców zagrożony upadkiem. Sieć Olimp karmiła dziesiątki tysięcy Polaków. Tarcze jej nie pomogły (2020). https://dziennikpolski24.pl/krakow-jeden-z-najwiekszych-pracodawcow-zagrozony-upadkiem-siec-olimp-karmila-dziesiatki-tysiecy-polakow-tarcze-jej-nie-pomogly/ar/c3-14951256 (Access: 21.01.2021).

Kaushal, V., Srivastava, S. (2021). Hospitality and tourism industry amid COVID-19 pandemic: Perspectives on challenges and learnings from India. *International Journal of Hospitality Management*, 92, pp. 1–9.

Koronawirus i branża outdoor (2020). https://4outdoor.pl/2020/03/17/koronawirus-i-branza-outdoor/ (Access: 25.01.2021).

Koronawirus. Uber zwolni 3 tys. osób i przewiduje, że to nie koniec (2020). www.money.pl/gospodarka/koronawirus-uber-zwolni-3-tys-osob-i-przewiduje-ze-to-nie-koniec-6512188139804289a.html (Access: 19.01.2021).

Koronawirus: Uber i Airbnb ogłaszają grupowe zwolnienia (2020). www.euractiv.pl/section/gospodarka/news/koronawirus-uber-i-airbnb-oglaszaja-grupowe-zwolnienia/ (Access: 19.01.2021).

Koronawirus uderzył w hotele Gołębiewski. "Trzy lata wychodzenia ze strat" (2020). www.money.pl/gospodarka/koronawirus-uderzyl-w-hotele-golebiewski-trzy-lata-wychodzenia-ze-strat-6507900920219777v.html (Access: 17.01.2021).

Koronawirus w Polsce. "Najemcy w biurowcach zostawieni sami sobie. Poważna luka w tarczy antykryzysowej" (2020). https://wiadomosci.wp.pl/koronawirus-w-polsce-najemcy-w-biurowcach-zostawieni-sami-sobie-powazna-luka-w-tarczy-antykryzysowej-6505159040678017a (Access: 21.01.2021).

Koronawirus wykończy Hotele Gołębiewski? Gołębiewski: zastawiłem cały majątek (2020). www.fakt.pl/pieniadze/biznes/koronawirus-wykonczy-hotele-golebiewski-golebiewski-zastawilem-caly-majatek/c63cbyw (Access: 17.01.2021).

Koronawirus. Właściciel znanego hotelu na Mazurach na skraju bankructwa (2020). www.olsztyn.com.pl/artykul,koronawirus-wlasciciel-znanego-hotelu-na-mazurach-na-skraju-bankructwa,31141.html (Access: 17.01.2020).

KPMG (2020). The implications of COVID-19 for the real estate industry. https://home.kpmg/content/dam/kpmg/nl/pdf/2020/services/the-implications-of-covid-19-for-the-real-estate-industry.pdf (Access: 7.01.2021).

Lloyds Bank and Pizza Hut cut more than 1,000 jobs (2020). www.bbc.com/news/business-54079002 (Access: 22.01.2021).

Long-struggling JC Penney files for bankruptcy as coronavirus crushes hopes for a quick turnaround (2020). www.cnbc.com/2020/05/15/jc-penney-bankruptcy-filing.html (Access: 21.01.2021).

LOTOS Komentarz Zarządu Grupy LOTOS S.A. do wyników skonsolidowanych za 2 kwartał 2020 roku (2020). https://inwestor.lotos.pl/192/raporty_i_dane/raporty_polroczne (Access: 3.01.2021).

LOTOS Skonsolidowane wyniki finansowe za 1 półrocze i 2 kwartał 2020 roku (2020). https://inwestor.lotos.pl/192/raporty_i_dane/raporty_polroczne (Access: 3.01.2021).

LPP na świecie (2021). www.lppsa.com/o-nas/lpp-na-swiecie (Access: 1.01.2021).

LPP podsumowuje wpływ epidemii Covid-19 na działalność spółki (2021). www.lppsa.com/informacje-prasowe/powrot-do-oczekiwanych-poziomow-sprzedazy-mozliwy-w-2021-roku-lpp-podsumowuje-wplyw-epidemii-covid-19-na-dzialalnosc-spolki (Access: 1.01.2021).

LPP w liczbach (2021). www.lppsa.com/o-nas/lpp-w-liczbach (Access: 1.01.2021).

M1 w Polsce (2020). www.metro-properties.pl/site/portfolio?section=m1 (Access: 22.01.2021).

McKinsey (2020). Oil and gas after COVID-19: The day of reckoning or a new age of opportunity? www.mckinsey.com/~/media/McKinsey/Industries/Oil%20and%20Gas/Our%20Insights/Oil%20and%20gas%20after%20COVID%2019%20The%20day%20of%20reckoning%20or%20a%20new%20age%20of%20opportunity/Oil-and-gas-after-COVID-19-v4.pdf (Access: 30.12.2020).

OECD (2020). Housing amid COVID-19: Policy responses and challenges. www.oecd.org/coronavirus/policy-responses/housing-amid-covid-19-policy-responses-and-challenges-cfdc08a8/ (Access: 7.01.2021).

Pizza Hut considers insolvency as Covid-19 crisis threatens jobs (2020). www.theguardian.com/business/2020/jul/29/pizza-hut-considers-insolvency-as-covid-19-crisis-threatens-jobs (Access: 22.01.2021).

Pizza Hut zaatakowana przez koronawirusa. Padło słowo "bankructwo" (2020). www.polsatnews.pl/wiadomosc/2020-07-03/pizza-hut-zaatakowana-przez-koronawirusa-padlo-slowo-bankructwo/ (Access: 22.01.2021).

PRCH szacuje, że 3 lockdowny oznaczają ok. 30 mld zł utraconych obrotów w handlu (2020). https://biznes.gazetaprawna.pl/artykuly/8063344,prch-3-lockdowny-straty-w-handlu.html (Access: 22.01.2021).

Raporty Spółek ESPI/EBI. Informacja poufna - wpływ rozprzestrzeniania się koronawirusa COVID-19 na działalnośćEmitenta FABRYKI MEBLI FORTE SPÓŁKA AKCYJNA (PLFORTE00012) (2020). www.gpw.pl/komunikat?geru_id=349218&title=informacja+poufna+-+wp%C5%82yw+rozprzestrzeniania+si%C4%99+koronawirusa+COVID-19+na+dzia%C5%82alno%C5%9B%C4%87Emitenta (Access: 23.01.2021).

Restructuring information (2020). https://jcprestructuring.com/ (Access: 21.01.2021).

Santander key facts and figures (2021). www.santander.com/en/about-us/key-facts-and-figures (Access: 5.01.2021).

Santander coronavirus: All information about Santander Group (2020). www.santander.com/en/press-room/specials/covid-19/general-information (Access: 5.01.2021).

Santander quaterly shareholder report (2020). https://santanderaccionistaseinversores.com/2T20/eng/index.php (Access: 29.01.2021).

Santander reports first quarter 2020 attributable profit of €331 million, after €1.6 billion reserve build related to covid-19 (2020). www.santander.com/en/press-room/press-releases/2020/04/1q-2020-results (Access: 5.01.2021).

Santander (2020). Results. https://santanderaccionistaseinversores.com/2T20/eng/resultados.php (Access: 29.01.2021).

Santander (2021). Where we are. www.santander.com/en/about-us/where-we-are (Access: 5.01.2021).

Second quarter 2020 results (2020). www.bp.com/en/global/corporate/news-and-insights/press-releases/second-quarter-2020-results.html (Access: 2.01.2021).

Sektor budownictwa w obliczu COVID-19 (2020). Polski Związek Pracodawców Budownictwa, Warszawa, https://pzpb.com.pl/2020/06/24/raport-pzpb-sektor-budownictwa-w-obliczu-covid-19/ (Access: 25.01.2021).

Simon property group reports first quarter 2020 results and provides business update (2020). https://investors.simon.com/news-releases/news-release-details/simon-property-group-reports-first-quarter-2020-results-and (Access: 7.01.2021).

Simon property group reports second quarter 2020 results (2020). https://investors.simon.com/news-releases/news-release-details/simon-property-group-reports-second-quarter-2020-results (Access: 7.01.2021).

Sprzedawcy, wypożyczalnie sprzętu narciarskiego apelują o pomoc do PFR (2020). www.money.pl/gielda/sprzedawcy-wypozyczalnie-sprzetu-narciarskiego-apeluja-o-pomoc-do-pfr-6599187596212353a.html (Access: 25.01.2021).

Sprzedaż mebli w tym roku może spaść o 35 proc. Pracę straci nawet 40 tys. osób (2020). https://businessinsider.com.pl/finanse/handel/koronawirus-wplyw-na-przemysl-meblowy-eksport-mebli-z-polski-praca/jc6fpgr (Access: 24.01.2021).

Szybka reanimacja budownictwa? Raport o stanie biznesu w czasie pandemii (2020). www.forbes.pl/biznes/sytuacja-branzy-budowlanej-w-polsce-w-czasie-epidemii-koronawirusa/w0s0qql (Access: 25.01.2021).

Tadeusz Gołębiewski zastawił swój majątek, by ratować hotele i miejsca pracy (2020). www.forbes.pl/biznes/hotele-golebiewski-w-czasie-koronawirusa-tadeusz-golebiewski-zastawil-majatek-by/dbnw4vj (Access: 17.01.2021).

The bp brand (2021). www.bp.com/en/global/corporate/who-we-are/our-brands/the-bp-brand.html (Access: 1.02.2021).

The coronavirus lockdown hit JCPenney even harder than we thought (2020). https://edition.cnn.com/2020/06/30/business/jcpenney-losses-bankruptcy/index.html (Access: 21.01.2021).

Uber rides take COVID-19 hit but food-delivery business doubles (2020). www.reuters.com/article/us-uber-results/uber-rides-take-covid-19-hit-but-food-delivery-business-doubles-idUSKCN25230X (Access: 18.01.2021).

Unctad (2020). Textile and garment supply chains in times of COVID-19: Challenges for developing countries. https://unctad.org/es/node/3024 (Access: 30.12.2020).

Will COVID-19 mark the end of department stores? (2020). https://nowfashion.com/will-covid-19-mark-the-end-of-department-stores-29775 (Access: 18.01.2021).

Wittchen – o firmie. (2021). www.wittchen.com/o-firmie (Access: 2.01.2021).

Wittchen Raport bieżący nr 21 (2020). www.wittchen.com/relacje-inwestorskie/wp-content/uploads/2020/10/RB_21_2020_Informacja-o-skonsolidowanych-przychodach-ze-sprzeda%C5%BCy-za-III-kwarta%C5%82-2020_RB-wys%C5%82any-o-godzinie-16_49.pdf (Access: 2.01.2021).

Wittchen Raport bieżący nr 5 (2020). www.wittchen.com/relacje-inwestorskie/wp-content/uploads/2020/03/Raport_bie%C5%BC%C4%85cy_5_2020.pdf (Access: 2.01.2021).

Wittchen Skonsolidowany Raport Roczny grupy kapitałowej Wittchen za 2019 rok (2020). www.wittchen.com/relacje-inwestorskie/wp-content/uploads/2020/03/Skonsolidowany-Raport-Roczny-Wittchen-S.A.-za-2019-rok.pdf (Access: 2.01.2021).

Wittchen zapłaci za usługi dla e-sklepu 200–300 tys. zł w 2020 roku (2020). www.dlahandlu.pl/detal-hurt/wiadomosci/wittchen-zaplaci-za-uslugi-dla-e-sklepu-200-300-tys-zl-w-2020-roku,85853.html (Access: 2.01.2021).

6 "Risk winners" during the COVID-19 pandemic

Case studies

6.1. Direct "medical" beneficiaries

6.1.1. Introduction

For some companies, the occurrence of the COVID-19 pandemic created prosaically greater opportunities for growth. Examples of enterprises that benefited from the pandemic include pharmaceutical companies, whose sales revenue increased impressively at the beginning of the pandemic and again at the end of 2020, in consequence of a multidemic, or the simultaneous occurrence of a few pandemics (Wpływ pandemii ..., 2020). In the pharmaceutical industry, the COVID-19 pandemic caused an intensification of research and development operations. Obviously, this was also influenced by the development of artificial intelligence, self-learning machines and gene therapies. Innovations became less costly and their profitability increased considerably. The developing Industry 4.0 integrates people, industrial machines and the internet, which will certainly speed up production processes. The business models of pharmaceutical companies are changing (Sektor farmaceutyczny ..., 2020). Obviously, activities related to the production of vaccines and COVID-19 drugs constitute the most spectacular market segment. The active participation of biotech companies in the fight against the virus (research, production of tests and vaccines) was reflected in the performance of their shares on stock exchanges (Firmy biotechnologiczne ..., 2020). At the same time, a number of biotech enterprises were gaining new, previously inaccessible, sources of funding as a result of the growing interest of external investors in such companies (Biotech ..., 2020).

The COVID-19 pandemic also significantly changed the profile of the medical device industry, forcing it to focus primarily on the manufacture of personal protective equipment. Masks, gloves and protective suits were particularly sought-after commodities, which resulted in a worldwide increase of more than 40% in sales of such products (Branża medyczna ..., 2020). At the same time, new business domains emerged for typical medical establishments, such as the performance of COVID-19 tests or vaccinations.

DOI: 10.4324/9781003131366-6

6.1.2. CVS Health and LuxMed case studies

6.1.2.1. CVS Health

CVS Health is a healthcare company with a portfolio of a few groups of services, for example, pharmacy services, health and wellness services, health plans, virtual care services and prescription drug coverage. Shortly after the onset of the COVID-19 pandemic in early 2020, the management prepared a business continuity plan that included a comprehensive approach comprising the following activities (Our actions ..., 2020):

- closely monitoring the global pharmaceutical environment and cooperation with suppliers to ensure that prescriptions can still be made up for pharmacy patients and plan members at CVS Health,
- balancing the growing interest in off-label use of certain prescription medications to treat COVID-19 pneumonia with the ongoing needs of patients and members who are prescribed these drugs to help manage chronic conditions,
- ensuring that retail pharmacies adhere to the dispensing guidelines for COVID-19 drugs approved for use in some states of the United States,
- PBM CVS Caremark's setting (with customers' approval) appropriate coverage limits for the quantities of such drugs for potential use in COVID-19 treatment.

The company also offered its patients the option to request a video visit in 40 states and Washington, DC. The implementation of the virtual medical care option, including video visits, proved to be an effective way to assess and treat viruses without leaving home, simultaneously minimizing exposure to other potentially contagious viruses (CVS Health response ..., 2020). In the financial report for the three quarters of 2020, the management identified the following four activities with the greatest impact on its current position (CVS Health reports ..., 2020):

- providing ongoing support to employees, consumers and communities across the country,
- doubling the number of test sites to more than 4,000 CVS Pharmacy locations nationwide,
- entering the sector of vaccine administration in long-term care facilities,
- improving the healthcare model oriented towards consumers and increasing access to products and services.

The implemented managerial measures allowed the company to achieve satisfactory financial results regarding growth in total revenue, operating profit and earnings per share. At the same time, the company carried out intensive investment activities.

6.1.2.2. LuxMed

The LuxMed Group is the largest player on the market of private healthcare services in Poland. LuxMed provides comprehensive care including outpatient, diagnostic, rehabilitation, hospital and long-term services for more than 2,200,000 patients. Patients have at their disposal 240 medical centres available to the general public or affiliated with particular companies, including outpatient and diagnostic facilities, hospitals, one care and rehabilitation centre and over 2,600 partner clinics. The company employs around 16,000 people, including 7,000 physicians and 4,000 nurses and paramedics (Placówki ..., 2021). Shortly after the onset of the pandemic, LuxMed took measures aimed at ensuring both service provision continuity and the safety of patients and the medical personnel. Emphasis was placed on telephone and online consultations, and direct contacts with physicians were limited to serious and justified cases, in strict compliance with established procedures (Korzystaj ..., 2020). Next LuxMed introduced new medical services in response to the COVID-19 pandemic. At the first stage, these services included (Koronawirus ..., 2020): online guides for patients explaining the possibilities of diagnosing the infection and its treatment, the possibility of performing tests, the possibility of donating plasma (in the case of patients who have recovered from the disease), and then also the administration of vaccines to patients qualified for the Polish national vaccination programme. LuxMed immediately started to offer its patients all available types of tests (Test ..., 2021), i.e. antigen tests, antibody tests, as well as RT PCR tests and RT PCR tests with a travel certificate.

An additional creative idea was the introduction of a service dedicated to those who had already suffered and recovered from the infection. Referred to as a post-COVID-19 health review, the service was launched in response to medical reports according to which alarming symptoms and long-term complications could occur in people whose course of the disease had been mild or even asymptomatic. Therefore, LuxMed offered a service including appropriate laboratory, functional and imaging examinations, a diagnosis of conditions and preparation of medical recommendations aimed at helping patients to achieve full recovery (Przegląd ..., 2020).

6.1.3. Pfizer and BioMaxima case studies

6.1.3.1. Pfizer

Established in New York in 1849 by Charles Pfizer, an American of German origin, Pfizer is an American pharmaceutical corporation. In the beginning, the company was to produce chemicals and its first product was santonin, a strong anthelmintic. During World War II, the company produced one of the most important antibiotics in history – penicillin. It was an important element of the equipment of American soldiers fighting on the Western European fronts. After the discovery of oxytetracycline in 1950, the company decided to transform from a manufacturer of typical chemicals into a pharmaceutical company specializing in research, as well as the development and manufacture of new drugs (Historia Pfizera ..., 2020). At present, Pfizer is one of the largest pharmaceutical corporations in the world. The 2019 revenue of USD 51.7 billion gave Pfizer the fourth place in the global pharmaceutical market (Historia Pfizera ..., 2020). At the beginning of 2020, Pfizer and BioNTech announced the signing of a letter of intent concerning the joint development and distribution (except of China) of a potential mRNA-based vaccine aimed at preventing COVID-19 infection. The companies signed a cooperation and material transfer agreement enabling them immediately to begin joint activities (Pfizer oraz BioNTech ..., 2020). Interestingly, the rapid progress of work on vaccine development was facilitated by their previous joint R&D activities initiated in 2018 for the purpose of developing an mRNA-based vaccine against seasonal influenza (Pfizer oraz BioNTech ..., 2020). That some managers were convinced of a possible success of the project can be confirmed by one of the statements made by Mikael Dolsten, Chief Scientific Officer and President of the Worldwide Research, Development and Medical Department of Pfizer, who said:

> We are proud that our ongoing, successful relationship with BioNTech gives our companies the resiliency to mobilize our collective resources with extraordinary speed in the face of this worldwide challenge. We believe that by pairing Pfizer's development, regulatory and commercial capabilities with BioNTech's mRNA vaccine technology and expertise as one of the industry leaders, we are reinforcing our commitment to do everything we can to combat this escalating pandemic, as quickly as possible.
>
> (Pfizer oraz BioNTech ..., 2020)

Opting for cooperation with BioNTech was like hitting the bullseye. This success was owed to the couple of German scientists with Turkish roots Ugur Sahin and Özlem Türeci. "Speed of light" was the name given in the middle of January 2020 by BioNTech to its project aimed at developing a vaccine against coronavirus in record time, which indeed turned out to be lightning fast. Usually it takes pharmaceutical corporations 8–10 years to invent a vaccine, but the scientists from Mainz needed just two years to get the research to the stage at which they were able to apply for a permit to launch their vaccine in the American market (Szczepionka z BioNTech, 2020). Not only was the vaccine the first in the world to be approved for use, it also turned out to be extremely effective (Pfizer ends ..., 2020). The success also translated into financial results. In 2021 alone, Pfizer plans to earn around USD 15 billion from the sale of the vaccine (Sprzedaż szczepionki ..., 2020). What adds spice to the matter is that on the day of the announcement of the breakthrough in the research on the vaccine against the coronavirus, Pfizer's CEO Albert Bourla sold 62% of his shares in the corporation, thus discounting his business position (Szczepionka na koronawirusa ..., 2020).

6.1.3.2. BioMaxima

BioMaxima is a Polish producer of microbiological substrates, reagents and equipment for *in vitro* diagnostics. The company is also a distributor of products manufactured by internationally recognized diagnostic companies such as Accelerated Diagnostics, Nova Biomedical, Mitsubishi Chemical, Technoclone, Kabe and Biolog. It is listed on NewConnect, an organized stock market operated outside the regulated market by the Warsaw Stock Exchange, in the form of an alternative trading system (Profil ..., 2020). In terms of sales channels, the company supplies customers in Poland as well as in international markets, cooperating with over 60 distributors on four continents. The company's product offering comprises numerous groups, for example, rapid diagnostic tests for the detection of infectious diseases, cancer markers, heart attack markers and addictive agent markers along with readers (Profil ..., 2020).

During the first phase of the pandemic, the company marketed COVID-19 detection tests from other manufacturers. However, it immediately initiated a research project aimed at developing its own test. The project was completed successfully in late 2020 and the company launched a new proprietary genetic test capable of detecting simultaneously several pathogens, including SARS-CoV-2 and influenza viruses. The company's press release read as follows:

> Already approved for marketing in Poland and other countries of the European Union, our latest SARS/Flu/RSV Real Time PCR LAB-KIT test is a state-of-the-art tool allowing a rapid diagnosis of upper respiratory tract infections and characterized by very high sensitivity and specificity.
>
> (BioMaxima wprowadziła ..., 2020)

The main advantage of the new test is that a simultaneous testing of a sample for several infectious diseases significantly reduces the resources required to perform tests and allows a faster diagnosis of patients suffering from an undetermined respiratory tract infection. The management of BioMaxima anticipates that the use of the test will not be limited to the pandemic, as combined testing is particularly appropriate for patients requiring a rapid diagnosis and appropriate treatment due to their severe condition and/or hospitalization, increased risk of complications, the simultaneous presence of several infections, immunosuppression or the presence of other chronic diseases (BioMaxima wprowadziła ..., 2020). For the company, the registration of its own test was also a breakthrough in terms of access to potential sales markets. While the company was allowed to distribute tests offered by other manufacturers only in Poland, it was able to sell its own tests all over the world (Prezes ..., 2020). The company's technological achievement also translated into a financial success. In 2020, the company doubled its revenue compared to its 2019 results, while total sales revenue in December 2020 was the best monthly result in the company's history (BioMaxima. Firma ..., 2021).

6.1.4 *Cardinal Health and Mercator Medical case studies*

6.1.4.1. Cardinal Health

Cardinal Health is a global manufacturer and distributor of medical and laboratory supplies, as well as a distributor of pharmaceutical products. During the pandemic, the company became an even more important link in healthcare supply chains. One of the company's strengths, critically needed during the COVID-19 pandemic, is actions characteristic of its operating model, such as (Manufacturing ..., 2020):

- conducting ongoing risk assessments of all finished goods and raw materials produced and sourced globally,
- assessing opportunities to insource products into own manufacturing network,
- exploring how to retrofit and add equipment to production lines in order to increase production of items in most need (face masks, gowns and other essential PPE),
- acquiring additional equipment to expand production of isolation gowns and face masks in facilities,
- aggressively evaluating additional suppliers to expand and diversify critical product options,
- expediting supplier validation and qualification processes,
- collaborating with government entities and industry partners to share knowledge, remove barriers and better align efforts.

What is noteworthy from a strategic perspective is the company's intensified efforts to work closely with suppliers, as well as groups including Health Industry Distributors Association, Healthcare Distribution Alliance, National Community Pharmacists Association, National Association of Chain Drug Stores, Healthcare Ready, and AdvaMed to respond to industry-wide challenges and customers, leading experts, and government officials to help deliver products where they are urgently needed (COVID-19 – Cardinal Health ..., 2020). One of the company's major business lines with high growth potential during the pandemic was the distribution of personal protective equipment (Personal ..., 2020). A particular expression of confidence in the company was the decision of the Ohio state government to select it as a distribution partner for COVID-19 vaccines in that state. Steve Mason, CEO of Cardinal Health's medical segment, commented:

> We are proud to provide our services to support our home state. A fully coordinated supply chain is critical to getting Americans safely vaccinated, and Cardinal Health is uniquely positioned to support Ohio's vaccination efforts so we can collectively begin to put COVID-19 behind us.
>
> (Cardinal Health chosen ..., 2020)

What turned out to be particularly valuable was the company's experience gained from its previous operations consisting in the distribution of flu vaccines as well as drugs and health products (Cardinal Health prepares ..., 2020). High operational and strategic agility resulted in a significant increase in the company's turnover in 2020 (COVID-19 Impact ..., 2020).

6.1.4.2. Mercator Medical

Mercator Medical is a Polish company and the largest manufacturer of protective gloves in Central Europe. The company was founded by Wiesław Żyznowski, who holds a doctoral degree in philosophy (Gracz ..., 2020). The company took perfect advantage of the situation in the global market for disposable protective and medical gloves, which favoured manufacturers and distributors of this product assortment. In each subsequent quarter of 2020, the Mercator Medical Group achieved a record level of operations and generated profits. The preliminary estimates of the results for the fourth quarter indicate improvement over the already extremely strong third quarter. Consolidated sales exceeded PLN 654 million, which was five times more than a year earlier. At the same time, the Mercator Medical Group's EBITDA for the period from October to December 2020 amounted to PLN 413.6 million, which translated into net profit of PLN 370 million. These are by far the best results in the company's history (Kolejne rekordowe ..., 2021). The achieved successes prompted Mercator Medical to expand its production capacities in Thailand. Thanks to a new manufacturing facility, it will be able to produce in excess of 3.9 billion gloves per year. This is how the company's good financial position and willingness to invest were described by Witold Kruszewski, Management Board Member for Finance:

> The investment will amount to around PLN 150 million and we will finance it entirely from our own resources. At the end of the third quarter of last year, we repaid all the investment loans (PLN 75.5 million) ahead of schedule, and at the end of the fourth quarter our net cash was more than PLN 0.5 billion. We are ready to invest and our potential is further supported by profit generated on an ongoing basis.
>
> (Mercator Medical wybuduje ..., 2021)

The beneficiaries of the situation are also the company's shareholders, who are paid generous dividends. One of several key factors determining the company's success turned out to be the optimization and cost-cutting measures undertaken in 2019 at the company's individual production facilities, which, combined with dynamically growing demand due to the COVID-19 pandemic, resulted in an improvement in production capacities and price competitiveness (Mercator Medical notuje ..., 2020). The company's success was appreciated so much that it was even hailed as the "pandemic king of the stock exchange" (Najlepsza spółka ..., 2021).

6.2. Replacing others

6.2.1. Introduction

The COVID-19 pandemic had an indirect positive impact on the operations of many enterprises. Such organizations can be referred to as the "unwittingly lucky ones", i.e. those that, due to lockdowns and restrictions imposed on the functioning of many sectors of the economy, were able to replace them and take over their previous customer bases. Consequently, in numerous cases such replacing others improved their positions in the market during COVID-19 and multiplied their profits. Such enterprises represent primarily the sectors of delivery services, e-commerce platforms and online grocery stores.

The pandemic triggered a globally visible increase in demand for all types of delivery services. Limitations caused by the lack of availability of brick-and-mortar shops and the focus of customers on safety caused them to opt strongly for contactless shopping, with home delivery. This, in turn, translated into long-lasting changes in customer behaviours, motivations and habits. It was enterprises providing logistics, postal and courier services that responded to the challenge resulting from such changes and the growing demand for such services. Shops with their own delivery systems enjoyed a major advantage over their competitors and started to increase their efficiency by extending their opening hours and developing their transport infrastructure. Enterprises unable to deliver their goods to customers on their own had to rely heavily on third-party delivery services as the main channel allowing them to reach customers during the pandemic (Deloitte, 2020a).

The aforementioned changes caused by COVID-19 were accompanied by a dynamic growth of e-commerce platforms. Research conducted in nine emerging and developed economies (Brazil, China, Germany, Italy, South Korea, Russia, South Africa, Switzerland and Turkey), shows that the pandemic had a considerable impact on changes in customer online shopping behaviours and a rapid acceleration in the usage of e-commerce platforms. Online shopping volumes increased by 6–10 percentage points in the majority of product categories, with the highest growth rates in cosmetics and personal care, digital entertainment, as well as agro food and beverages (Unctad, 2020).

The pandemic had a particular impact on the market of staple products, thus increasing the dynamics of online grocery shopping. A case in point is the United States, where online grocery sales amounted to USD 1.2 billion in August 2019 and as much as USD 7.2 billion in June 2020. Over the same period, the number of online customers grew from 16.1 million to 45.6 million (Morgan, 2020).

6.2.2. Deutsche Post DHL Group and DPD Polska case studies

6.2.2.1. Deutsche Post DHL Group

DHL is the global leader in the logistics industry. It specializes in international deliveries, courier services and transport. The company employs around 380,000 people in over 220 countries around the world (DHL about us, 2021). Thanks to increased demand for the company's services, it managed to not only maintain its financial results, but also improve them during COVID-19. In the second quarter of 2020, revenue rose by 3.1% compared to the same period in 2019. At the same time, profit from operating activities (EBIT) increased by 18.6%. In the first half of 2020, revenue increased by 2% compared to 2019 (DHL

Half ..., 2020). The global COVID-19 pandemic allowed DHL and its worldwide network providing logistics services to play a significant role in delivering necessities to private customers, as well as shipping medical equipment and supplies for healthcare professionals. Against the backdrop of a global pandemic, the company's operations are being constantly adapted to identified changes in the business environment. As a globally operating company, DHL analyses pandemic risk scenarios as an integral part of its risk planning process. It employs a holistic management process that enables its business units to serve customers in the best possible way, even in emergency situations. In order to closely monitor and manage the COVID-19 situation, a special unit – the Deutsche Post DHL Group Coronavirus task force – was established with the aim of coordinating actions with international organizations such as the WHO, CDC, ECDC and Robert Koch Institute. The task force makes efforts to ensure that the company's branches worldwide comply with the regulations and legal requirements related to the pandemic. Furthermore, the newly developed business continuity policy contains global guidelines for the company's operations in 220 countries. Also, each business unit developed and implemented additional measures corresponding to specific needs of a particular country or specific requirements of a given branch (DHL Our response ..., 2020).

6.2.2.2 DPD Polska

DPD Polska is the leader of the Polish courier market and the domestic branch of the French global shipping company DPDgroup. In 2019, the company recorded revenue of almost PLN 2.1 billion and delivered 157 million parcels. DPD Poland employs more than 6,500 couriers (O DPD Polska, 2021). In 2020 the COVID-19 pandemic allowed DPD Polska to increase the volume of delivered parcels by around 15% in comparison to that of 2019. The greatest volumes were recorded in April and May 2020. On 20 April alone the number of dispatched parcels exceeded 1 million compared to 0.6 million the year before. The year 2020 also witnessed more than 20 days with more than 750,000 parcels, while in 2019 there were only two such days. According to DPD statistics, during the lockdown period, the share of parcels sent to individual customers increased to 82.5% (in 2019 it was 65%), which, according to DPD Polska managers, was mainly triggered by a huge number of orders placed by customers buying equipment necessary for remote work and learning, as well as other goods that could not be purchased directly due to lockdown restrictions and closures of brick-and-mortar shops. At that time, DPD Polska also recorded a significant rise in the share of non-cash payments. However, the company was well prepared for the aforementioned increase in the number of orders. It had developed procedures for such situations and each year applied them consistently during the hectic pre-Christmas season. As part of these procedures and preparations for the peak season, each year the company employs approximately 1,000 new couriers. Following the rise in demand for courier services, among other projects, DPD Polska put into service a new regional package sorting facility. The facility is to handle ultimately about 300,000 parcels per day, optimizing delivery processes in the southern part of Poland. This was another stage in the implementation of a new logistics model providing for the decentralization of logistics processes. Its aim is to increase the company's operational potential in line with the growing dynamics of e-commerce, as well as to shorten transport routes and reduce CO_2 emissions. During periods of increased demand for courier services such as the COVID-19 crisis, the smooth operation of the new facility was ensured by approximately 300 employees (Nowa ..., 2020; Kurierzy ..., 2020).

6.2.3. *Amazon and Allegro case studies*

6.2.3.1. *Amazon*

Amazon is one of the largest retailers in the world, operating one of the most popular e-commerce platforms. It is a marketplace for products offered by approximately 1.7 million small and medium-sized businesses around the world. Amazon has pioneered many products and services; for example, Prime, Fulfilment by Amazon, AWS, Kindle Direct Publishing, Kindle, Fire tablets, Fire TV, Amazon Echo, and Alexa (Amazon Who ..., 2021; Amazon Store, 2021). Global trends related to the surge in online commerce during the COVID-19 pandemic resulted in a significant improvement in Amazon's performance. The company's results for the third quarter of 2020 indicated that operating cash flows had increased by 56% in the last 12 months compared to the same period in 2019. In the same period, net sales were 37% higher than a year earlier. In its report for the third quarter of 2020, Amazon announced the creation of hundreds of thousands of new jobs all over the world due to, among other things, the opening of a hundred new operations buildings across North America, the creation of seasonal jobs with Amazon Air, logistics, fulfilment centres, sortation centres and global speciality fulfilment teams in the United States and Canada, the creation of corporate and technology jobs in Bellevue, Washington as well as new permanent jobs in the United Kingdom. Moreover, in India, Amazon announced the expansion of its operations network with new fulfilment centres, sortation centres, delivery stations and seasonal jobs to meet customer demand during the holiday season and increased online shopping caused by the pandemic. This significant increase in the number of jobs in a period difficult for the whole world was a huge success for Amazon. Jeff Bezos, Amazon founder and CEO, commented: "Offering jobs with industry-leading pay and great healthcare, including to entry-level and front-line employees, is even more meaningful in a time like this, and we're proud to have created over 400,000 jobs this year alone". In light of the dynamic development of the pandemic and the associated states of uncertainty about the future of the enterprise, Amazon keeps constant track of the following: actions taken by national governments and businesses in response to the pandemic, the impact of the pandemic on the global and regional economies, workforce staffing, productivity, consumer demand and spending patterns, as well as the consequences of COVID-19 for suppliers, creditors and third-party vendors. It also actively monitors and analyses risks related to inventory management, seasonality, trade agreements, strategic transactions, new products, services and technologies, possible system disruptions, government regulations, taxes, fraud, as well as payments risks, risks of fulfilment throughput and productivity. All of this is done to adequately respond to changes in current circumstances, adapt to them and ensure the company's ability to continue operations in affected areas (Amazon.com Announces ..., 2020; Amazon's COVID-19 ..., 2020).

6.2.3.2. Allegro

Allegro is the largest e-commerce marketplace platform in Poland, with more than 117,000 trading enterprises, most of which are small and medium-sized businesses based in Poland. The company employs approximately 2,200 people. Each month Allegro is visited by 20 million customers (O Allegro, 2021). During the COVID-19 pandemic, the company experienced increased demand for its e-commerce services, which allowed it to improve its operating and financial results. Summarizing the company's position, John Eastick, Allegro CFO, said: "Following the Allegro Group's exceptionally rapid growth in the first half of 2020, we strengthened our position in the third quarter and achieved 48.7% GMV growth and a positive adjusted margin". This means that the gross value of merchandise sold on the Allegro.eu Group platform in the third quarter of 2020 was 48.7% higher than in the same period of 2019. Also in the third quarter of 2020, net revenue increased by 49.7% compared to the third quarter of 2019. The number of active buyers increased by 1.4 million during this period compared to the same period a year earlier (+12.9%). This period also saw an increase in the frequency and value of customer purchases, with average spending per shopper increasing by 7.4% in the third quarter of 2020. There was also a record number of customers joining the SMART loyalty programme (during the three peak months of the pandemic in Poland, programme participants were able to enjoy free delivery of orders). During the pandemic, the company undertook a number of initiatives in response to the rise in the number of customers and orders, aimed at increasing the number of offers and ensuring competitive prices for consumers and the best possible shopping experience. Furthermore, the logistics infrastructure was prepared to handle the growing internet traffic resulting from the national quarantine and lockdown. Despite the prevalence of work performed on a remote basis, the company managed to maintain satisfactory productivity levels and uninterrupted online recruitment of the necessary personnel. It also increased capital expenditures in the IT area with a view to securing its system resources during COVID-19 and ensuring its ability to support the trading platform ecosystem during the pandemic. Marketing activities were also developed and changes in customer behaviours caused by the pandemic were continuously monitored. The impact of COVID-19 on the Group's business was also monitored on a cyclical basis and analyses were conducted with respect to possible credit losses and goodwill impairment. A number of assistance programmes for both sellers and buyers were also implemented (Allegro Komunikat ..., 2020; Allegro.eu III ..., 2020; Raport kwartalny ..., 2020).

6.2.4. Ocado Group and Frisco.pl case studies

6.2.4.1. Ocado Group

Ocado is the world's largest dedicated online supermarket. With a quarter of a million active customers, it has a 15% share of the UK online grocery market. Besides classic online shopping, the company offers the Ocado Zoom hourly grocery shopping service that allows customers to receive groceries in less than 60 minutes or at a time of their choice on the same day (Ocado Who ..., 2021). Ocado recorded a marked increase in demand for its online grocery shopping services during the COVID-19 pandemic. Responding to the significantly increased number of orders, the company reacted quickly and adequately, thus managing to serve a significantly higher number of customers than before, even in the international market, despite disruptions caused by the pandemic. The reported 27% increase in retail revenue in the first half of 2020 (compared to the same period in 2019) confirmed the company's ability to meet the unprecedented and sustained demand for online groceries. Ocado Retail achieved these levels of growth without sacrificing profitability. The first half of 2020 also saw a 28% growth in basket value (compared to the same period in 2019). In order to cope technically with the handling of the increasing number of online orders, additional solutions were introduced to ensure network capacity and development of new systems. Also, the company carried out quick and targeted range optimizations, using data from the fulfilment and order processes. The company also implemented flexible solutions to support its partners. For example, Customer Fulfilment Centres (CFCs) for Sobeys in Canada and Groupe Casino in France were launched. Along with its CFCs for Ocado Retail in the United Kingdom, the company strove to increase its capacities as quickly as possible in response to the changes brought about by the global COVID-19 pandemic. Ocado also improved its logistics, order handling, technological and engineering solutions to enable its partners to provide the best customer services under unprecedented circumstances. Commenting on the company's situation, the Chairman of Ocado Group said: "At Ocado, our role is to enable our partners to grow faster, delivering to all customers an outstanding experience, through a flexible ecosystem of CFCs, micro-fulfilment centres and store pick in the most economic and environmentally sustainable way" (Ocado Group 1H20 ..., 2020; Ocado Group Results ..., 2020; Ocado Group Our Response ..., 2020).

6.2.4.2. Frisco.pl

Frisco.pl is an online supermarket operating in Poland and offering a full range of food and non-food products. It is one of the leaders of the Polish e-grocery market (Frisco o nas, 2021). Associated with the COVID-19 pandemic, the increased interest in online grocery shopping had a clear influence on Frisco's turnover and profit. The upward trend could be observed, for example, in net sales, which for the nine months of 2020 amounted to PLN 154.9 million, compared to PLN 114.3 million for the whole year 2019. Furthermore, the number of daily online orders during the first wave of the pandemic in Poland (March–May 2020) increased by 6% compared to the pre-pandemic level (January–February 2020). During the second wave (October 2020), this rate increased to 27% compared to the pre-pandemic level. The average basket value also rose by 48% during the first wave of the pandemic compared to the period before its onset. There was also an increase in the share of loyal customers from 45% before the pandemic to 59% during the second wave. The second quarter of 2020 also saw a significant increase in basket value, in relation to not only the level before the pandemic, but also the corresponding period in 2019 – an increase of 50%. The proven business model allowed Frisco to handle the rapidly growing number of orders triggered by the pandemic, which was a manifestation of surging demand for online grocery shopping, without compromising the quality of the order fulfilment and delivery process or the speed of delivery. The model is ready to be scaled and introduced into new markets. This is confirmed by the achieved quality complaint rate of only 1%. In contrast, the order completeness rate was 99.5%. Also, during the COVID-19 pandemic, the company changed the order placement procedure, which made it possible to deliver purchases to a greater number of customers, as well as to broaden the range of available products (Frisco.pl Nr 1 ..., 2020).

6.3. Opportunity catchers

6.3.1. Introduction

Among the enterprises that profited from the COVID-19 pandemic there are groups that experienced an unprecedented increase in demand for their products or services. Such enterprises seized emerging opportunities, adjusting their activities to the identified rapid growth in customer numbers. This allowed them to achieve marked improvements in their financial results. These groups of companies belonged primarily to the IT, consulting, as well as media and entertainment sectors.

Due to the massive shift to remote working or learning during COVID-19, the demand for products and services offered by enterprises from the IT sector grew at an unprecedented pace. This mainly applies to companies offering software, platforms and tools for remote communication and work, Internet providers, companies combating and preventing cyber-attacks, as well as manufacturers and vendors of ICT infrastructure. The demand for the products and services of these companies was strengthened, among other things, by the announcement of the transition of schools and universities in 191 countries worldwide to online teaching and learning by mid-April 2020 (World Economic Forum, 2020). Another contributing factor was an enormous increase in the number of employees working on a remote basis all over the world during the COVID-19 pandemic. Research carried out by Deloitte (2020b) indicates that in 2020 around 50% of people employed or self-employed worked from home.

The situation resulting from the global pandemic also changed the position of consulting companies. Dynamic economic and social changes caused, among other things, increased demand for consulting and assistance services, as well as statistical and analytical studies in various areas of social and business life. The main trend of changes in the functioning of consulting companies during the pandemic was an increase in demand mainly for technological, business and management consulting, particularly in the areas of strategic planning, crisis management, business processes, customer cooperation or adaptation to remote work (Columbia University, 2020).

Due to pandemic-related quarantines, isolations, lockdowns and a sharp decline in social contacts resulting in much more leisure time, there was a huge increase in demand for services offered by media and entertainment companies operating primarily in the online space. They include, for example, streaming platforms, computer game manufacturers, social media or television stations (KPMG, 2020; Capgemini, 2020).

6.3.2. Microsoft and NTT System case studies

6.3.2.1. Microsoft

Microsoft is an American IT corporation with a global reach, a manufacturer of operating systems, office software, cloud solutions (Microsoft Azure), as well as remote work and communication tools, such as the MS Teams platform. The company has 166,475 employees worldwide (Facts about …, 2021). During the COVID-19 pandemic, Microsoft actively supported enterprises and individuals in their digital transformation processes carried out in the business, educational and social spheres, helping them to build resilience in the face of an unprecedented crisis. Therefore, it continued to develop dynamic tech intensity, i.e. adopting the best digital tools and platforms to enhance and improve the products and services offered to customers. Thanks to these actions in response to the increased demand for IT solutions during the pandemic, in 2020 Microsoft managed to improve its financial results in comparison to those of 2019. During the year ended 30 June 2020, revenue grew by almost 14%, operating income by over 23% and total assets by over 5%. Furthermore, commercial cloud surpassed USD 50 billion in revenue for the first time – up 36% year-over-year. Microsoft Teams reached 115 million daily active users during the pandemic. This growth reflects the continued demand for Teams as the lifeline for remote and hybrid work and learning during the pandemic, helping people and organizations in every industry stay agile and resilient in this new era. The company also notes that the continued impact of the COVID-19 pandemic on its business will be conditioned by the following factors: the duration of the pandemic; actions taken by governments, businesses and individuals in response to the pandemic and potential for recession and financial market instability, all of which could adversely affect customer, business and government expenditures on IT solutions and their ability to pay for Microsoft products and services. Accordingly, the company continually monitors pandemic developments and changes caused by it, proactively manages identified risk factors and takes measures aimed at protecting its business. Pandemic-related uncertainty also affects Microsoft management's accounting estimates and assumptions, which could result in greater variability in a variety of areas that depend on these estimates and assumptions, including investments, receivables and forward-looking guidance (Microsoft Annual ..., 2020; Microsoft Teams ..., 2020; How Microsoft ..., 2020).

6.3.2.2. NTT System

NTT System is Poland's largest manufacturer of desktop computers sold under both its own brand and contract brands. The company is one of the leading distributors of computer accessories, components and peripherals in Poland. It employs over 120 people (NTT System o nas, 2021). During the course of the COVID-19 pandemic, the company recorded increased demand for computer hardware as well as tools facilitating remote work and learning. In addition, the demand for computers triggered increased demand for computer components, accessories and peripherals. These trends are clearly visible in NTT System's results for the first half of 2020. Sales revenue increased by more than 23% compared to the same period in 2019, while operating profit rose by more than 66%. To meet the challenges of the pandemic, NTT System monitored its operating cost structure on an ongoing basis and adjusted its inventories to changes occurring in the market and increased demand for its products. If the pandemic were to last much longer, the company takes into consideration the possibility of a fall in demand caused by deterioration in customers' purchasing power and risks on the supply side resulting from disruptions in the continuity of supplies and reduced production capacities. However, the supply chain risk is regarded as low, due to the gradual recovery of the logistics sector in Europe and beyond to its normal mode of operation. Similarly, the company also recognizes risks on the sales side as low. Admittedly, the closure of shopping centres, including retail outlets of some of NTT System's customers, resulted in reduced sales to many customers. However, the majority of NTT System's retail segment customers use commercial premises with surface areas that were not subject to pandemic restrictions. Furthermore, the company cooperates with enterprises running very efficient online shops, so in the opinion of the management, if the logistics facilities function smoothly, sales in this channel should be characterized by growing interest on the part of customers and high growth potential. Another opportunity for growth emerges also in the company's actions aimed at increasing the volume of sales and rental of mobile equipment to business enterprises and public sector institutions obliged to make such equipment available to employees working on a remote basis. During COVID-19, NTT System also launched its Blue Bolt, a temperature measuring device installed at an entry to a building and preventing anybody whose temperature exceeds the set limit from entry. Blue Bolt is operated via smartphones (NTT System Sprawozdanie ..., 2020; NTT System Śródroczne ..., 2020; Aktualności NTT System, 2020).

6.3.3. Deloitte and PwC Polska case studies

6.3.3.1 Deloitte

Deloitte is an international consulting firm with approximately 245,000 employees in 150 countries around the world. Its business areas include audit and assurance, consulting, risk and financial advisory, risk management, tax and legal, and related services (About Deloitte, 2021). During the COVID-19 pandemic, Deloitte recorded an improvement in its financial results due to, among other factors, increased demand for advisory services, particularly in the areas of risk management, crisis management, strategic management and corporate adaptation to the legal and regulatory environment shaped by the pandemic. Total revenue increased to USD 47.6 billion, of which the Consulting business area contributed the most at USD 19.8 billion (compared to 2019 total revenue of USD 46.2 billion, including USD 18.7 billion generated by Consulting). Other business areas, for example Risk Advisory and Tax and Legal, also recorded increases in revenue. Also in 2020, the total headcount rose by 7.3% as compared to that of 2019. During COVID-19, Deloitte focused on identifying ways to support employees, clients and other members of communities in dealing with the pandemic crisis and helping them to prepare to function in the post-pandemic world. Despite the temporary closure of all Deloitte University facilities following pandemic-related restrictions, the company continued to provide training opportunities for its professionals and experts by launching Cura, a virtual platform to deliver customized learning content instantly to approximately 330,000 Deloitte people. Moreover, all the while during COVID-19 Deloitte also maintained its commitment to professional development and promotion programmes, understanding that building leaders for the future was more important than ever. During the pandemic, Deloitte actively assisted companies in managing the unexpected, anticipating the impact of COVID-19 and adapting to long-term trends of change. A case in point in this respect is the Deloitte COVID-19 Global Recovery Navigator, which consolidates and enables analysis of key health, social, and economic data to inform government and private sector decision-making and activities based on actions taken by others around the world. In addition, The Deloitte Global Security Office (GSO) monitored the effects of the pandemic on the company on an ongoing basis, developed recovery strategies and assisted in reviewing Deloitte's business continuity and response plans with clients. Also, comprehensive security plans were developed and proactive steps were taken to mitigate the overall impact of the COVID-19 risk on Deloitte Global's risk profile (Deloitte Global Impact Report, 2020).

6.3.3.2. PwC Polska

PwC Polska is the Polish branch of PwC, a global firm providing professional consultancy services. In Poland, PwC has seven operational offices located in major cities, as well as Financial Crime Units in Gdańsk and Warsaw, Shared Service Centres in Katowice and Opole and a PwC IT Services Unit in Lublin. The PwC companies in Poland employ over 6,100 people (PwC Polska o nas, 2021). The company supports entrepreneurs in the areas of business transformation, auditing, legal and tax issues and the use of new technologies. The year 2020 was different for all consulting firms all over the world. During that time, PwC Polska actively supported businesses in meeting the challenges of the COVID-19 pandemic and significantly increased the scale of its social engagement. In this respect, the company provided financial and consultancy support to 9,531 individuals, 144 NGOs and social enterprises and ten hospitals. The increased demand for consultancy services during the pandemic resulted in PwC Polska's increasing its gross revenue by 18% on a year-over-year basis in the financial year ended 30 June 2020. During the pandemic, the company made significant investments in new technologies, developed business continuity procedures and remote and hybrid work models, and was thus able to conduct its operations despite COVID-19 issues. The company's digital transformation process was significantly accelerated and numerous measures were taken to strengthen the digital competencies of employees, clients and individuals whose position in the market may be at risk due to skills mismatches with the changing reality in the aftermath of the pandemic (e.g. in the areas of data analytics, process automation, artificial intelligence and robotization). In addition, the human capital planning process was updated by building appropriate training and workshop programmes. PwC Polska also developed plans for rapid response and business adaptation to contingencies resulting from the COVID-19 pandemic and kept abreast of pandemic-induced changes in customer behaviours and expectations, as well as in the legal and regulatory environment. To meet increased client demand for consultancy services, PwC Legal experts operated a toll-free, 24/7 hotline where clients could seek advice on issues related to COVID-19 (PwC Polska rok …, 2020).

6.3.4. Netflix and Cyfrowy Polsat case studies

6.3.4.1. Netflix

Netflix is the world's leading streaming entertainment service with 204 million paid memberships in over 190 countries enjoying TV series, documentaries and feature films across a wide variety of genres and languages (Netflix Company …, 2021). During the pandemic, the previously high global interest in Netflix products and services continued to grow dynamically due to the TV watching and streaming surge during the lockdown. This trend was reflected in the company's financial results. In 2020, the company's revenue rose on a year-over-year basis as follows (Netflix Four …, 2020):

- close to 14% in the UCAN area (United States and Canada),
- over 40% in the EMEA area (Europe, Middle East and Africa),

- almost 13% in the LATAM area (Latin America),
- over 60% in the APAC area (Asia-Pacific).

Furthermore, Netflix registered 15.77 million new subscribers in the first quarter of 2020 and 10.09 million in the second quarter. This was the biggest jump in the number of subscribers in the company's history. From the very beginning of the pandemic the company was analyzing current developments, identifying material risks and taking proactive measures to mitigate operational, employee and other risks to business associated with the pandemic. Referring to the company's activities during COVID-19, Jay C. Hoag, Lead Independent Director, said:

> We are focused on health and safety, and the general welfare of those around us. We are working to protect the well-being of our employees, and are taking steps to assist those directly impacted, while ensuring that we continue to operate our business as best we can under these difficult circumstances.
>
> (Netflix 2020 ..., 2021)

During the pandemic, Netflix temporarily slowed production operations, which caused an improvement in its profit margins. Aware of the uncertainties generated by the global pandemic, the company took measures aimed at the following: maintaining its ability to attract new members and retain existing members, maintaining and improving its ability to compete effectively, maintaining and expanding device platforms for streaming, preventing adverse fluctuations in consumer usage of service, preventing service interruptions, mitigating production risks associated with the pandemic, monitoring competitors and changes in consumer adoption of different modes of viewing in-home filmed entertainment (Netflix 2020 ..., 2021; Netflix Letter ..., 2020; Netflix Subscriber, 2020).

6.3.4.2. Cyfrowy Polsat

Cyfrowy Polsat is Poland's largest and Europe's fourth largest satellite platform. It is the parent company of the Polsat Group, i.e. one of the largest Polish corporations and the leading media and telecommunications group in the region, with 5.6 million customers receiving in total 17.4 million services (Grupa Polsat o nas, 2021). During the COVID-19 pandemic the Cyfrowy Polsat Group maintained a high level of demand for its communications and home entertainment services, including premium content (pay-TV), which did not suffer despite the temporary closure of part of the sales network. It also managed to continuously generate a wide stream of cash flows, which ensured security in terms of ongoing liquidity. The company ended the third quarter of 2020 with results that exceeded the expectations of market analysts. During this period, sales revenue increased by 3.8% compared to the third quarter in 2019. In addition, the third quarter also saw a strong increase in the number of contract services by 581,000, up 4% compared to the same period last year. The customer defection rate was also reduced to 6.1%, which indicates high levels of customer satisfaction with the quality of provided services. Negative changes observed during the pandemic included, among others, a contraction in the television advertising market (especially in the second quarter of 2020). During the pandemic, Cyfrowy Polsat immediately took a number of steps to ensure business continuity and limit the impact of negative changes caused by the pandemic. It turned out that the strategy, nature and diversity of the business of the Cyfrowy Polsat Group made it resistant to the negative effects of the pandemic. Mirosław Błaszczyk, President of the Cyfrowy Polsat Management Board, commented:

> The nature and diversity of our business activities have made us resistant to the situation in which we all have found ourselves. At the same time, the third quarter allowed us to rebuild the results of the media segment, which was most severely affected by the spring lockdown. Having a stable financial situation, with a view to further development of the Group, we conducted large investment projects.
>
> (Grupa Cyfrowy Polsat podsumowuje ..., 2020)

The diversified and subscription-based business model provided the company with stable and predictable revenue streams during the pandemic. Revenue in the retail segment was also positively impacted by changes in the prices of mobile services. During the lockdown, the company made efforts to replace direct sales channels with remote ones and then significantly intensified sales through its network of retail outlets, which had been under lockdown until May 2020. To adapt the business to the conditions resulting from the COVID-19 pandemic, cost-cutting initiatives were also implemented in the areas of distribution, marketing, as well as customer service and retention. The result was a 3.6% fall in such costs in the third quarter of 2020, as compared to the same period in 2019. The company also decided to increase its inventories of end user equipment as security against the risk of interruptions in supply chains in consequence of the COVID-19 pandemic (Grupa Kapitałowa Cyfrowy Polsat S.A. Rozszerzony ..., 2020; Grupa Cyfrowy Polsat podsumowuje ..., 2020; Grupa Kapitałowa Cyfrowy Polsat S.A. Wyniki ..., 2020; Cyfrowy Polsat S.A. Podsumowanie ..., 2020).

6.4. Creative despite adversities

6.4.1. Introduction

For companies in some sectors, the COVID-19 pandemic reduced business opportunities and worsened operating conditions, leaving, however, some niches allowing such enterprises to distinguish themselves. The insurance sector is a case in point. Sharing the opinion about numerous challenges faced by this sector, Deloitte analysts also draw attention to a catalogue of opportunities resulting from the pandemic, for example (Deloitte, 2020c): the possibility of recovery in health and life insurance, the broadening of product offers, the simplification of processes and procedures, technological leaps and new innovative solutions. The catering industry was hit by restrictions similar to, or even more severe than those experienced by the insurance sector. Quite often heavily indebted already before the pandemic, many catering businesses had to fight factually for survival after its onslaught (Gastronomia walczy ..., 2020). However, even in this highly competitive sector there are examples of creative attitudes based on the belief in success and personal determination (Jak w pandemii ..., 2020). The big losers of the pandemic are also mountain regions and the ski industry (Regiony górskie ..., 2020). But even in this sector there was space for creative entrepreneurs.

6.4.2. Allstate and PZU case studies

6.4.2.1. Allstate

Allstate is an American insurance company with very rich traditions. Founded in 1931, it was one of the pioneers of the insurance industry and has continued to this day to protect Americans' assets and property. Allstate is headquartered in Northbrook, Illinois and is the largest publicly traded personal insurance provider in the US (Allstate History ..., 2020). In response to the COVID-19 pandemic, the company launched a special programme, Allstate Benefits, which included the following components (Allstate Benefits ..., 2020):

- commitment to support employees, partners and customers during the unprecedented pandemic,
- advanced business continuity planning to ensure 100% uptime,
- ensuring the best service from the customer service and claims handling teams,
- coverage of claims related to COVID-19 by a wide range of insurance products,
- adjusting settlement processes to the constraints faced by customers financially affected by the pandemic.

It is worth noting that Allstate decided to demonstrate its social responsibility during the pandemic. The company's mission for that difficult period was formulated as "helping our customers and communities to cope" (Allstate is ..., 2020). Specific actions taken included, for example, paying back USD 1 billion to customers through Shelter-in-Place Payback, as well as donating millions of dollars to various community outreach and other initiatives. In its communications, the company emphasized that such a philosophy of social sensitivity had always constituted an element of its corporate culture. The company also strongly promoted its Allstate mobile application allowing customers to view policy information, file claims, provide proof of insurance or obtain roadside assistance (Allstate is ..., 2020). Allstate also placed particular emphasis on the promotion of life insurance, arguing that COVID-19 was a condition covered under Allstate Benefits and voluntary life insurance policies. This contributed to increased sales of these insurance products (Allstate Benefits ..., 2020).

6.4.2.2. PZU

The PZU Group is Poland's largest insurance corporation. PZU's history dates back to the 1920s. Following the political transformation after 1989, the state-owned enterprise Państwowy Zakład Ubezpieczeń was transformed into a joint stock company, with the State Treasury as its sole shareholder. In December 1991, PZU established its subsidiary PZU Życie and transferred there its portfolio of life insurance contracts. At present, the PZU Group also comprises other financial entities (Historia PZU, 2020). Following the outbreak of the COVID-19 pandemic, many insurance company customers learned that their policies did not cover pandemic risk. However, in its March 2020 announcement, PZU informed its customers as follows:

> PZU Życie SA provides its customers with insurance cover also in the case of an epidemic or pandemic. This means that contracting COVID-19, as well as the consequences of the disease, are covered by standard insurance protection. We will pay the costs of a hospital stay, provided that the insurance contract conditions are met, including: medical documentation is available, a hospital stay had a minimum required duration, the diagnosed disease is included in the contract, the disease has been treated in hospital (being quarantined does not constitute a basis for the payment of an indemnity).
>
> (Ubezpieczenie w PZU ..., 2020)

With such an attitude, the company gained increased customer confidence. Another very good move was the introduction of the new "Remote COVID Care" service as a programme targeted at people with suspected SARS-CoV-2 coronavirus infection or with a confirmed COVID-19 result and quarantined at home. PZU also provided patients who had previously purchased the medical package with pulse oximeters, thanks to which they were able to monitor their pulse and blood oxygen levels. In addition, the insurer provided free consultations with internal medicine specialists and psychologists (Opieka ..., 2020). This service was complemented by PZU with different types of guidebooks with medical recommendations for customers directly affected by the virus (Poradnik ..., 2020). Although PZU did not achieve all its business objectives in 2020, it managed to maintain its growth potential and ensure the stability of its financial security, especially its solvency ratio (PZU ..., 2020).

6.4.3. *Fisza Concept by Marcin Budynek and Ptak-Team Ski School case studies*

6.4.3.1. *Fisza Concept by Marcin Budynek*

Fisza Concept by Marcin Budynek is a restaurant located in the city of Augustów, Poland, which is a typical tourist city. It was founded by Marcin Budynek, a famous Polish chef who had previously worked in many well-known restaurants and appeared in numerous television programmes. Among other things, he currently runs his own culinary academy (Akademia ..., 2020). Before the onset of the COVID-19 pandemic, Fisza operated in an absolutely traditional way, serving dishes on site. After the onset of the pandemic, in view of the long periods of closure of the catering industry in Poland, Fisza completely changed its previous approach to running a restaurant business. As a first step, the restaurant owner focused on dramatically strengthening communication with customers, using his Facebook profile. Subsequent Facebook posts informed customers about novelties introduced by Fisza. The numerous and very creative actions aimed at keeping the restaurant afloat included the following (Tawerna ..., 2020):

- broadening the offer with occasional gifts to celebrate the Mother's Day, religious holidays, St. Valentine's Day and other special days such as birthdays and name days,
- using various events, such as Augustów Days, to promote the restaurant's offer,
- introducing dynamic changes in the menu, particularly a weekly lunch menu and dishes based on seasonal produce,
- introducing a breakfast menu during the holiday season,
- introducing and intensively promoting festivals of different foods,
- inviting celebrity chefs specializing in the preparation of specific dishes for one-day performances and providing customers with video instruction,
- broadening the offer with packaged food with a longer shelf life (e.g. pâtés, jams, cakes, snacks) and launching a new brand "Fisza to go",
- launching the production and sale of semi-finished products for final preparation at home, supplemented by instructional videos for customers,
- informing customers of various awards and distinctions received by the owner, e.g. on Tripadvisor,
- extending opening hours to allow customers to buy take-away products more easily,
- establishing cooperation with restaurateurs in other cities to broaden the scope of promotional activities,
- introducing catering services and occasional menus dedicated to particular holidays,
- developing cooperation with courier companies to ensure the shipment of products to customers,
- introducing various promotions,
- launching a new brand "Party Box" in connection with a separate line of products for home parties.

These numerous and highly imaginative measures allowed the restaurant to not only survive, but also develop intensively.

6.4.3.2. Ptak-Team Ski School

Ptak-Team Ski School is an enterprise based in Zakopane, the winter capital of Poland. Its offer for customers includes, for example, ski training programmes conducted mainly in Italian mountains, training in sports skiing, organization of sports events and competitions, daily ski training events at the Suche and Rusin-ski stations, as well as summer camps for children and adults. Ptak-Team Ski School is one of few such enterprises in Poland holding official authorizations granted by the Polish Ski Association to organize qualified courses for ski demonstrators, ski assistant instructors and ski instructors. The school is also authorized to conduct examinations for candidates wishing to obtain the aforementioned qualifications (Szkoła ..., 2020). The owner of the enterprise is Bartłomiej Ptak, the best ski instructor in Poland in 2016. The introduction of very high restrictions in the functioning of the ski sector in Poland and the majority of other European countries forced the owner to introduce changes in the previously used business model. The newly introduced measures included the following (Ptak-Team ..., 2020):

- intensifying communication with a broad base of customers acquired in previous years by means of Facebook,
- recognizing the possibilities to conduct sports ski training despite the existing restrictions; yet in compliance with the applicable regulations (in consultation with the Polish Ski Association),
- informing customers of the possibilities to participate in ski training based on preparations for ski sports competitions and possession of required sports licences,
- maintaining cooperation with Suche Ski u Jędrola, one of few ski stations open in Poland, a specialist in the organization of sports training events,
- introducing additional services such as ski maintenance, agency in purchasing ski equipment,
- introducing promotions in the form of ski training passes,
- adjusting ski training hours to customers' preferences and the ski station's capacity.

Consequently, thanks to the owner's ingenuity, during the winter season 2020/2021, Ptak-Team Ski School was one of very few ski schools in Poland that managed to maintain the continuity of its business. This resulted in a high increase in customers' interest in other services offered again from mid-February 2021 after the relaxation of restrictions in the ski sector.

6.5. The key success factors of the analyzed enterprises during the COVID-19 pandemic

Based on the analysis of the risk management practices presented above, we identified and grouped the key success factors (Figure 6.1). The 44 identified success factors were divided into seven groups. The majority of the groups related to management processes followed in the enterprises under examination and comprising strategy, business model, resources, operational flexibility, products or services and relations with customers. Four of the identified factors were related to the business environment of the analyzed enterprises.

6.5.1. Strategy

In some of the discussed enterprises, factors related to operational strategies turned out to be key success factors. These are primarily factors that directly

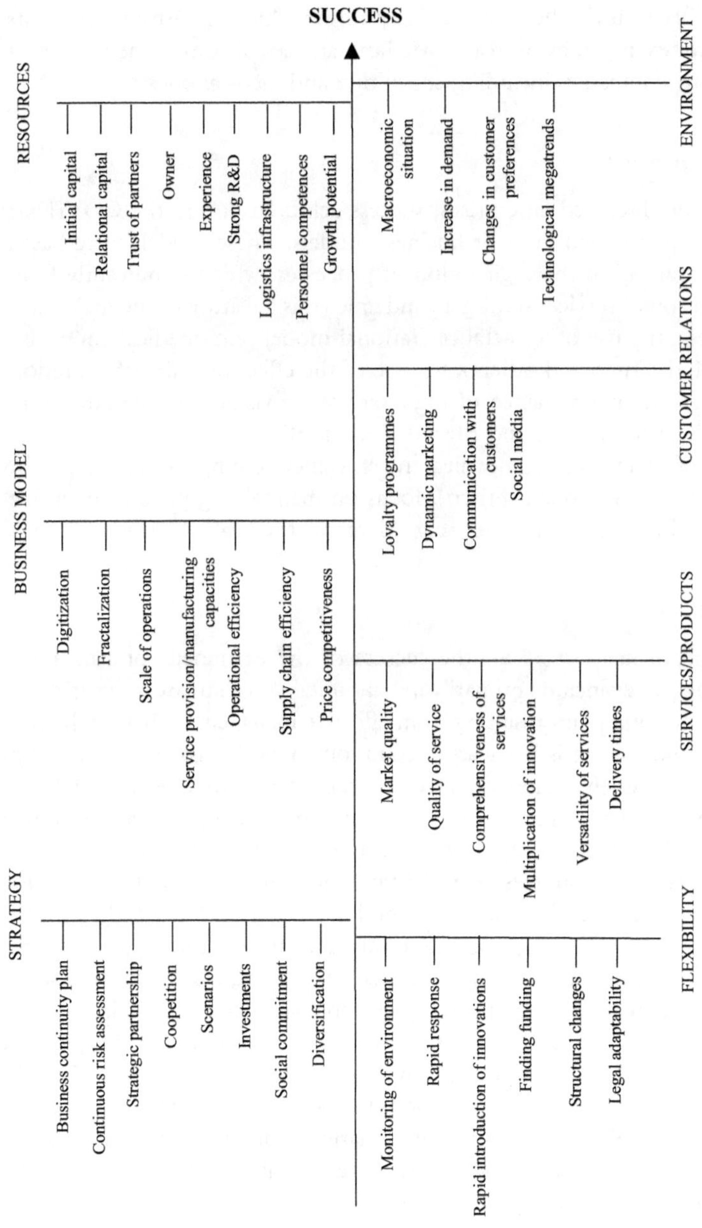

Figure 6.1 Factors determining the success of the enterprises under analysis during the COVID-19 pandemic

demonstrate the functioning of professional strategic risk management, such as using business continuity plans (e.g. CVS Health and Allstate), conducting a continuous risk assessment (e.g. Cardinal Health), using scenario management (typical of courier companies) or diversification visible in the media and entertainment sector. The vision and ability to cooperate within the framework of a strategic partnership (especially in the case of Pfizer and BioNTech), as well as the ability to coopetition (visible particularly in the case of the Fisza enterprise), were very important too. The strategic factors also include intensive investments, represented, for example, by Mercator Medical, and social commitment, demonstrated by many companies including consulting and medical ones.

6.5.2. Business model

For many of the discussed enterprises, success achieved during the COVID-19 pandemic was determined by their business models. These models were based, among other things, on the digitization of processes, which significantly facilitates the provision of services during a pandemic (it is a feature of the majority of the companies), the use of a fractal operational model (e.g. medical enterprises such as LuxMed, Frisco and others), the use of the effect of scales of operations (e.g. Amazon), the maintenance of high service provision and manufacturing capacities (primarily Amazon and Mercator Medical), the operational efficiency characteristic of all analyzed companies, the efficiency of supply chains (e.g. CVS Health, the Ocado Group and Frisco), focus on maintaining price competitiveness through optimization measures (e.g. Mercator Medical).

6.5.3. Resources

Another group of key factors for the success of the examined companies was resource factors. They include primarily initial capital that in many respects determined a good starting point resulting from effective management before the outbreak of the pandemic (this is a feature common to all discussed companies) as well as previous experience allowing the companies to accelerate the availability of products with high demand during the pandemic (particularly the cases of Pfizer and BioMaxima). Relational capital and trust of partners constitute other success factors related to resources (e.g. Allstate and Cardinal Health). For some enterprises, particularly small ones (e.g. Fisza, Ptak-Team Ski School) the owner's personal commitment, his vision and determination turned out to be of crucial importance for success. Another important factor is strong R&D. In the cases of Pfizer and BioMaxima, it allowed the relatively rapid launching of such impatiently expected products as tests and vaccines. Some of the companies relied heavily on excellent logistics infrastructure (especially courier companies, Cardinal Health, Amazon). Due to the combination of various factors and circumstances, the enterprises referred to as direct "medical" beneficiaries, replacing others and opportunity catchers had a considerable growth potential during the pandemic. The feature common to all the analyzed enterprises was highly competent personnel.

6.5.4. *Flexibility*

Flexibility turned out to be an important category of success factors during the COVID-19 pandemic. In this group, the following factors emerged: monitoring the environment to support the decision-making process (very characteristic of Amazon), responding quickly to changing business conditions (a feature common to all examined companies, but especially those referred to as creative despite adversities), introducing novelties quickly as a means of attracting and retaining customers (e.g. Fisza), the ability to obtain financing for planned projects, implementing organizational changes aimed at adjusting the management system to the pandemic conditions (e.g. Deutsche Post DHL Group) and the ability to adapt to frequently changing legal regulations (e.g. Fisza and Ptak-Team Ski School).

6.5.5. *Services/products*

During the COVID-19 pandemic, traditional sources of success directly linked to provided services and products, as well as their perception by customers, also proved their worth. These include the market quality of services or products perceived by customers as an important strength (the feature common to all discussed enterprises), the quality of provided services (e.g. the medical companies and Frisco), the complexity of services offered in a particular field (e.g. the medical companies, Ptak-Team Ski School), the multiplication of innovations allowing a company to distinguish itself in the market (Fisza's spectacular achievements), the universal character of offered services resulting in the maintenance of high demand for them during the COVID-19 pandemic (e.g. consulting firms) and delivery times, very important for such companies as Deutsche Post DHL Group, DPD Polska, Amazon, Allegro, Ocado Group and Frisco.

6.5.6. *Customer relations*

A very important role in the activities of the analyzed enterprises was also played by customer relations, which facilitate ensuring customers' interest in offered products and services, stimulate their purchase behaviours and strengthen their loyalty. This group contains the following four factors: the use of loyalty programmes (e.g. Allegro), dynamic marketing aimed at promoting companies as well as their products and services (visible especially in the case of the companies offering consumer goods), communication with customers by means of modern channels (visible in the case of the insurance and medical companies, Fisza and the Ptak-Team Ski School), and a high level of activity in social media, especially Facebook.

6.5.7. *Environment*

Besides the previously discussed factors shaped by the enterprises under analysis, there are also those that have their source in the environment. These include:

a favourable macroeconomic situation characteristic of the sales markets of the enterprises, an increase in demand for their services and products as a direct result of the pandemic (especially the companies referred to as direct "medical" beneficiaries and replacing others), favourable changes in customer preferences, already apparent before the COVID-19 pandemic and strengthened during its course (especially the courier companies, Amazon, Allegro and Netflix), as well as megatrends with a technological basis, such as the development of the internet, the growing number of non-cash transactions and the development of e-commerce, which were advantageous for many of the enterprises, particularly the courier companies, Amazon, Allegro, Ocado Group, Frisco, Netflix and Cyfrowy Polsat.

Similarly to the case of factors determining failure (Chapter 5), the conducted research revealed a very numerous and diverse set of success factors. These factors in different configurations contributed to the success of the examined enterprises during the COVID-19 pandemic. The research also allowed the identification of the enterprises' diversified profiles of behaviours during the course of the pandemic. Due to the nature of provided services or manufactured goods, some of them became direct beneficiaries of the pandemic, others (referred to as replacing others) employed a substitution strategy by replacing those competitors in the sector whose business approach was not adequate for the challenges of COVID-19. Still other enterprises followed a management philosophy incorporating openness to opportunities. And last but not least, there was a group of companies demonstrating exceptional creativity despite the adverse impact of external business conditions.

References

About Deloitte. Learn about our global network of member firms (2021). www2.deloitte.com/an/en/footerlinks/about-ddc.html (Access: 23.01.2021).

Akademia kulinarna Marcina Budynka (2020). http://marcinbudynek.pl/ (Access: 10.02.2021).

Aktualności NTT system (2020). https://ntt.pl/aktualnosci/ (Access: 22.01.2021).

Allegro.eu III kwartał 2020 Prezentacja wyników (2020). www.allegro.eu/static-files/e19345ef-b42f-4652-922e-fc2a8c70950c (Access: 19.01.2021).

Allegro Komunikat prasowy (2020). www.allegro.eu/static-files/70cf80af-ad04-4081-8e16-8a8b079bb650 (Access: 19.01.2021).

Allstate benefits COVID-19 update (2020). www.allstatevoluntary.com/covid19/ (Access: 10.02.2021).

Allstate history & timeline (2020). www.allstate.com/about/history-timeline.aspx (Access: 10.02.2021).

Allstate is here to help (2020). www.allstate.com/covid.aspx (Access: 10.03.2021).

Amazon.com announces third quarter results (2020). https://press.aboutamazon.com/news-releases/news-release-details/amazoncom-announces-third-quarter-results/ (Access: 19.01.2021).

Amazon's COVID-19 blog: Updates on how we're responding to the crisis (2020). www.aboutamazon.com/news/company-news/amazons-covid-19-blog-updates-on-how-were-responding-to-the-crisis (Access: 19.01.2021).

Amazon store (2021). www.aboutamazon.com/what-we-do/amazon-store (Access: 19.01.2021).

Amazon who we are (2021). www.aboutamazon.com/about-us (Access: 19.01.2021).

BioMaxima. Firma od testów na COVID-19 zarobiła krocie (2021). www.money.pl/gielda/biomaxima-firma-od-testow-na-covid-19-zarobila-krocie-6594776812346144a.html (Access: 3.02.2021).

BioMaxima wprowadziła nowy test genetyczny wykrywający m.in. SARS-CoV-2 (2020). www.bankier.pl/wiadomosc/BioMaxima-wprowadzila-nowy-test-genetyczny-wykrywajacy-m-in-SARS-CoV-2-8028309.html (Access: 3.02.2021).

Biotech nie boi się pandemii, inwestorzy też. Koronawirus uderzył w nierówny sposób (2020). www.forbes.pl/technologie/spolki-biotechnologiczne-na-celowniku-polskich-inwestorow-w-czasie-koronawirusa/hmd4b41 (Access: 2.02.2021).

Branża medyczna w obliczu COVID-19 (2020). https://biznes.newseria.pl/biuro-prasowe/zdrowie/branza-medyczna-w-obliczu,b1783262025 (Access: 2.02.2021).

Capgemini (2020). COVID-19 outbreak global outlook. Media & Entertainment Industry. www.capgemini.com/wp-content/uploads/2020/06/Covid-19-Impact-on-Media-Entertainment-industry.pdf (Access: 13.01.2021).

Cardinal health chosen to distribute COVID-19 vaccines in Ohio (2020). https://drugstorenews.com/cardinal-health-chosen-distribute-covid-19-vaccines-ohio (Access: 6.02.2021).

Cardinal health prepares to distribute coronavirus vaccines (2020). https://eu.dispatch.com/story/business/2020/11/05/cardinal-sets-aside-1-billion-opioid-litigation/6166784002/ (Access: 7.02.2021).

Columbia University (2020). COVID-19's effects on the consulting industry. www.careereducation.columbia.edu/news/june-2020/covid-19s-effects-consulting-industry (Access: 13.01.2021).

COVID-19 – Cardinal health global preparedness (2020). www.cardinalhealth.com/en/cmp/ext/corp/cardinal-health-covid-19-response-plan.html (Access: 5.02.2021).

COVID-19 impact on Cardinal Health Inc.'s revenue and operations (2020). https://store.globaldata.com/report/gdhc008ci--covid-19-impact-on-cardinal-health-inc-s-revenue-and-operations-medical-devices/ (Access: 5.02.2021).

CVS health reports third quarter results with diversified assets delivering strong enterprise performance (2020). https://cvshealth.com/news-and-insights/press-releases/cvs-health-reports-results-2020-q3 (Access: 2.02.2021).

CVS health response to the COVID-19 outbreak (2020). https://cvshealth.com/news-and-insights/press-releases/cvs-health-response-to-the-covid-19-outbreak (Access: 2.02.2021).

Cyfrowy Polsat S.A. Podsumowanie wyników za 3Q 2020 r. dla analityków i inwestorów (2020). https://grupapolsat.pl/sites/default/files/documents/brief_3q20_pl.pdf (Access: 22.01.2021).

Deloitte (2020a). Last mile delivery after COVID-19: A world of things to solve. www2.deloitte.com/global/en/pages/about-deloitte/articles/covid-19/last-mile-customer-delivery-after-covid-19.html (Access: 12.01.2021).

Deloitte (2020b). How Covid-19 contributes to a long-term boost in remote working. www2.deloitte.com/ch/en/pages/human-capital/articles/how-covid-19-contributes-to-a-long-term-boost-in-remote-working.html (Access: 13.01.2021).

Deloitte (2020c). Wpływ pandemii COVID-19 na działalność ubezpieczeniową: szanse i zagrożenia. www2.deloitte.com/pl/pl/pages/financial-services/articles/

wplyw-pandemii-COVID-19-na-dzialalnosc-ubezpieczeniowa-szanse-i-zagrozenia.html (Access: 9.02.2021).

Deloitte global impact report (2020). www2.deloitte.com/content/dam/Deloitte/global/Documents/About-Deloitte/about-deloitte-global-report-full-version-2020.pdf (Access: 23.01.2021).

DHL half-year report (2020). www.dpdhl.com/content/dam/dpdhl/en/media-center/investors/documents/interim-reports/2020/DPDHL-Half-year-Report-2020.pdf (Access: 14.01.2021).

DHL about us (2021). www.dhl.com/global-en/home/about-us.html (Access: 14.01.2021).

DHL our response to Covid-19 (2020). www.dhl.com/global-en/home/global-news-alerts/global-messages/coronavirus.html (Access: 14.01.2021).

Facts about Microsoft (2021). https://news.microsoft.com/facts-about-microsoft/#About (Access: 21.01.2021).

Firmy biotechnologiczne rosną na wirusie. To już bańka? (2020). https://cyfrowa.rp.pl/technologie/46159-firmy-biotechnologiczne-rosna-na-wirusie-to-banka (Access: 2.02.2021).

Frisco o nas (2021). www.frisco.pl/stn,o_nas (Access: 20.01.2021).

Frisco.pl Nr 1 na warszawskim rynku e-zakupów spożywczych (2020). https://grupaeurocash.pl/assets/media/frisco-draft-pol-final.pdf (Access: 20.01.2021).

Gastronomia walczy o przetrwanie. Zadłużenie sektora było duże już przed pandemią (2020). www.wiadomoscihandlowe.pl/artykul/gastronomia-walczy-o-przetrwanie-zadluzenie-sektora-bylo-duze-juz-przed-pandemia (Access: 9.02.2021).

Gracz w rękawicach. Dzięki pandemii dołączył do grona najbogatszych Polaków (2020). www.forbes.pl/biznes/mercator-medical-pandemia-postawila-producenta-rekawic-w-dwuznacznej-sytuacji/whfm6yk (Access: 5.02.2021).

Grupa Cyfrowy Polsat podsumowuje III kwartał. Komunikat prasowy (2020). https://grupapolsat.pl/sites/default/files/documents/2020-11-10_grupa_cyfrowy_polsat_podsumowuje_iii_kwartal_2020_komunikat_prasowy.pdf (Access: 22.01.2021).

Grupa Kapitałowa Cyfrowy Polsat S.A. Rozszerzony skonsolidowany raport półroczny za okres trzech miesięcy zakończony 30 września 2020 roku (2020). https://grupapolsat.pl/sites/default/files/documents/cps_raport_kwartalny_za_3_kw:2020.pdf (Access: 22.01.2021).

Grupa Kapitałowa Cyfrowy Polsat S.A. Wyniki finansowe 3Q'2020 r. (2020). https://grupapolsat.pl/sites/default/files/documents/prezentacja_3q_2020_pl_fv.pdf (Access: 22.01.2021).

Grupa Polsat o nas (2021). https://grupapolsat.pl/pl/nas/w-skrocie (Access: 22.01.2021).

Historia Pfizera - koncernu, który wywołał euforię informacją o szczepionce na koronawirusa (2020). https://businessinsider.com.pl/firmy/strategie/pfizer-co-to-za-firma-szczepionka-na-koronawirusa-a-wczesniej-viagra-i-penicylina/sdft7sb (Access: 5.02.2021).

Historia PZU (2020). www.pzu.pl/relacje-inwestorskie/o-grupie/historia (Access: 9.02.2021).

How Microsoft is responding to the COVID-19 pandemic in Washington state (2020). https://news.microsoft.com/on-the-issues/2020/04/17/microsoft-covid-19-washington-state/ (Access: 21.01.2021).

Jak w pandemii kreatywnie radzi sobie gastronomia – studium najciekawszych przypadków (2020). https://krytykakulinarna.com/gastronomia-w-czasach-pandemii/ (Access: 10.02.2021).

Kolejne rekordowe wyniki Grupy Mercator Medical: spółka szacuje 414 mln zł wyniku EBITDA w Q4 2020 (2021). https://pl.mercatormedical.eu/media/informacje-prasowe/kolejne-rekordowe-wyniki-grupy-mercator-medical-spolka-szacuje-414-mln-zl-wyniku-ebitda-w-q4-2020/ (Access: 6.02.2021).

Koronawirus SARS-CoV-2 (2020). www.luxmed.pl/dla-pacjentow/zdrowie-w-4-krokach/zdrowie-na-co-dzien/koronawirus.html (Access: 3.02.2021).

Korzystaj bezpiecznie (2020). www.luxmed.pl/dla-pacjentow/otaczamy-opieka/korzystaj-bezpiecznie.html (Access: 3.02.2021).

KPMG (2020). Media and entertainment sector in the era of COVID-19. https://home.kpmg/in/en/home/insights/2020/09/media-and-entertainment-report-kpmg-india-2020-year-off-script/covid-19-impact-media-and-entertainment-2020.html (Access: 13.01.2021).

Kurierzy nie przeszli na pracę zdalną. Prezes DPD Polska o tym, jak epidemia wpłynęła na liczbę paczek (2020). https://businessinsider.com.pl/firmy/zarzadzanie/koronawirus-a-przesylki-kurierskie-komentarz-prezesa-dpd-polska/8mseeqy (Access: 15.01.2021).

Manufacturing and sourcing of critical medical supply inventory (2020). www.cardinalhealth.com/en/cmp/ext/corp/cardinal-health-covid-19-response-plan/manufacturing-and-sourcing-of-critical-inventory.html (Access: 5.02.2021).

Mercator Medical notuje rekordy przez koronawirusa (2020). www.parkiet.com/Medycyna-i-zdrowie/305199936-Mercator-Medical-notuje-rekordy-przez-koronawirusa.html (Access: 4.02.2021).

Mercator Medical wybuduje trzecią fabrykę rękawic jednorazowych (2021). https://pl.mercatormedical.eu/media/informacje-prasowe/mercator-medical-wybuduje-trzecia-fabryke-rekawic-jednorazowych/ (Access: 7.02.2021).

Microsoft annual report 2020 (2020). www.microsoft.com/investor/reports/ar20/index.html (Access: 21.01.2021).

Microsoft teams reaches 115 million DAU - Plus, a new daily collaboration minutes metric for Microsoft 365 (2020). www.microsoft.com/en-us/microsoft-365/blog/2020/10/28/microsoft-teams-reaches-115-million-dau-plus-a-new-daily-collaboration-minutes-metric-for-microsoft-365/ (Access: 21.01.2021).

Morgan (2020). 3 Lasting changes to grocery shopping after Covid-19. *Forbes*, www.forbes.com/sites/blakemorgan/2020/12/14/3-lasting-changes-to-grocery-shopping-after-covid-19/?sh=2e0825d054e7 (Access: 12.01.2021).

Najlepsza spółka pandemii zarobiła 274 razy więcej niż rok temu (2021). https://businessinsider.com.pl/najlepsza-spolka-pandemii-zarobila-274-razy-wiecej-niz-rok-temu/lf8chgj (Access: 7.02.2021).

Netflix 2020 proxy statement (2020). https://s22.q4cdn.com/959853165/files/doc_financials/2019/ar/Netflix-2020-Proxy_Updated.pdf (Access: 22.01.2021).

Netflix company profile (2021). https://ir.netflix.net/ir-overview/profile/default.aspx (Access: 22.01.2021).

Netflix four quarter earnings. Financial statements (2020). https://ir.netflix.net/financials/quarterly-earnings/default.aspx (Access: 22.01.2021).

Netflix letter to shareholders (2020). https://s22.q4cdn.com/959853165/files/doc_financials/2020/q4/FINAL-Q420-Shareholder-Letter.pdf (Access: 22.01.2021).

Netflix subscriber growth slows after surging during pandemic (2020). www.forbes.com/sites/joewalsh/2020/10/20/netflix-subscriber-growth-slows-after-surging-during-pandemic/?sh=5cc693f7244e (Access: 22.01.2021).

Nowa sortownia DPD Polska w Rudzie Śląskiej (2020). www.dpd.com/pl/pl/2020/11/04/nowa-sortownia-dpd-polska-w-rudzie-slaskiej/ (Access: 15.01.2021).

NTT System o nas (2021). https://ntt.pl/o-nas/ (Access: 22.01.2021).

NTT System Sprawozdanie Zarządu z działalności Grupy Kapitałowej NTT System S.A. za I półrocze 2020 r. (2020). https://ntt.pl/wp-content/uploads/2020/10/sprawozdanie-zarzadu-30_06_2020_GK-NTT-1.pdf (Access: 22.01.2021).

NTT System Śródroczne Skrócone Skonsolidowane Sprawozdanie Finansowe Grupy Kapitałowej NTT System za okres od 1 stycznia 2020 do 30 czerwca 2020 r. (2020). https://ntt.pl/wp-content/uploads/2020/10/SkroconeSrodroczneSkonsolidowaneSprawozdanieMSSF-30-06-2020_GK-NTT_k.pdf (Access: 22.201.2021).

O Allegro (2021). www.allegro.eu/pl/o-nas/poznajmy-sie (Access: 19.01.2021).

O DPD Polska (2021). www.dpd.com/pl/pl/o-dpd/o-firmie/ (Access: 15.01.2021).

Ocado group plc 1H20 results (2020). www.ocadogroup.com/sites/ocado-corp-v2/files/documents/fy20-half-year-results-presentation.pdf (Access: 20.01.2021).

Ocado group results centre (2020). www.ocadogroup.com/investors/result-centre (Access: 20.01.2021).

Ocado group our response coronavirus (COVID-19) (2020). www.ocadogroup.com/coronavirus-response (Access: 20.01.2021).

Ocado who we are (2021). https://ocadoretail.com/who-we-are/ (Access: 20.01.2021).

Opieka medyczna bez wychodzenia z domu (2020). www.pzu.pl/zdalnaopiekacovid (Access: 9.02.2021).

Our actions in response to COVID-19 (2020). https://cvshealth.com/covid-19/cvs-health-actions (Access: 2.02.2021).

Personal protective equipment supply updates (2020). www.cardinalhealth.com/en/cmp/ext/corp/cardinal-health-covid-19-response-plan/personal-protective-equipment-supply-updates.html (Access: 5.02.2021).

Pfizer ends COVID-19 vaccine trial with 95% success rate (2020). www.aljazeera.com/economy/2020/11/18/pfizer-ends-covid-19-vaccine-trial-with-95-success-rate (Access: 5.02.2021).

Pfizer oraz BioNTech pracują nad rozwojem potencjalnej szczepionki na COVID-19 (2020). www.pfizer.com.pl/o-firmie/press-room/pfizer-oraz-biontech-pracuj%C4%85-nad-rozwojem-potencjalnej-szczepionki-na-covid-19 (Access: 5.02.2021).

Placówki Grupy LUX MED (2021). www.luxmed.pl/dla-pacjentow/centra-medyczne-grupy-lux-med.html\ (Access: 3.02.2021).

Poradnik o zdrowiu (2020). www.pzuzdrowie.pl/poradnik-o-zdrowiu/koronawirus-covid-19/informacja-dla-pacjenta (Access: 10.02.2021).

Ptak-Team Szkoła Narciarska (2020). www.facebook.com/ptak.team (Access: 10.02.2021).

Prezes BioMaxima: Covid to gorący temat na świecie, trzeba się z własnym wyrobem przebić (2020). www.bankier.pl/wiadomosc/Prezes-BioMaxima-Covid-to-goracy-temat-na-swiecie-trzeba-sie-z-wlasnym-wyrobem-przebic-7991164.html (Access: 3.02.2021).

Profil działalności (2020). www.biomaxima.com/7-profil-dzialalnosci.html (Access: 3.02.2021).

Przegląd zdrowia po przebyciu COVID-19 (2020). www.luxmed.pl/dla-pacjentow/oferta/przeglad-zdrowia-po-przebyciu-covid-19.html (Access: 3.02.2021).

PwC Polska o nas (2021). www.pwc.pl/pl/o-nas.html (Access: 25.01.2021).

PwC Polska rok inny niż wszystkie (2020). www.pwc.pl/pl/publikacje/rok-inny-niz-wszystkie-podsumowanie-roku-finansowego-2019-2020-w-pwc-polska.html (Access: 25.01.2021).

PZU z powodu COVID-19 może nie zrealizować niektórych celów strategii do 2020 (2020). www.money.pl/gielda/pzu-z-powodu-covid-19-moze-nie-zrealizowac-niektorych-celow-strategii-do-2020-6552515067693185a.html (Access: 10.03.2021).

Raport kwartalny Grupy Allegro.eu za III kwartał 2020 r. (2020). www.allegro.eu/static-files/c0d16d25-dbd9-4612-b45f-fbf810e9effb (Access: 19.01.2021).

Regiony górskie i branża narciarska – wielcy przegrani drugiej fali pandemii koronawirusa? (2020). www.euractiv.pl/section/bezpieczenstwo-i-obrona/news/koronawirus-pandemia-narciarstwo-osrodki-kurorty-narciarskie-zima-sezon-narty-niemcy-wlochy-francja-austria-szwajcaria/ (Access: 9.02.2021).

Sektor farmaceutyczny w czasie koronawirusa (2020). https://przemyslfarmaceutyczny.pl/artykul/sektor-farmaceutyczny-w-czasie-koronawirusa (Access: 2.02.2021).

Sprzedaż szczepionki na koronawirusa. Pfizer podał szacunkowe kwoty na 2021 r. (2020). https://businessinsider.com.pl/wiadomosci/pfizer-sprzedaz-szczepionki-na-koronawirusa-covid-19-w-2021-r-szacunkowe-dane/y0f9rww (Access: 5.02.2021).

Szczepionka na koronawirusa. Szef Pfizera sprzedał swoje akcje w dniu ogłoszenia sukcesu (2020). www.money.pl/gielda/szczepionka-na-koronawirusa-szef-pfizera-sprzedal-swoje-akcje-w-dniu-ogloszenia-sukcesu-6574455732935552a.html (Access: 5.02.2021).

Szczepionka z Biontech: sukces potomków imigrantów (2020). www.dw.com/pl/szczepionka-z-biontech-sukces-potomk%C3%B3w-imigrant%C3%B3w/a-55557039 (Access: 5.02.2021).

Szkola narciarska (2020). https://ptak-team.pl/ (Access: 10.03.2021).

Tawerna Fisza concept by Marcin Budynek (2020). www.facebook.com/TawernaFisza/ (Access: 10.02.2021).

Test na koronawirusa (2021). www.luxmed.pl/dla-pacjentow/oferta/test-na-koronawirusa.html (Access: 3.02.2021).

Ubezpieczenie w PZU Życie chroni także w przypadku zakażenia koronawirusem (2020). www.pzu.pl/grupa-pzu/o-nas/aktualnosci/szczegoly/ubezpieczenie-w-pzu-zycie-chroni-takze-w-przypadku-zakazenia-koronawirusem (Access: 9.02.2021).

Unctad (2020). COVID-19 has changed online shopping forever, survey shows. https://unctad.org/news/covid-19-has-changed-online-shopping-forever-survey-shows (Access: 12.01.2021).

World Economic Forum (2020). 10 technology trends to watch in the COVID-19 pandemic. www.weforum.org/agenda/2020/04/10-technology-trends-coronavirus-covid19-pandemic-robotics-telehealth/ (Access: 13.01.2021).

Wpływ pandemii COVID-19 na rynek farmaceutyczny (2020). www.cyfrowyszpital.pl/wplyw-pandemii-covid-19-na-rynek-farmaceutyczny/ (Access: 2.02.2021).

7 Building enterprises' resilience to crisis

Lessons learned during the COVID-19 pandemic

7.1. Reducing threats and combating weaknesses

Enterprises' risk management in times of crisis should first and foremost relate to attempts at reducing threats in their environment and eliminating their own weaknesses. A hint as to the directions of possible actions is provided by the troubles of enterprises considered to be losers during the COVID-19 pandemic, the case studies of which are presented in Chapter 5. The directions in reducing threats and combating weaknesses are illustrated in Figure 7.1.

7.1.1. Limiting the negative impact of the macro-environment during the crisis

The further environment has traditionally been perceived in management as a source of risks on which enterprises have limited influence. Research on the negative impact of the environment on enterprises during the COVD-19 pandemic identifies the following challenges:

- the need for adaptive business management when business restrictions due to pandemic regulations are not uniform across countries and regions (Van Assche and Lundan, 2020),
- ensuring continuity of work during a pandemic and organizing a return to regular work, in particular by taking measures aimed at inhibiting the transmission of the virus among workers (Bernes and Sax, 2020),
- attempting to influence national governments to improve support programmes targeted at businesses in times of a pandemic, particularly in the form of feedback on identified flaws and deficiencies (Eklund, 2021),
- measures aimed at providing balance between compliance with sanitary restrictions and possibilities to conduct business activities, partly by designing necessary transformations (Ibn-Mohammed et al., 2021),
- the necessity to ensure the safety of enterprises' financial assets in a situation of interest rate volatility (Goy and van den End, 2020).

DOI: 10.4324/9781003131366-7

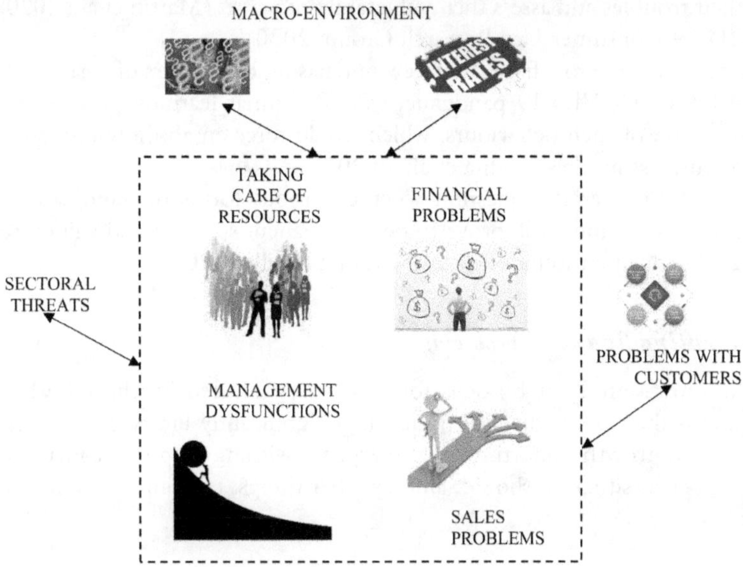

Figure 7.1 Directions in reducing threats and combating weaknesses in enterprises affected by the COVID-19 pandemic

7.1.2. Reducing sectoral threats

Besides the macro-environment, it was particular sectors that turned out to be areas where enterprises had to deal with emerging threats during the COVID-19 pandemic. In relation to sectoral risks, the following measures prove to be desirable:

- addressing the problem of falling prices and margins, especially through stabilization strategies and structural diversification (Troster and Küblböck, 2020),
- reducing enterprises' exposure to supply and demand shocks by selecting business domains characterized by lower vulnerability to such shocks (del Rio-Chanona et al., 2020),
- implementing preventive policies to reduce the vulnerability of supply chains to disruptions, based in part on experience gained during other disruptions, such as natural disasters (Grida et al., 2020).

7.1.3. Responding to problems with customer relations

The COVID-19 pandemic distinctly confirmed that, for businesses, customers are the most important stakeholder allowing enterprises to generate financial revenues. Thus, problems with customer relations constitute a serious problem during a crisis situation. In order to reduce them, enterprises should pay attention to the following:

- the need to monitor the situation of customers on a permanent basis, anticipate their troubles and assess their vulnerability to crisis (Martin et al., 2020; COVID-19-Consumer Law Research Group, 2020),
- the need to analyse to what extent new purchasing behaviours of customers, forced by the COVID-19 pandemic, will affect their learning process and consolidation of such behaviours, which would force an absolute modification of business models (Mehta et al., 2020),
- the need to answer the question whether various forms of remote work imposed on customers will prove to be a permanent solution and will cause changes in collaboration models in the future (Phillips, 2020).

7.1.4. Preventing financial problems

One of the most significant burdens for enterprises affected by the COVID-19 pandemic is their poor financial position. It significantly limits their defensive abilities and growth opportunities. Enterprises wishing to prevent financial problems in a crisis situation should, among other things, take into account the following:

- designing financial management in such a way as to reduce enterprises' dependence on long-term debt and ensuring the maintenance of liquidity (Almeida, 2021),
- the need to ensure a situation of equilibrium in terms of all types of business costs, i.e. fixed and variable as well as direct and indirect costs of the crisis (Mandel and Veetil, 2020).

7.1.5. Taking care of resources

Obviously, all types of resources are necessary for businesses to operate. The COVID-19 pandemic revealed a wide variety of strategies followed by enterprises with respect to their resources. Research conducted among pandemic-affected enterprises shows that human resource policies are the most problematic (Carnevale and Hatak, 2020). Specific dilemmas requiring a resolution include the following (Carnevale and Hatak, 2020):

- the need to strike a balance between resource vigilance consisting of caution about staffing levels and adjustment of the number of employees to the typical scale of operations,
- the need to strike a balance between the social responsibility of an enterprise to employ its staff under normal contracts and the value resulting from the use of flexible forms of employment,
- the need to find a compromise between the desire to retain employees despite problems and the courage to rationally assess the chances of survival and sometimes the need to downsize personnel in times of crisis in order to rebuild it later.

7.1.6. Reducing management dysfunctions

A huge impact on the troubles of enterprises during the COVID-19 pandemic was exerted by various management errors and inadequacies. Among numerous challenges that managers have to face, attention can be drawn to the following:

- redesigning strategies towards their adjustment to high levels of uncertainty and optionality of action, as well as subordinating such strategies to existential goals (Etemad, 2020; Liguori and Pittz, 2020),
- the need to overcome weaknesses in forecasting, rejecting the statement that a crisis is an "uncharted territory" for the company and it has to come to terms with it, as well as beginning to use professional forecasting methods and tools (Nikolopoulos, 2020),
- improving the ways in which decisions are made in times of crisis, particularly eliminating the dysfunction of procrastination in making necessary decisions (Karnon, 2020),
- the need to reconfigure global value chains and to introduce alternatives in localization strategies (Strange, 2020).

7.1.7. Improving a sales strategy

For many enterprises, the source of serious problems during the COVID-19 pandemic was a bad configuration of sales channels. The pandemic situation forced a completely different view of relationships between traditional and digital sales. In this context, the challenges for managers include the following:

- a quick and deep reflection on the future of traditional sales in brick-and-mortar establishments in the enterprise's markets, possibilities of their reconfiguration in terms of location, format and potential for replacement by digital sales (Pantano et al., 2020),
- a permanent digital transformation involving the work of salespeople, their social relations, marketing, sales and technologies used, as well as the development of new digital services (Almeida, 2020).

7.2. Exploiting opportunities and developing strengths

During a crisis situation, risk management should also focus on making the most of opportunities arising in the business environment and developing enterprises' strengths that previously had ensured a stable market position and competitiveness. In this respect, points of reference can be measures taken by enterprises regarded as winners during the COVID-19 pandemic, the case studies of which are presented in Chapter 6. The directions in the exploitation of opportunities and development of strengths are illustrated in Figure 7.2.

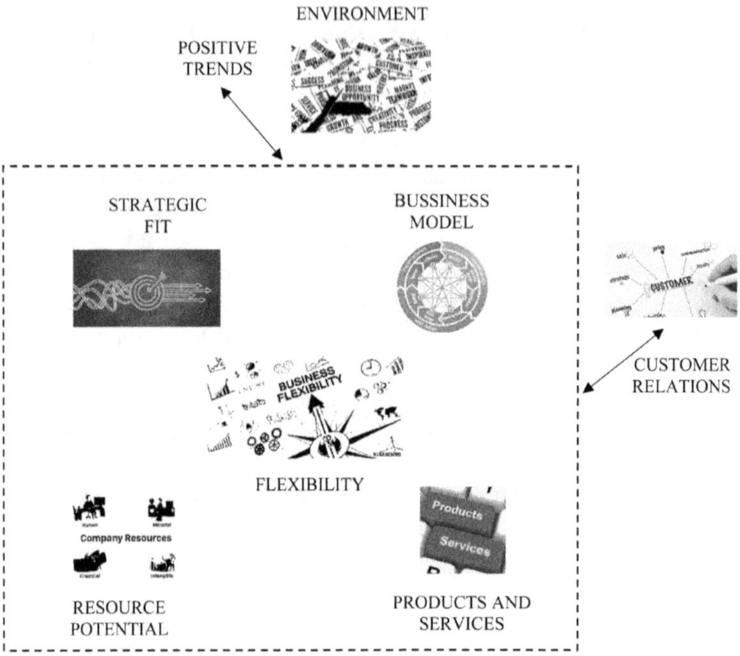

Figure 7.2 Directions in exploiting opportunities and developing strengths in enterprises during the COVID-19 pandemic

7.2.1. Exploring the strategic fit

It turned out that one of the most significant strengths of enterprises during the COVID-19 pandemic was their strong business strategies providing for actions aimed at minimizing negative and maximizing positive impacts of crises on their business, as well as implementing rapid crisis preparedness and adaptation measures. These measures include the following:

- having the organizational capacity to respond adequately to crises, which is crucial from the perspective of planning, ensuring business continuity and providing managers with comprehensive information allowing them to define response strategies (Margherita and Heikkila, 2021),
- conducting a methodically sound assessment of macroeconomic risks associated with the occurrence of a specific crisis situation, enabling the implementation of effective control mechanisms (Boldog et al., 2020),
- using various forms of strategic business partnerships (e.g. strategic alliances) that enable a faster response to crisis changes and better protection than separation measures (Cojoianu et al., 2020),
- using relationships based on coopetition activities with a view to balancing the risks and benefits of a crisis situation. During COVID-19, in many cases,

coopetition strategies proved to be more effective than actions taken within the framework of individual business models, for example among retailers, pharmaceutical companies, technology giants or charitable organizations (Crick and Crick, 2020),

- analyzing different scenarios for crisis development in order to build resilience and plan contingency actions adequate to particular scenarios. Scenario analyses proved to be one of the primary sources for assessing the insurability risks related to the COVID-19 pandemic (Richter and Wilson, 2020),
- mapping the dynamics of corporate financial management during a crisis, with a particular focus on opportunities for investments and measures mitigating uncertainty associated with entrepreneurship under crisis conditions (Brown and Rocha, 2020),
- a strong CSR strategy supporting the groups most affected by the unprecedented public health and economic crisis and constituting one of the dimensions of corporate strategic management during COVID-19 (Lee, 2020),
- diversification activities that build resilience. It appears that during COVID-19 such activities enabled enterprises to maintain a balance between the development of entrepreneurship in crisis conditions and the risks associated with such conditions (Korsgaard et al., 2020).

7.2.2. Exploiting the advantages of business models

Another advantage enjoyed by enterprises and contributing to their success during the COVID-19 was their existing business models, which enabled them to adapt extremely quickly to a radically different situation and ensured their undisturbed operation (and sometimes even surprising growth) despite the global crisis. This success was possible thanks to the fact that their business models included the following elements:

- the broadly understood digitization of work, sales channels, customer relations and business cooperation, which translated into increased productivity, efficiency and revenue in many companies during COVID-19. Digitization also played a considerable role in dealing with the aftermath of the crisis and ensuring business continuity (Papadopoulos et al., 2020),
- preparing for above-average turnover by providing infrastructure and resources to ensure manufacturing or service provision capacities to adapt to increased pandemic demand for specific products and services, as well as cooperating in supply chains under new rules (Paul and Chowdhury, 2020),
- changes in sustainable production/consumption patterns developed for emergency and crisis situations to ensure operational efficiency and implemented in both emergency strategies and internal procedures (Kumar et al., 2020),
- preventive policies aimed at protecting supply chains operating under pandemic uncertainty and ensuring their efficiency (Grida et al., 2020),

- flexible adaptation of pricing strategies to crisis changes both in the existing customer market in a given sector and from the perspective of global changes in the Consumer Prices Index (Blundell et al., 2020).

7.2.3. Exploiting the potential of resources

A substantial role in risk management during COVID-19 was played by stimulating the developmental potential of resources held by enterprises. The following activities proved to be most beneficial for enterprises representing different sectors of the economy:

- using the developed relational capital (especially between employees and the owner or between the enterprise and its external stakeholders) to design anti-crisis measures, mainly oriented towards preventing the negative effects of the crisis and developing proactive intervention strategies, which in many companies translated into reducing their vulnerability to the crisis (Walecka, 2021),
- proactively managing business-to-business relationships during the pandemic, which allows many businesses to maintain increased productivity and profitability and helps them to meet urgent short-term needs and exploit long-term opportunities (Obal and Gao, 2020),
- using past experience, R&D investments and innovation as opportunities for survival, stronger growth and improved profitability during COVID-19 (Roper and Turner, 2020),
- paying special attention to human resource development during the crisis, with particular focus on leadership competencies, digital competencies and retraining the personnel in COVID-19 adaptation activities (Dirani et al., 2020),
- exploiting growth potential based on different groups of resources during the pandemic: strategic, physical, financial, human and organizational resources and treating firm growth as the expansion of this resource system during the crisis (Lim et al., 2020).

7.2.4. Discounting flexibility

Flexibility is another attribute that, for many enterprises, constituted a critical factor determining the achievement of success during the global pandemic. Thus, flexibility supporting risk management processes and building resilience during a crisis should be considered in terms of the following:

- the introduction of innovations, new technologies, new product groups, new services, offers, marketing activities and other new initiatives that, by creating organizational agility, allow enterprises to adapt quickly and adequately to global crisis changes and develop resilience (George et al., 2020),

- active management of organizational designs (understood as optimal levels of differentiation and integration given relevant internal and external contingencies), as COVID-19 crisis events often force structural changes (Foss, 2020),
- agile, flexible and rapid adaptive management adjusting enterprises to regulatory changes introduced in connection with the global pandemic (Janssen and van der Voort, 2020).

7.2.5. Competing on the basis of products and services

The COVID-19 pandemic also highlighted the phenomenon of competition based on products and services that recorded unprecedented growth in demand. Consequently, for many businesses, multifaceted competition became a source of success in the market. However, in order to make success possible, many enterprises undertook a number of initiatives to strengthen the extra-price advantages of their products/services, for example:

- improving the quality of customer service processes and the comprehensiveness of services, which had a positive impact on customer loyalty, satisfaction and trust, and customer retention became one of the main business concepts applied by enterprises during the pandemic (Alketbi et al., 2020),
- ensuring timely deliveries to customers despite disruptions in global supply chains, and sometimes speeding up delivery processes as one of the factors of competitiveness among enterprises offering substitutes for the most desirable products during the pandemic (Gruenwald, 2020).

7.2.6. Benefiting from customer relations

Maintaining positive, uninterrupted relationships with customers during COVID-19 is another aspect through which enterprises were able to stimulate their growth during the crisis. In this area of activity, companies placed particular emphasis on the following:

- improved marketing strategies and policies enabling businesses to communicate effectively with new customers and reach new customer groups (Hoekstra and LeeFlang, 2020),
- intensified use of remote tools and platforms for customer communication (mainly through social media), also in such sectors as healthcare where this form of customer contact had been previously used minimally or not at all (Wong et al., 2020).

7.2.7. Taking advantage of positive changes in the environment

During the global pandemic both the macroeconomic and microeconomic environments became areas of growth for enterprises representing certain sectors.

However, if changes in the economic environment were to be turned into sources of success, enterprises had to exercise creativity in their adaptation activities, including the following:

- adapting resources, infrastructure and organizations to increasing demand for particular products and services, changes in customer behaviours and preferences in order to ensure the sustainability of business models (Donthu and Gustafsson, 2020; Mehta et al., 2020),
- aligning operations with global, technological megatrends transforming the previous ways of managing businesses, social relations, marketing and sales (Almeida et al., 2020).

7.3. A model of an enterprise's resilience to crisis

The above considerations on mitigating weaknesses and reducing threats, as well as discounting strengths and exploiting opportunities during the COVID-19 pandemic, included numerous courses of action recommended for enterprises in different, winning or losing, positions. Nevertheless, a model of an enterprise's resilience in the face of a crisis such as the COVID-19 pandemic can refer to the three core concepts that indicate how to build resilience to crises. Such a framework is presented in Figure 7.3.

An enterprise's resilience to crisis is understood as its ability to restore a state that guarantees its survival and the acquisition of skills necessary to conduct activities under destructive conditions. Xiao and Cao (2017) attribute the following characteristics to resilience understood in this way: it is a non-continuous capability, it emphasizes survival as well as the ability to adapt and grow in a difficult situation, it is multi-level in nature and maintains connections with resources, processes and procedures. From an organizational perspective, building resilience, an enterprise focuses precisely on its unique capabilities that should be developed to ensure preparedness for uncertain situations (Ma et al., 2018).

Figure 7.3 A framework of an enterprise's resilience to crisis

Morales et al. (2019) are of the opinion that resilience refers to the category of system (especially ecological, economic, social and organizational systems) and means the ability to return to normal conditions after a destructive event that changes the state of such systems. Some researchers (e.g. Ledesma, 2014) refer to compensatory, provocation, protective and vulnerability models of resilience. Such an approach is rather debatable. After all, an enterprise's resilience model should be universal. Proag (2014) proposes an interesting approach that differentiates between hard resilience (the direct strength of an enterprise's structures) and soft resilience (the ability of systems to absorb problems and recover from negative impacts). Resilience also has several domains. Hillmann and Guenther (2020) distinguish three complementary domains guaranteeing stability of an enterprise: the behavioural domain, the growth domain and the performance domain. Duchek (2020), on the other hand, segments the resilience abilities into anticipatory, coping and adaptive. Kantur and İşeri-Say (2015) indicate increasing chaos in the business environment as the main source of growing demand for enterprises' resilience.

Ultimately, the features determining an enterprise's resilience should include the following (Erol et al., 2010):

- redundancy, absorbing capability, recovery capability,
- situation awareness, management of keystone vulnerabilities, adaptive capacity,
- risk intelligence, agility,
- awareness, preparedness, flexibility,
- diversity, efficiency, adaptability, cohesion,
- collaboration, risk management culture, visibility.

However, the development of these features needs to be based on the three pillars of resilience shown in Figure 7.3.

7.3.1. Culture of preparedness

A culture of preparedness is important in building enterprises' resilience to crisis. Appleby-Arnold et al. (2018) argue that cultural aspects of an enterprise remain in a close relation with how it perceives risk. According to FEMA (2019), a culture of preparedness is based on four key principles: building trust, inclusion of stakeholders, efficiency of communication (including cross-cultural communication) and support for bottom-up practices and the desire to succeed. The same authors propose an interesting approach to building and developing a culture of preparedness based on the key role of professionally prepared people referred to as "culture brokers". Importantly, the successful long-term implementation of a culture of preparedness strengthens an enterprise's social legitimacy by improving its perception by its environment (Fowler et al., 2007). Carmeli and Schaubroeck (2008) have proven that the extent to which an enterprise succeeds in implementing a culture of preparedness has a direct impact on how it responds to crisis situations, especially because it is capable of receiving early warning signals. A culture of preparedness can also be the result of an enterprise's learning process based on its own or external examples of crisis situations (Kapucu, 2008).

7.3.2. Business continuity

Business continuity planning can be a strategically important procedure used to promote organizational resilience by enhancing an enterprise's ability to survive and sustain business operations during a crisis (Tracey et al., 2017). Business continuity is critically important for ensuring the availability of products and services, maintenance of infrastructure, efficiency in supply chains and stability at the micro and macro levels. The most popular definition of business continuity included in the ISO 22300:2018 standard shows this construct as "the capability of an organization to continue the delivery of products or services at acceptable predefined levels following a disruption" (Mathenge, 2020). Business continuity maintains a close semantic relationship with organizational resilience, which, according to the ISO 22316:2017 standard means "the ability of an organization to absorb and adapt in a changing environment to enable it to deliver its objectives and to survive and prosper" (Mathenge, 2020). The vast area of business continuity management delineates a cyclical process including the provision of information on risk, the formulation of continuity plans, the implementation of necessary preparedness measures and effective corrective actions and coordination among stakeholders, which ultimately improves an organization's ability to maintain effective business continuity (Baba et al., 2014). Sawalha et al. (2015) point out that a major threat to the effectiveness of continuity plans is insufficient testing, training, maintenance and updating, which can make such plans irrelevant and insufficient. It is also worth noting that nowadays business continuity management should be an immanent component of business models. Activities typical of business continuity can provide criteria for assessing the resilience of business models to a variety of disruptions (Niemimaa et al., 2019).

7.3.3. Disaster resilience

Disaster resilience reflects a measure of the ability of systems to absorb changes in state variables, control variables and parameters as well as to continue to stay alive (Parker, 2019). Among other things, researchers specializing in this issue point out that it is particularly important for microenterprises, which are more than likely to be affected by various types of disruptions, especially disasters that cause shocks to supply chains (Prasad et al., 2014). Such enterprises are also less able to obtain formal assistance in various types of markets, such as banking and insurance markets. Abeling et al. (2018) claim that the technical and environmental dimensions of disaster resilience are already well identified. However, this is not the case for social resilience, which requires scientific and practical penetration. Among the threats to corporate resilience, the previously mentioned disasters are of great importance. Resilience to them depends especially on the extent to which an organization's social system acquires the ability to learn from past disasters (Sertyesilisik, 2017). Interestingly, striving to develop disaster resilience can also take place at an informal level. What is particularly important in this context is efforts aimed at strengthening relationships, changing mindsets and building trust (Hunt and Eburn, 2018).

7.4. Procedure for implementing a model of an enterprise's resilience to crisis

If the enterprise crisis resilience model presented in Figure 7.3 is to fulfil its alleged function, it needs to be implemented according to a carefully planned procedure. First of all, the implementation of the resilience model should not be just an episodic programme of an enterprise, developed only in the case of an immediate threat, but a permanent component of a business model and strategy. A universal resilience model implementation procedure (dedicated to all enterprises, regardless of size or business profile) is presented in Figure 7.4. The starting point for the implementation of the resilience model is the assumption that the enterprise has a functioning risk management system, which is a pillar for building resilience to crises and an initiator for subsequent steps in the implementation of the resilience model. The resilience model implementation procedure is divided into three stages: shaping a culture of preparedness, planning business continuity and building disaster resilience.

7.4.1. Shaping a culture of preparedness

The first step in shaping a culture of preparedness should be its permanent integration into the enterprise's strategy (e.g. at the level of one of strategic objectives), in such a way that the planning of preparedness measures is an ongoing process with a long-term perspective. Therefore, building a culture of preparedness is increasingly being treated as one of strategic plans (FEMA, 2019). Another extremely important step in building a culture of preparedness is developing techniques for assessing the enterprise's vulnerability to both internal and external crises (the latter being beyond an enterprise's control). For this purpose, enterprises use various techniques of predicting and estimating risks to which they are exposed. In line with the risk exposure assessment methodology used by the World Economic Forum (2020), these techniques include an assessment of the likelihood of the occurrence of particular risks and an assessment of their impact on the enterprise should they materialize. The next implementation step should be an analysis of crises experienced by the enterprise or entities in its environment in the past, as well as crises to which the enterprise is potentially exposed. Such designing of hypothetical crisis solutions is an extremely important component of learning in the process of building organizational resilience. The importance of identifying and analyzing potential crisis threats is also emphasized by Kalbassi (2016). In the procedure of planning and implementing preparedness measures, an important element is the development and planning of actions

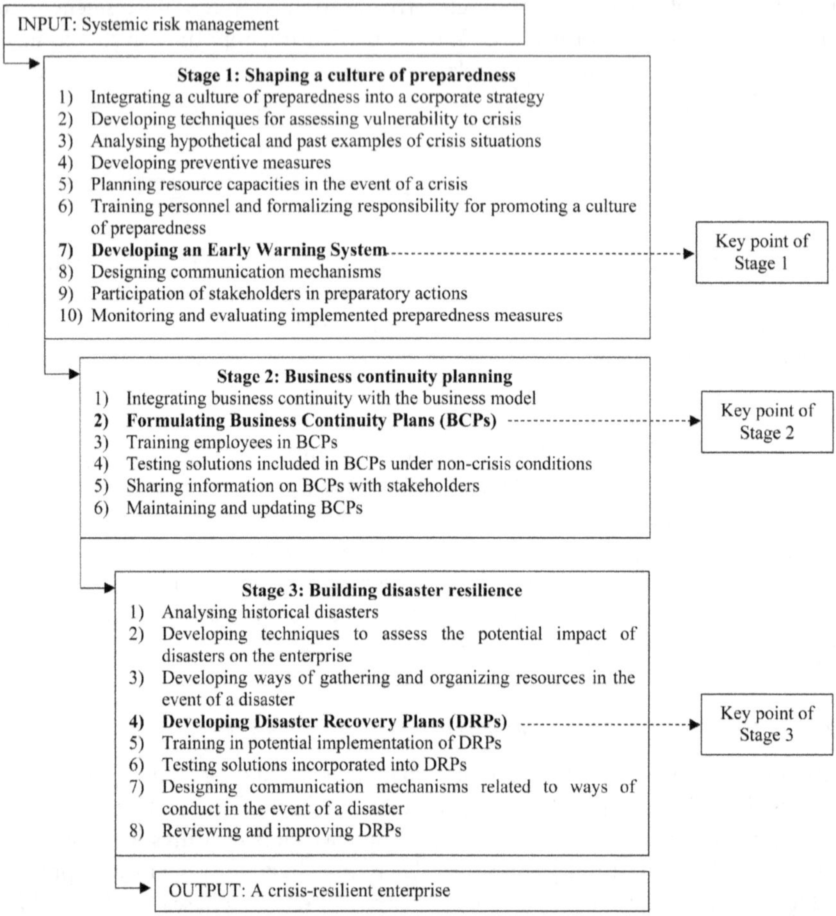

Figure 7.4 A procedure for implementing a model of an enterprise's resilience to crisis

aimed at preventing threats whose emergence can be prevented or whose negative consequences can be eliminated by taking specific countermeasures. Such preventive actions are the pillar of a proactive approach to managing a crisis before it occurs (Pop, 2017). One of the most important steps in shaping a culture of preparedness is plans regarding a resource base to be used in the event of a crisis situation. Such a base should comprise financial, infrastructural, human and knowledge resources. Building and maintaining such resources is necessary for the effective use of preventive measures (Mikušová and Horváthová, 2019). When implementing preparedness measures, it is also necessary to train employees, with a special focus on formalizing responsibility for promoting a culture of preparedness within an enterprise, for example, by creating positions responsible for crisis preparedness management (FEMA, 2019). A key point in the procedure for implementing a culture of preparedness in an enterprise is the development of an early warning system providing information on the occurrence of symptoms of crisis events. Detecting and exploiting early signals plays an important role in crisis prevention (Simola, 2005). Besides, what can be observed nowadays is the high effectiveness of early warning systems in preventing economic or business crises with the simultaneous provision of systematic forecasts of adverse events (Klopotan et al., 2018). Designing communication mechanisms at all levels of the organizational structure also plays a substantial role in the crisis preparedness shaping process. What is particularly important in this context is strategies in crisis communication (Noratikah et al., 2017), which are relevant for both preventing possible crises and responding to those that have already occurred. Stakeholder participation in preparedness activities is the next step in building a culture of preparedness in an enterprise. The multi-stakeholder approach is treated as one of the forms of building resilience (Adekola et al., 2020). However, in order for the developed culture of preparedness to fulfil its presumed function, it is necessary to continuously monitor and evaluate the implemented preparedness measures and improve the developed actions based on the results of such an evaluation.

7.4.2. Business continuity planning

Business continuity planning is the second of the three main stages in the implementation of the enterprise crisis resilience model. The starting point should be the integration of business continuity with an enterprise's business model. Such integration makes it possible to significantly strengthen the business model's resilience to crises. For this purpose, it is recommended to implement Strategic Business Continuity Management, which allows the enterprise, firstly, to maintain the continuity of the business model (value preservation) and, secondly, to evaluate and modify the business model (value creation) (Niemimaa et al., 2019). The key element of this stage of building resilience is the formulation of Business Continuity Plans (BCPs), which significantly help to maintain the functionality and continuity of the enterprise when crises arise in consequence of risks that could not have been avoided. Furthermore, comprehensive BCPs help to mitigate disruptions to the functioning of business systems (Cerullo and Cerullo, 2004). In view of the fact that the development of BCPs often results in new responsibilities for many employees (mainly managers), what becomes necessary is dedicated training, mainly due to the fact that continuity planning requires strategic skills to enable the planning of organizational success, preservation of future competitiveness and maintenance of organizational performance (Wong, 2009). A very important moment in the implementation of the resilience model is the testing of solutions included in BCPs in non-crisis conditions. By developing possible scenarios of solutions, such testing allows enterprises to prepare for various threats indicating a potential crisis. Examining also enables continuous improvements of BCPs based on obtained test results (Fani and Subriadi, 2019). In the effective implementation of BCPs, it is also necessary to provide information on developed plans to both internal and external stakeholders, whose role in Business Continuity Management Practices is also recognized by Järveläinen (2020). BCPs have to be maintained as a permanent component in the resilience building process. It is also necessary to update them periodically in response to changing external threats and internal transformations within the enterprise.

7.4.3. Building disaster resilience

Building disaster resilience is the final stage in the implementation of a crisis resilience business model, following the introduction of a culture of preparedness and the implementation of business continuity planning. Building disaster resilience should start with learning through experience, i.e. drawing conclusions from a historical analysis of disasters. The importance of this type of analysis in assessing vulnerability and resilience to disasters is emphasized, among others, by Kelman et al. (2016). An important element of implementing the model at this stage is to develop techniques to assess the potential impact of disasters on the enterprise. In order to improve the methodology in the area of disaster impact analysis and mitigation, disaster impact analysis models can be used, such as the one proposed by Oh et al. (2010), consisting of the following four stages: the level-of-service measurement, conversion to the level-of-damage, the impact measurement (on each industry) using the inter-relationship and the overall impact on the community (or industries as a whole). The next step in the disaster resilience building process should be the development of ways to gather and organize resources to be used in the event of a disaster. The importance of organizing and rationally allocating such resources is emphasized, for example, by Preston et al. (2016). A key point in the third stage of building resilience to crisis is the development of Disaster Recovery Plans (DRPs) allowing for scenario-based planning to restore the enterprise's normal functionality after a potential disaster experience. This is because developed recovery plans support business continuity and significantly increase the level of adaptive resilience (Tiernan et al., 2018). Developing effective DRPs also requires training employees in their potential implementation, as highlighted by Kadlec and Shropshire (2010). The content of such training should include, among other elements, disaster identification and notification methods as well as the creation of recovery procedures. It is also extremely important to test solutions included in DRPs in order to make sure that they are feasible, and thus to obtain confirmation of their continued effectiveness (Conrad, 2011). The next implementation step should be designing mechanisms of communicating procedures that have to be followed in the event of a disaster. This is so because communication is considered an integral part of decision-making processes in disaster management (Palttala et al., 2012). If DRPs are to fulfil their role, they have to be reviewed periodically and improved continuously, in response to changes observed in the environment.

The final point of the implementation procedure for the model of an enterprise's resilience to crisis outlined above is the formation of a crisis-resilient enterprise, i.e. an enterprise possessing all the characteristic features of resilience. The implementation of the model in the proposed configuration and sequence of consecutive stages in any enterprise may contribute to the achievement of resilience to crisis.

References

Abeling, T., Huq, N., Chang-Seng, D., Birkmann, J., Wolfertz, J., Renaud, F., Garschagen, M. (2018). Understanding disaster resilience: The emBRACE approach [in:] H. Deeming, M. Fordham, C. Kuhlicke, L. Pedoth, S. Schneiderbauer, C. Shreve (eds.), *Framing Community Disaster Resilience: Resources, Capacities, Learning, and Action*. Hoboken NJ, Chichester: John Wiley & Sons.

Adekola, J., Fischabcher-Smith, D., Fischabcher-Smith, M. (2020). Inherent complexities of a multi-stakeholder approach to building community resilience. *International Journal of Disaster Risk Science*, 11, pp. 32–45.

Alketbi, S., Alshurideh, M., Al Kurdi, B. (2020). The influence of service quality on customers' retention and loyalty in the UAE hotel sector with respect to the impact of customer' satisfaction, trust, and commitment: A qualitative study. *International Journal of Innovation, Creativity and Change*, 14(7), pp. 734–754.

Almeida, F., Santos, J.D., Monteiro, J.A. (2020). The challenges and opportunities in the digitalization of companies in a post COVID-19 world. *IEEE Engineering Management Review*, 48(3), pp. 97–103.

Almeida, H. (2021). Liquidity management during the Covid-19 pandemic. *Asia-Pacific Journal of Financial Studies*, 50(1), pp. 1–18.

Appleby-Arnold, S., Brockdorff, N., Jakovljev, I., Zdravković, S. (2018). Applying cultural values to encourage disaster preparedness: Lessons from a low-hazard country. *International Journal of Disaster Risk Reduction*, 31, pp. 37–44.

Baba, H., Watanabe, T., Nagaishi, M., Matsumoto, H. (2014). Area business continuity management, a new opportunity for building economic resilience. *Procedia Economics and Finance*, 18, pp. 296–303.

Bernes, M., Sax, P.E. (2020). Challenges of "Return to Work" in an ongoing pandemic. *NEJM Group Public Health Emergency Collection*, 383(8), pp. 779–786.

Blundell, R., Griffith, R., Levell, P., O'Connell, M. (2020). Could COVID-19 infect the consumer prices index? *Fiscal Studies. The Journal of Applied Public Economics*, 41(2), pp. 357–361.

Boldog, P., Tekeli, T., Vizi, Z., Dénes, A., Bartha, F.A., Röst, G. (2020). Risk assessment of novel coronavirus COVID-19 outbreaks outside China. *Journal of Clinical Medicine*, 9(571), pp. 1–12.

Brown, R., Rocha, A. (2020). Entrepreneurial uncertainty during the Covid-19 crisis: Mapping the temporal dynamics of entrepreneurial finance. *Journal of Business Venturing Insights*, 14, e00174.

Carmeli, A., Schaubroeck, J. (2008). Organisational crisis-preparedness: The importance of learning from failures. *Long Range Planning*, 41(2), pp. 177–196.

Carnevale, J.B., Hatak, I. (2020). Employee adjustment and well-being in the era of COVID-19: Implications for human resource management. *Journal of Business Research*, 116, pp. 183–187.

Cerullo, V., Cerullo, M.J. (2004). Business continuity planning: A comprehensive approach. *Information Systems Management*, 2(3), pp. 70–78.

Cojoianu, T.F., Haney, A.B., Meiring, A. (2020). Strategic alliances as treatment for COVID-19 and beyond. Oxford Smith School of Enterprise and the Environment. *Working Paper* No. 20-04.

Conrad, E. (2011). *Business Continuity and Disaster Recovery Planning*. Eleventh Hour CISSP Study Guide, pp. 89–107.

COVID-19-Consumer Law Research Group., Alderman, R., De Franceschi, A. et al. (2020). Consumer law and policy relating to change of circumstances due to the COVID-19 pandemic. *Journal of Consumer Policy*, 43, pp. 437–450.

Crick, J., Crick, D. (2020). Coopetition and COVID-19: Collaborative business-to-business marketing strategies in a pandemic crisis. *Industrial Marketing Management*, 88, pp. 206–213.

del Rio-Chanona, R.M., Mealy, P., Pichler, A., Lafond, F., Farmer, J.D. (2020). Supply and demand shocks in the COVID-19 pandemic: An industry and occupation perspective. *Oxford Review of Economic Policy*, graa033, pp. 1–44.

Dirani, K., Abadi, M., Alizadeh, A., Barhate, B., Garza, R.C., Gunasekara, N., Ibrahim, G., Majzun, Z. (2020). Leadership competencies and the essential role of human resource development in times of crisis: A response to Covid-19 pandemic. *Human Resource Development International*, 23(9), pp. 1–15.

Donthu, N., Gustafsson, A. (2020). Effects of COVID-19 on business and research. *Journal of Business Research*, 117, pp. 284–289.

Duchek, S. (2020). Organizational resilience: A capability-based conceptualization. *Business Research*, 13, pp. 215–246.

Eklund, M.A. (2021). The COVID-19 lessons learned for business and governance. *SN Business & Economics*, 1(25), pp. 1–9.

Erol, O., Sauser, B.J., Mansouri, M. (2010). A framework for investigation into extended enterprise resilience. *Enterprise Information Systems*, 4(2), pp. 111–136.

Etemad, H. (2020). Managing uncertain consequences of a global crisis: SMEs encountering adversities, losses, and new opportunities. *Journal of International Entrepreneurship*, 18, pp. 125–144.

Fani, S.V., Subriadi, A.P. (2019). Business continuity plan: Examining of multi-usable framework. *Procedia Computer Science*, 161, pp. 275–282.

FEMA. (2019). *Building Cultures of Preparedness: A Report for the Emergency Management Higher Education Community*. Washington, DC: FEMA.

Foss, N.J. (2020). The impact of the Covid-19 pandemic on firms' organizational designs. *Journal of Management Studies*, 58(81), pp. 270–274.

Fowler, K.L., Kling, N.D., Larson, M.D. (2007). Organizational preparedness for coping with a major crisis or disaster. *Business & Society*, 46(1), pp. 88–103.

George, G., Lakhani, K.R., Puranam, P. (2020). What has changed? The impact of covid pandemic on the technology and innovation management research agenda. *Journal of Management Studies*, 57(8), pp. 1754–1758.

Goy, G., van den End, J.W. (2020). The impact of the COVID-19 crisis on the equilibrium interest rate. https://voxeu.org/article/impact-covid-19-crisis-equilibrium-interest-rate (Access: 18.02.2021).

Grida, M., Mohamed, R., Zaied, A.N.H. (2020). Evaluate the impact of COVID-19 prevention policies on supply chain aspects under uncertainty. *Transportation Research Interdisciplinary Perspectives*, 8, p. 100240.

Gruenwald, H. (2020). Parcel delivery services boom during COVID-19. Project: logistics in Asia. www.researchgate.net/publication/343674544_Parcel_Delivery_Services_boom_during_Covid-19 (Access: 18.02.2021).

Hillmann, J., Guenther, E. (2020). Organizational resilience: A valuable construct for management research? *International Journal of Management Reviews*, 23(1), pp. 7–44.

Hoekstra, J.C., Leeflang, P.S.H. (2020). Marketing in the era of COVID-19. *Italian Journal of Marketing*, 2020, pp. 249–260.

Hunt, S., Eburn, M. (2018). How can business share responsibility for disaster resilience? *Australian Journal of Public Administration*, 77(3), pp. 482–491.

Ibn-Mohammed, T, Mustapha, K.B., Godsell, J., Adamu, Z., Babatunde, K.A., Akintade, D.D., Acquaye, A., Fujii, H., Ndiaye, M.M., Yamoah, F.A., Koh, S.C.L. (2021). A critical analysis of the impacts of COVID-19 on the global economy and ecosystems and opportunities for circular economy strategies. *Resources, Conservation and Recycling*, 164, p. 105169.

Janssen, M., van der Voort, H. (2020). Agile and adaptive governance in crisis response: Lessons from the COVID-19 pandemic. *International Journal of Information Management*, 55, p. 102180.

Järveläinen, J. (2020). Understanding the stakeholder roles in business continuity management practices – A study in public sector. *Conference: Hawaii International Conference on System Sciences*, Maui, Hawaii, USA, January 7–10, 2020.

Kadlec, C., Shropshire, J. (2010). Best practices in IT disaster recovery planning among US Banks. *Journal of Internet Banking and Commerce*, 15(1), pp. 1–11.

Kalbassi, C. (2016). Identifying crisis threats: A partial synthesis of the literature on crisis threat assessment with relevance to public administrations. *Journal of Risk Analysis and Crisis Response*, 6(3), pp. 110–121.

Kantur, D., İşeri-Say, A. (2015). Organizational resilience: A conceptual integrative framework. *Journal of Management & Organization*, 18(6), pp. 762–773.

Kapucu, N. (2008). Culture of preparedness: Household disaster preparedness. *Disaster Prevention and Management*, 17(4), pp. 526–535.

Karnon, J. (2020). A simple decision analysis of a mandatory lockdown response to the COVID-19 pandemic. *Applied Health Economics and Health Policy*, 18, pp. 329–331.

Kelman, I., Gaillard, J.C., Lewis, J., Mercer, J. (2016). Learning from the history of disaster vulnerability and resilience research and practice for climate change. *Natural Hazards*, 82, pp. 129–143.

Klopotan, I., Zaroja, J., Meško, M. (2018). Early warning system in business, finance, and economics: Bibliometric and topic analysis. *International Journal of Engineering Business Management*, 10, pp. 1–12.

Korsgaard, S., Hunt, R.A., Townsend, D.M., Ingstrup, M.B. (2020). COVID-19 and the importance of space in entrepreneurship research and policy. *International Small Business Journal: Researching Entrepreneurship*, 38(8), pp. 697–710.

Kumar, A., Luthra, S., Mangla, S.K., Kazançoğlu, Y . (2020). COVID-19 impact on sustainable production and operations management. *Sustainable Operations and Computers*, 1, pp. 1–7.

Ledesma, J. (2014). Conceptual frameworks and research models on resilience in leadership. *SAGE Open*, 4(3), pp. 1–8.

Lee, S. (2020). Corporate social responsibility and COVID-19: Research implications. *Tourism Economics*, OnlineFirst, pp. 1–7.

Liguori, E.W., Pittz, E.G. (2020). Strategies for small business: Surviving and thriving in the era of COVID-19. *Journal of the International Council for Small Business*, 1(2), pp. 106–110.

Lim, D.S.K., Morse, E.A., Yu, N. (2020). The impact of the global crisis on the growth of SMEs: A resource system perspective. *International Small Business Journal: Researching Entrepreneurship*, 38(6), pp. 492–503.

Ma, Z., Xiao, L., Yin, J. (2018). Toward a dynamic model of organizational resilience. *Nankai Business Review International*, 9(3), pp. 246–263.

Mandel, A., Veetil, V. (2020). The economic cost of COVID Lockdowns: An out-of-equilibrium analysis. *Economics of Disasters and Climate Change*, 4, pp. 431–451.

Margherita, A., Heikkila, M. (2021). Business continuity in the COVID-19 emergency: A framework of actions undertaken by world-leading companies. *Business Horizons*, 1733, pp. 1–32, https://doi.org/10.1016/j.bushor.2021.02.020".

Martin, A., Markhvida, M., Hallegatte, S., Walsh, B. (2020). Socio-economic impacts of COVID-19 on household consumption and poverty. *Economics of Disasters and Climate Change*, 4, pp. 453–479.

Mathenge, J. (2020). Business continuity vs business resiliency: What's the difference? www.bmc.com/blogs/business-continuity-vs-resiliency/ (Access: 20.02.2021).

Mehta, S., Saxena, T., Purohit, N. (2020). The new consumer behaviour paradigm amid COVID-19: Permanent or transient? *Journal of Health Management*, 22(2), pp. 291–301.

Mikušová, M., Horváthová, P. (2019). Prepared for a crisis? Basic elements of crisis management in an organisation. *Economic Research-Ekonomska Istraživanja*, 32(1), pp. 1844–1868.

Morales, S.N., Martínez, L.R., Gómez, J.A.H., López, R.R., Torres-Argüelles, V. (2019). Predictors of organizational resilience by factorial analysis. *International Journal of Engineering Business Management*, 11, pp. 1–13.

Niemimaa, M., Järveläinen, J., Heikkilä, M., Heikkilä, J. (2019). Business continuity of business models: Evaluating the resilience of business models for contingencies. *International Journal of Information Management*, 49, pp. 208–216.

Nikolopoulos, K., Punia, S., Schäfers, A., Tsinopoulos, C., Vasilakis, C. (2020). Forecasting and planning during a pandemic: COVID-19 growth rates, supply chain disruptions, and governmental decisions. *European Journal of Operational Research*, 290, pp. 99–115.

Noratikah, M.A., Aizza Maisha, D.A.A., Mus Chairil, S. (2017). Crisis response strategy and crisis types suitability: A preliminary study on MH370. Paper presented at the *International conference on communication and media: An international communication association regional conference (i-COME'16)*, Kuala Lumpur, Malaysia.

Obal, M., Gao, T. (2020). Managing business relationships during a pandemic: Conducting a relationship audit and developing a path forward. *Industrial Marketing Management*, 88, pp. 247–254.

Oh, E.H., Deshmukh, A., Hastak, M. (2010). Disaster impact analysis based on inter-relationship of critical infrastructure and associated industries. *International Journal of Disaster Resilience in the Built Environment*, 1(1), pp. 25–49.

Palttala, P., Boano, C., Lund, R., Vos, M. (2012). Communication gaps in disaster management: Perceptions by experts from governmental and non-governmental organizations. *Journal of Contingencies and Crisis Management*, 20(1), pp. 1–12.

Pantano, E., Pizzi, G., Scarpi, D., Dennis, C. (2020). Competing during a pandemic? Retailers' ups and downs during the COVID-19 outbreak. *Journal of Business Research*, 116, pp. 209–213.

Papadopoulos, T., Baltas, K.N., Balta, M.E. (2020). The use of digital technologies by small and medium enterprises during COVID-19: Implications for theory and practice. *International Journal of Information Management*, 55, p. 102192.

Parker, D.J. (2019). Disaster resilience – A challenged science. *Environmental Hazards*, 19(1), pp. 1–9.

Paul, S.K., Chowdhury, P. (2020). A production recovery plan in manufacturing supply chains for a high-demand item during COVID-19. *International Journal of Physical Distribution & Logistics Management*, 51(2), pp. 104–125.

Phillips, S. (2020). Working through the pandemic: Accelerating the transition to remote working. *Business Information Review*, 37(3), pp. 129–134.

Pop, S. (2017). Prevention and crisis management. *International Conference KNOWLEDGE-BASED ORGANIZATION*, 23(1), pp. 246–250.

Prasad, S., Su, H-C., Altay, N., Tata, J. (2014). Building disaster-resilient micro enterprises in the developing world. *Disasters*, 39(3), pp. 447–466.

Preston, J., Chadderton, C., Kitagawa, K., Edmonds, C. (2016). Community response in disasters: An ecological learning framework. *International Journal of Lifelong Education*, 34(6), pp. 727–753.

Proag, V. (2014). The concept of vulnerability and resilience. *Procedia Economics and Finance*, 18, pp. 369–376.

Richter, A., Wilson, T.C. (2020). COVID-19: Implications for insurer risk management and the insurability of pandemic risk. *The Geneva Risk and Insurance Review*, 45, pp. 171–199.

Roper, S., Turner, J. (2020). R&D and innovation after COVID-19: What can we expect? A review of prior research and data trends after the great financial crisis. *International Small Business Journal: Researching Entrepreneurship*, 38(6), pp. 504–514.

Sawalha, I.H.S., Anchor, J.R., Meaton, J. (2015). Continuity culture: A key factor for building resilience and sound recovery capabilities. *International Journal of Disaster Risk Science*, 6, pp. 428–437.

Sertyesilisik, B. (2017). Building information modeling as a tool for enhancing disaster resilience of the construction industry. *Transactions of the VSB - Technical University of Ostrava, Safety Engineering Series*, 12(1), pp. 9–18.

Simola, S. (2005). Concepts of care in organizational crisis prevention. *Journal of Business Ethics*, 62, pp. 341–353.

Strange, R. (2020). The 2020 COVID-19 pandemic and global value chains. *Journal of Industrial and Business Economics*, 47, pp. 455–465.

Tiernan, A., Drennan, L., Nalau, J., Onyango, E., Morrissey, L., Mackey, B. (2018). A review of themes in disaster resilience literature and international practice since 2012. *Policy Design and Practice*, 2(1), pp. 53–74.

Tracey, S., O'Sullivan, T.L., Lane, D.E., Guy, E., Courtemanche, J. (2017). Promoting resilience using an asset-based approach to business continuity planning. *SAGE Open*, 7(2), pp. 1–15.

Troster, B., Küblböck, K. (2020). Unprecedented but not unpredictable: Effects of the COVID-19 crisis on commodity-dependent countries. *The European Journal of Development Research*, 32, pp. 1430–1449.

Van Assche, A., Lundan, S. (2020). From the editor: COVID-19 and international business policy. *Journal of International Business Policy*, 3, pp. 273–279.

Walecka, A. (2021). The role of relational capital in anti-crisis measures undertaken by companies - Conclusions from a case study. *Sustainability*, 13(2), pp. 1–16.

Wong, A., Ho, S., Olusanya, O., Antonini, M.V., Lyness, D. (2020). The use of social media and online communications in times of pandemic COVID-19. *Journal of the Intensive Care Society*, 0(0), pp. 1–6, https://journals.sagepub.com/doi/pdf/10.1177/1751143720966280 .

Wong, W.N. (2009). The strategic skills of business continuity managers: Putting business continuity management into corporate long-term planning. *Journal of Business Continuity & Emergency Planning*, 4(1), pp. 62–68.

World Economic Forum. (2020). The global risks report 2020. www3.weforum.org/docs/WEF_Global_Risk_Report_2020.pdf (Access: 1.08.2020).

Xiao, L., Cao, H. (2017). Organizational resilience: The theoretical model and research implication. *ITM Web of Conferences*, 12(18), p. 04021.

Conclusions

Risk management has never been an easy task because a considerable proportion of risks that business enterprises have to deal with in practice is resistant to the simple and easily available risk mitigation tools such as insurance. Crisis situations affecting enterprises additionally compound managerial problems, imposing uncertainty, complexity and stress on managers responsible for risk mitigation. Even for experienced crisis managers, a crisis such as the one caused by the COVID-19 pandemic poses a significant challenge due to its unique specificity and dissimilarity to other previously occurring types of crisis such as an economic crash or natural disaster.

Presented in Chapters 1, 2 and 3, the latest research on risk management and crisis management reveals the existing body of knowledge of these areas of management sciences. This knowledge constitutes some kind of "initial capital" to be used in responding to the challenges of the COVID-19 pandemic. The accumulated knowledge and experience relating to risk management allow a better understanding of different types of risk, as well as strategies, concepts and methods of handling risk, including those codified in the form of official standards.

The occurrence of COVID-19 exposed certain types of risk, particularly visible during the course of the pandemic. Our research identified the following types of risk as being particularly prominent during the pandemic: (1) financial risks (liquidity risk, insurance risk, price risk, credit risk), (2) organizational risks (legal risk, personnel risk), (3) strategic risks (business continuity risk, reputational risk, investment risk), (4) global risks (global supply chain risk, technological risk).

We conducted empirical research on a group of several dozen global and local enterprises representing various sectors of the economy. In the entire population of the selected enterprises, we distinguished two groups: those that lost and those that won during the COVID-19 pandemic. The conducted case studies made it possible to identify various categories of enterprises reflecting their profiles and starting positions, as well as patterns of conduct and philosophy of crisis management adopted for the period of the pandemic. Thus, in the group of enterprises classified as losers, we distinguished the following categories: (1) blocked by restrictions, (2) too inert to protect themselves, (3) too traditional to change, (4) opportunity wasters. On the other hand, the group of so-called "winners" consisted of the following categories: (1) direct "medical"

DOI: 10.4324/9781003131366-102

beneficiaries, (2) replacing others, (3) opportunity catchers, (4) creative despite adversities.

A particularly important research finding was the identification of key failure factors (for companies considered as losers) and key success factors (for companies considered as winners). The various failure factors were eventually divided into seven categories: (1) law and economics, (2) sector, (3) customers, (4) finances, (5) resources, (6) management, (7) sales. It can be clearly seen that these factors, on the one hand, have an internal origin, and on the other hand, to a considerable extent have their sources in the business environment. Some of them are universal, while others are typical of the entire sector in which a given enterprise operates. The key success factors were also divided into seven categories, but different from those of the failure factors: (1) strategy, (2) business model, (3) resources, (4) flexibility, (5) services/products, (6) customer relations, (7) environment. Thus in the case of the winning enterprises, these factors were predominantly rooted in a strategically aligned, flexible and effective management model that had often been in place some time before the COVID-19 pandemic and turned out to be a valuable asset after its outbreak. Dependence on the environment is much smaller in the case of the winners, which would confirm their reliance on proactive, effective and creative policies. The category of resources represents a case of a managerial paradox. The same category may be a source of either a failure or a success, depending on resources' current condition and adjustment to requirements of a crisis situation.

The guidelines for the building of enterprises' resilience to crisis situations are pragmatic and represent some potential in terms of theory creation. They are based on various enterprises' crisis management experience gained from previous crises as well as recent observations made during the COVID-19 pandemic. At the outset, we identified blocks of actions necessary in this regard. Actions concerning reducing threats and combating weaknesses should pursue the following objectives: limiting a negative impact of the macro-environment during a crisis, reducing sectoral threats, responding to problems in relations with customers, preventing financial problems, taking care of resources, reducing managerial dysfunctions and improving sales strategies. Actions oriented towards the exploitation of opportunities and the development of strengths should focus on the following aims: exploring the strategic fit, exploiting the advantages of business models, exploiting the potential of resources, discounting flexibility, competing on the basis of products and services, benefiting from customer relations and taking advantage of positive changes in the environment.

On the basis of the conducted research, we constructed our own original model of an enterprise's resilience to crisis supplemented with a procedure for its implementation. The framework is based on the following pillars: (1) a culture of preparedness, (2) business continuity and (3) disaster resilience. Taking actions relating to the respective pillars may lead to the development of features of resilience, for example redundancy, adaptive capacity, agility, flexibility, diversity and efficiency. The presented model implementation procedure provides a hint for managers on how to implement in practice this complex and multidimensional approach to crisis management.

The conducted literature review, empirical research and – last but not least – modelling of solutions for management under crisis conditions generate a number of advantages and implications. What should be emphasized on the theoretical ground is the enrichment of knowledge about management in crisis, based on previously unavailable experience that was gained during the course of the global COVID-19 pandemic. On the empirical ground, attention should be paid to the research result in the form of identified "bad" and "good" practices followed during the pandemic. The former may serve as a warning for managers and protect them from making similar mistakes, while the latter constitute unique benchmarks worthy of imitation or replication. Nevertheless, both types of practices form a basis for the processes of organizational learning under crisis conditions. Our research also has methodological implications. The proposed model of an enterprise's resilience to crisis constitutes a comprehensive approach to building a model of an enterprise that will not tumble down under the pressure of a crisis, will be prepared for possible disturbances and will be able to survive a crisis situation or even take advantage of it as a lever for development.

Index

Note: Page locators in italics refer to figures and bold refer to tables.

For Product Safety Concerns and Information please contact our EU representative GPSR@taylorandfrancis.com
Taylor & Francis Verlag GmbH, Kaufingerstraße 24, 80331 München, Germany

www.ingramcontent.com/pod-product-compliance
Lightning Source LLC
LaVergne TN
LVHW021124300926
849160LV00010B/850
9780367674557